The Hermits of Big Sur

Paula Huston

With a Foreword by Pico Iyer

LITURGICAL PRESS
Collegeville, Minnesota

www.litpress.org

Cover design by Ann Blattner. Cover art by Arthur Poulin, OSB Cam, *Night Symphony*.

"The Coast Road," in *The Collected Poetry of Robinson Jeffers*, Volume 2, 1928–1938 by Robinson Jeffers, edited by Tim Hunt © 1938, renewed 1966 by Donnan Jeffers and Garth Jeffers. "Evening Ebb," in *The Selected Poetry of Robinson Jeffers* by Robinson Jeffers, edited by Tim Hunt © 2001 by Jeffers Literary Properties. All rights reserved. Used by permission of Stanford University Press.

1   2   3   4   5   6   7   8   9

Library of Congress Cataloging-in-Publication Data

Names: Huston, Paula, author.
Title: The Hermits of Big Sur / Paula Huston ; with a foreword by Pico Iyer.
Description: Collegeville, MN : Liturgical Press, [2021] | Includes bibliographical references and index. | Summary: "Based on notes kept for over sixty years by an early American novice at New Camaldoli Hermitage, The Hermits of Big Sur tells the story of what unfolds within this small and idealistic community when medievalism comes to terms with modernism"— Provided by publisher.
Identifiers: LCCN 2021022395 (print) | LCCN 2021022396 (ebook) | ISBN 9780814685068 (paperback) | ISBN 9780814685303 (epub) | ISBN 9780814685303 (pdf)
Subjects: LCSH: Hermits—California—Big Sur. | Monastic and religious life—California—Big Sur. | New Camaldoli Hermitage (Big Sur, Calif.)
Classification: LCC BX2847.U6 H87 2021 (print) | LCC BX2847.U6 (ebook) | DDC 255.009794/76—dc23
LC record available at https://lccn.loc.gov/2021022395
LC ebook record available at https://lccn.loc.gov/2021022396

"What an extraordinary gift Paula Huston's *The Hermits of Big Sur* has revealed itself to be. Who would have thought a seventy-year history of a Camaldolese monastery that rose in the wilds of the California coast could turn out to be such a page-turner! There's so much history here—world history, the major movements from Mussolini, Hitler, and Stalin to the opening dialogues between East and West, the aftermath of Vatican II, hippydom, and radical feminism. And at the heart of it all, the need to find that necessary solitude and solace and true companionship which only the interior Mystery at the still point can provide."

—Paul Mariani, biographer, poet, and author of *Thirty Days: On Retreat with the Exercises of St. Ignatius* and *The Mystery of It All*

"In *The Hermits of Big Sur*, author Paula Huston uses her exceptional literary skills to introduce us to individuals who are hidden to us but who nevertheless pray for us constantly. Deftly, she weaves together the thousand-year history of the Camaldoli order with intimate details of monastic life at Big Sur. Above all Huston shows us the deep Christ-like community these hermits have been able to develop."

—Richard J. Foster, author of *Celebration of Discipline* and *Sanctuary of the Soul*

"This story of how one monastic community found its place on earth and in the evolving church will certainly appeal to those who already recognize monasteries as spiritual oases. Huston offers an intimate glimpse into the complex community life, life-giving humor, and humble wisdom of men who know something about love the rest of us can't afford to forget."

—Marilyn McEntyre, author of *Caring for Words in a Culture of Lies* and *Word by Word*

"Paula Huston's very readable history of the Camaldolese monastery at Big Sur gives a very clear picture of the challenges faced and overcome in establishing an eremitical monastery on the coast of California. She tells the story by focusing on the people involved, how they discovered monastic life, and how the unique experience of each has contributed to the unfolding of the community's charism. The result is a realistic and very human portrayal of this distinctive chapter of monastic history."

—Michael Casey, OCSO, author of *Balaam's Donkey: Random Ruminations for Every Day of the Year*

"Absolutely fascinating, gorgeously written, frequently brilliant. In her story of how an ancient monastic order found a home in California, and how the author found a home with them, Paula Huston offers us an invitation into a world that few see, but all will want to experience."

—James Martin, SJ, author of *Learning to Pray*

"*The Hermits of Big Sur* is a remarkable book. Meticulous in research and engaging in tone, it explores some of the most significant and turbulent moments in the history of Italy and America through the lens of the thousand-year-old Camaldolese order in the mountains of Tuscany and the order's sometimes challenging relationship with its younger daughter house in California. More than a fascinating introduction to the rich and complex history of eremitical monasticism, this book is also an invitation to drink from monastic spirituality's deep, life-giving springs."

> —Deborah Smith Douglas, Oblate OSB Cam, is the author of
> *The Praying Life: Seeking God in All Things*

"Paula Huston's history of the founding of New Camaldoli Hermitage reads like a novel, recounting the tumultuous story of planting the seeds of a thousand-year-old tradition on fresh but wild American soil. Told with obvious love as well as unflagging dedication to research, this work is sure to delight monks and oblates and serve as a warm introduction to the unique spirit of an incredible place on the edge of the continent."

> —Cyprian Consiglio, OSB Cam, Prior, New Camaldoli Hermitage and
> author of *The God Who Gave You Birth*

"This is a wonderfully affectionate and informative look at the holy ground that has been a source of prayer, revelation, and grace for so many."

> —Ron Hansen, Santa Clara University, author of *Mariette in Ecstasy* and
> *Hotly in Pursuit of the Real*

"Like a family history, with diverse characters ranging from the chemist to the guitarist, Paula Huston tells the story of the Camaldolese hermits of Big Sur. Having co-founded more than one hermitage at the same time as New Camaldoli, I can attest to the authenticity of the hermits' struggles to survive in the wilderness in a true spirit of 'derring-do.'"

> —Tessa Bielecki, co-founder of the Spiritual Life Institute and the Nada/
> Nova Nada hermitages and co-director of the Desert Foundation and
> the author of *Holy Daring, Season of Glad Songs*, and *Desert Visions*

"T. S. Eliot once said of a sacred place: 'You are here to kneel where prayer has been valid.' In Paula Huston's graceful, engrossing narrative history of New Camaldoli, she has given us privileged access to another such place. Even if you can't go there yourself, this book will enrich your sense of what contemplative prayer and the monastic life offer to every living soul."

> —Gregory Wolfe, author of *Beauty Will Save the World*

Contents

Foreword by Pico Iyer ix

Chapter 1 1

Chapter 2 6

Chapter 3 14

Chapter 4 21

Chapter 5 28

Chapter 6 35

Chapter 7 43

Chapter 8 50

Chapter 9 58

Chapter 10 67

Chapter 11 75

Chapter 12 84

Chapter 13 93

Chapter 14 102

Chapter 15 110

Chapter 16 119

Chapter 17 128

Chapter 18 136

Chapter 19 144

Chapter 20 154

Chapter 21 163

Chapter 22 173

Afterword 183

Chronology 193

Notes 204

Bibliography 217

Index 225

Bench at New Camaldoli Hermitage (photograph by Kayleigh Meyers)

Foreword

My life was transformed the minute I set foot in New Camaldoli, thirty years ago today. A smiling monk in the monastery bookstore led me down to the small but comfortable room in which I was to spend the next three nights. I stepped into the dazzling sunlight, saw a white chair in the private walled garden beyond the desk, took in the ocean stretching out in every direction thirteen hundred feet below, and knew I'd come home. The feeling was as sudden, as impossible to argue away, as when you encounter the person who will become your lifelong love.

Almost instantly, all the worries and fears that had been cutting me in two on the four-hour drive up to Big Sur were gone. And just as thousands, from every background, have felt on meeting the Hermitage, I realized that I was in a place that I could trust and that recalled to me a truth, a self—a freedom from self—I too often forget amidst the clatter of the freeway and the shopping mall. The fact I'd lost my family home—and everything I own—in a wildfire eight months earlier made me even more grateful for an inner home that felt so deep, so lasting, beyond the reach of every flame. The fact I wasn't Christian—and in fact had had my fill of hymns and crosses, so I thought, during sixteen years of Anglican schooling in England—came to seem the least important detail of all.

I started returning to this source, again and again, and I came to see, as Paula Huston reminds us with such radiant clarity in this book, how very diverse and unexpected it is. Many of the re-treatants I met were women and soon there'd be women in residence imparting a special grace on every flower they left behind in the rooms they prepared for us. Quite a few of the other visitors turned out to be Buddhist or Sufi or maybe nothing at all. I was working at the time as an essayist for *Time* magazine, having recently escaped from a 25th floor office in Midtown Manhattan; many of the quiet new friends I made along the monastery road were lawyers and teachers and software engineers who were even more familiar with the world far below.

In time, as Paula describes here, I'd also come to see what a re-markably talented group of monks had assembled in this spot. The current Prior practices yoga and has a strong association with a Zen *sangha*; when once I watched an obscure Shakespeare play in the Enclosure, the two monks beside me knew it better than professors at Oxford might. Everything I thought I knew about Catholicism and worship was turned on its head in the course of almost a hun-dred retreats, sometimes for as long as three weeks each. I started taking my wife, my friends, urging imaginative young men I know to try the *ora et labora* program that would allow them to live with the monks for a while in return for doing odd jobs around the property.

When first I arrived, it was the rare beauty of the place, the puls-ing silence, the freedom from telephone and television and internet that liberated me. I could read or write or, most remarkably of all, do nothing at all. I could take walks above the ocean, try to count the stars at night, follow an impulse to write a long letter to a friend I hadn't seen for years. Gradually, though, as this beautiful book makes clear, I came to realize how much my solitude could deepen, and be deepened by, community. Every soul I met along the road above the sea had come in search of more or less the same silence, which meant that all of us were joined by the deepest of shared interests and commitments.

As you'll read in the pages to come, the Camaldoli order has been cultivating sanctuary and contemplative practice for more than a thousand years now. But has the world ever been so full of rush and distraction as now? If you're reading these words, you're likely one of those who takes in more data in one day than Shakespeare did in a lifetime. Does that make us wiser than he was? I fear it might be the opposite.

As I go about my job as a journalist—the year I arrived at New Camaldoli, I'd just returned from Tibet and North Korea and Paris and London, and was on my way to Vietnam and a dozen other places—my greatest fear is that I'll forget what's true and what lies deepest inside me. The danger with a cluttered mind is the same as with a cluttered desk: in a moment of need, you can't put your hand on what really sustains you. But then I think of the drive along the ever more pristine highway to the sign that leads to the winding road that leads to the top of the mountain.

So long as I have that place and its people inside me, I never feel alone or lost or without substance. A little of the clarity and the peace of the Hermitage will be with me even in the most stressful of moments. I'm deeply grateful for this book, which offers so much historical and human detail I'd never have known otherwise. I'm no less grateful for the community it commemorates, which sometimes seems to have been my salvation for almost half a lifetime now. For this Hindu-born traveler long based in Buddhist Japan, the Benedictine hermits of Big Sur have been my guiding teachers, inspirations, and role models. For them, and for their story, as given here, I feel—to use the word on which Paula ends, so perfectly—profoundly "blessed."

Pico Iyer

Nara, Japan

February 15, 2021

1

The view was spectacular, one of the most beautiful he'd ever seen, and he'd been in beautiful places all his life. Before him lay the sea, a 180 degree spread of it glittering in an immense bay beneath the noonday sun. Behind him rose the mountains, fold after endless fold for miles to the north and south, and above all of it, a piercingly blue summer sky. The wilderness he'd been seeking for so long.

He stood near a fence line, his long beard and white cowl ruffled by the sea breeze. The real estate agent waited down by the car parked on the dirt ranch road, knowing enough to leave him alone while he surveyed the land. Four thousand acres, if they could afford it, Klinglesmith had said in his letter, but six hundred should suffice—the entire face of a mountain with enough level ground to plant olives, vines, fruit orchards, vegetables. Grassy meadows, summer gold in June, but the winter rains are almost tropical in their intensity, Klinglesmith insisted: you can run cattle, keep milk cows, whatever you need to sustain yourself so far from civilization. True, it wouldn't be so easy to fish—the crashing of the breakers against the rocky cliffs 1,300 feet below roared up the mountain face toward him like the voice of God—but it could be done. With enough hard work, it could be done.

He turned and waved to the agent. It was time to look at the old ranch house and outbuildings, at whether there was already enough in place that could be adapted for the postulants he knew would come flocking once the word was out. Their needs were simple, but still—they'd require a bunkhouse until they could build real cells, a building that could double as a chapel until the church could be constructed. They'd need a refectory for meals, and a kitchen.

They'd need a shed to store tools—these future postulants had no idea how many wheelbarrows full of rock and sand and concrete they'd be pushing before the hermitage was completed—but he knew they could do it. This would be the first American foundation birthed from the thousand-year-old Italian order to which he belonged. Here on this wild California coast with its canyons full of redwoods, they would start anew, away from the political tensions that still seethed back at home.

If only he were younger. After so many years of apostolic ministry—India, Australia, Italy—he was sixty-one and feeling his age. He'd been a monk since 1950—not long, compared to his decades as a Jesuit on the global stage. In 1953, he'd finally gotten permission to go into reclusion, but less than five years later, here he was, negotiating with American bishops, fund-raising among the celebrities of Hollywood, visiting potential building sites with real estate agents. He was at one and the same time Dom Agostino Modotti, hermit, and Fr. Ugo Modotti, former Jesuit, and this American expedition would require every ounce of energy he had and all the diplomatic and social skills he'd acquired during his long years in foreign lands. It helped that, unlike his Italian brothers, he spoke flawless English. But this was not an assignment he'd sought out on his own, and if it hadn't been for the still unhealed conflict back home, he would have tried his best to get out of it. In the end, he'd agreed to give up his recluse cell in the ancient Sacro Eremo of Camaldoli and to lead this mission "under obedience." However, now that he was here and seeing what he was seeing—the great sea glittering in the sun, the screaming hawks wheeling overhead—he was filled with joy. He'd done it. He'd found the place.

The Big Sur coast of California is one of America's last true wildernesses. Highway 1, a narrow ribbon twisting its vertiginous way along the sea cliffs in the shadow of looming, unstable mountains, provides the only access, but the road is regularly cut off by landslides and devastating wildfires. The hardy souls who live here are used to drivers plunging off cliffs, basketball-sized rocks suddenly littering the road ahead of them, flooding creeks and washed-out bridges. The nearest town in either direction is a death-defying hour's drive away. And there is no cell service, no internet, no way to call for help if you need it. In 1958, the coast was even wilder and more isolated than it is now. So why would a world traveler like Modotti be so drawn to this daunting place?

Writer Belden Lane maintains that the wilderness exerts a mysterious power over the imagination that can lead to a transformative spiritual experience. Both dangerous and unpredictable, it quickly demolishes the illusion that we are in control. We are forced to pay close attention to what is happening around us—where is that ominous black cloud headed? what's that rumbling sound? is that a mountain lion track?—which means we expend unusually high levels of energy when we are in these places. We are awake, alert, focused in ways that comfortable circumstances do not inspire in us. "Fierce landscapes," says Lane, "serve as metaphorical maps of the life of the spirit. Deserts and mountains of the psyche can be traced throughout the history of mythology, the writings of the mystics, and the work of psychologists exploring landscape symbols in folklore and dreams."[1] No wonder, then, that the first impulse for people being called on a serious spiritual journey is to head for some version of the wilderness, even if only for a short time and even if the wilderness is strictly metaphorical.

In early Christian times, the wilderness meant the pitiless deserts of Syria, Palestine, and Egypt, and those who fled there either died quickly or found ways not only to survive but to flourish. Between the third and fifth centuries, these wilderness dwellers were known as the Desert Fathers and Mothers, and their cryptic, koan-like sayings, born of the pressure of their circumstances, still challenge and intrigue us. Some of them chose the strictly "eremitical," or hermit, life, lived out in an isolated cave or mud hut, while others congregated in what became the first Christian monasteries. Both were driven by "fuga mundi," the overwhelming longing to flee the world.

While these early Christians certainly did not invent this kind of arduous spiritual quest—there seems to be an archetypal spiritual journey in every faith tradition, often involving wilderness—enough Christians spent enough time in harsh landscapes during those early centuries that, even today, the image of a solitary hermit hut in the wilds has the power to compel. What were these people doing out there? What did they think they were accomplishing?

For many Christians throughout the ages, the answer has been . . . exactly nothing. Withdrawal from "normal" life—a life of endless, busy productivity—indicates, at best, the triumph of idealism over reality. Take away marriage, money, the marketplace, and what out there could possibly be worth living for? The eighteenth-century British historian Edward Gibbon was famously appalled by the notion of *fuga mundi* and the hermits and monks who disappeared into the desert in pursuit of the knowledge it could teach. "They seriously renounced the business and the pleasures of the age; abjured the use of wine, of flesh, and of marriage; chastised their body, mortified their affections, and embraced a life of misery, as the price of eternal happiness." More than that, it was this single-minded pursuit of whatever these lunatics were pursuing (Gibbon certainly couldn't say what *that* was) that he believed responsible for "the gradual corruption of Christianity."[2]

For the desert Christians, however, the allure of the wilderness lay in the fact that it was emphatically *not* the world of commerce and contracts and combat; not the world of sound and fury, signifying nothing. The very harshness of the wilderness was reassuring to them. Worldly people would not follow them there. They would be free to seek God with all that was in them. Their goal was contemplation, or a clarified vision made possible by a purified heart. They believed that the contemplative monk lives in the continual presence of the Divine and sees, as Wordsworth put it, into the life of things. In the presence of a true contemplative, people miraculously lose their self-consciousness and reveal everything, especially that which has burdened them with guilt or shame. And then they wait for a life-changing *word*, a penetrating insight from the holy elder. This word is not guaranteed. It sometimes comes and sometimes doesn't. This is because the contemplative, who is a master of patient waiting, does not speak unless prompted to by God.

You do not become a contemplative overnight. In fact, to become holy and full of wisdom in this way requires years of slow, painful un-selfing. Desires must be dealt with. Passions must be tamed. The mind must be trained. Humility must become second nature, a way of life. The Christian monastic tradition calls the outcome of this un-selfing process *puritas cordis*, or purity of heart. On a practical level, this means you are no longer plagued by obsessive thoughts about sex, food, possessions, comfort, money, power, status, safety, ambition, winning, being "right," taking vengeance, or passing acerbic judgments on the foibles and failing of others—everything, in short, that Edward Gibbon thought made life worth living. All this has somehow been reduced in importance so that it no longer has the power to blur your vision or block God's voice. Your heart is at peace, your mind is open, your spirit has developed the capacity to love the world and all its suffering and evil, the world that you once fled.

But first comes fuga mundi. And as you might imagine, the road you take during your headlong flight is littered with potential traps. You might, for example, be a natural-born introvert who is not so much seeking God as hiding out. You might believe, as Sartre so slyly put it, that "hell is other people." Or you might be leaving the world of bosses and social obligations and stop signs at the corner so as to liberate yourself from rules and regulations; *nobody* can tell you what to do anymore. You might even be fleeing because you cannot deal with change, and the world is ever-changing.

At least, however, when you've removed yourself from the world, you've spared it a terrible fate: the imposing upon it of your own utopian fantasies. The twentieth century saw the rise of the great political religions known as fascism and communism. These totalitarian ideologies and the brutal dictatorships they spawned were rooted not in fuga mundi but in a dangerous form of *contemptus mundi*: disgust for a broken society made up of disappointing human beings coupled with an unquenchable thirst to master and reshape all this in one's own image.

Modotti, who had lived through the nightmare unleashed by these political religions, thought he had finally found the wilderness he longed for in the ancient eremo of Camaldoli. But the world was there too, and he was soon caught back up in it. Maybe—he prayed that it would be so—this mountain ranch in Big Sur would prove to be the place he had been seeking.

2

"If I am lucky and no one is there, I share the delicious solitude with the rocks, the sea otters, a passing whale, the drifting clouds, mist and fog, the floating islands of kelp and the screeching gulls. If the tide is out, I commune with a two-faced rock out of which the blazing sun and pounding surf have sculpted a king and queen of the Ptolemaic line."[1] Thus writes Henry Miller, a delightful and eccentric literary genius whose own version of *fuga mundi* took place in 1946 and lasted for eighteen years. *Big Sur and the Oranges of Hieronymus Bosch* is set fourteen miles north of Modotti's paradise. Partway between them is Slate's Springs, a natural source of abundant hot water, where Miller is currently floating in one of the many tubs that overlook the sea.

Miller has chosen Big Sur for a reason. He has achieved enough notoriety to last him a lifetime (several of his best-selling books are banned in the US), and his fans won't leave him alone. Maybe, he thinks, if I go to the wilderness, one that's nearly impossible to access, I will be at peace and have time to write and be a better father to my kids. So he moves his family first to Partington Ridge, a few miles north of Slate's, and then, several years later, to Anderson Creek, an abandoned camp that housed convict labor during the building of Highway 1 in the 1930s. In time, he winds up back on Partington Ridge. What he realizes very quickly is that 1) he is not the first artist to think of moving to Big Sur, and 2) his fans are indefatigable and will find him anywhere.

Both types—fans and would-be artists—begin showing up at his cabin door almost as soon as he arrives on the coast. The ones who most interest him, however, are the young men with artistic aspirations just coming out of the service after World War II. Miller understands their longings, even though he knows that the vast majority will never become real writers: "They were all filled with a desire to escape the horrors of the present and willing to live like rats if only they might be left alone and in peace."[2] More, he recognizes that they are in some way prescient about the stupendous cultural shifts about to take place in American society. "These young men," he says, "are now roaming about in our midst like anonymous messengers from another planet."[3] What message do they bear? Miller thinks it is very simple: That it is possible to live a far better life than most post-war Americans are currently living. That the only thing keeping them from this better life is fear of whatever sacrifices might be demanded of them in order to achieve it. Many give up soon and drift off to try their luck in some other, less challenging, environment. But Miller is surprised by how many do persist and manage to make a go of it on the coast, whether or not they ever become artists. He is even more impressed by what happens to them in the process: "The most important thing I have witnessed since coming here, is the transformation people have wrought in their own being."[4]

Transformation is no small thing and also fairly rare. So how does he account for this phenomenon being relatively common in Big Sur? Miller thinks that it must be the "grandeur and nobility" of the setting. "The place itself is so overwhelmingly bigger, greater, than anyone could hope to make it that it engenders a humility and reverence not frequently met with in Americans. There being nothing to improve on in the surroundings, the tendency is to set about improving oneself."[5]

But Big Sur is not only astonishingly beautiful; it also manifests what the nineteenth-century British Romantics would call "the Sublime." By this term, they meant that the full power of uncontrolled nature is on display, and humans can only stand before the spectacle in awe. Religious philosopher Rudolf Otto coined a word to describe this phenomenon; he called it an experience of the "numinous," and believed that without this underlying awareness of what lies beyond human understanding or command, religion is mere "morality touched with emotion."[6] Belden Lane agrees that the shock of the numinous has the power to change us: "A vast expanse of jagged stone, desert sand, and towering thunderheads has a way of challenging all the mental constructs in which we are tempted to take comfort and pride, thinking we have captured the divine."[7] No wonder, then, that so many artists and spiritual seekers have made their way to Big Sur over the decades. In 1962, only four years after Modotti's first look at the ranch that would become a hermitage, Henry Miller's beloved hot tubs at Slate's Springs became part of a new phenomenon, the human potential movement. Michael Murphy, a member of the family who owned the property, graduated from Stanford with a degree in psychology, as did his friend Richard Price. Fascinated by the current breakthroughs in their chosen field, they conceived the idea of inviting cutting-edge psychologists and spiritual teachers to give seminars. And thus humble Slate's Springs, where nineteenth-century mountain men once washed out their underwear and fifty years later, Henry Miller bobbed happily in his tub overlooking the Pacific, became the famed Esalen Institute.

The name "Esalen" was meant to honor the Indigenous inhabitants of the Big Sur coast, the rather mysterious Esselen. The first Esalen seminar was offered by Alan Watts, interpreter of Zen Buddhism for a Western audience. In 1951, one year after Modotti entered the Sacro Eremo of Camaldoli, Watts published *The Wisdom of Insecurity*, which attempted to explain the peculiar phenomenon Henry Miller had noticed in *Big Sur and the Oranges of Hieronymus Bosch*: intelligent young men with "good futures ahead of them" who instead of taking corporate jobs were fleeing to the wilderness of Big Sur to live without running water or electricity. The problem, thought Watts, lay in our Western perspective: "[F]or most human beings the past and the future are not *as* real, but *more* real, than the present. The present cannot be lived happily unless the past has been 'cleared up' and the future is bright with promise."[8] Not only are we incapable of actually living in the moment but we are so burdened by the past, and so overly focused on the future, that we are doomed to deep unhappiness: "[M]odern civilization is in almost every respect a vicious circle. It is insatiably hungry because its way of life condemns it to perpetual frustration."[9] For Watts, the starting place toward a real life, one worth living, begins with our rejecting the illusion that we can ever achieve the security we crave.

Another early visitor to the institute was religious historian Aldous Huxley, a founding board member of the Harvard Psilocybin Project run by Timothy Leary. The project was launched to, in part, determine if mescaline could facilitate the experience of profound religious states. Huxley first took the drug in 1953, the same year Modotti went into reclusion at the Sacro Eremo, and he wrote his famous *The Doors of Perception* a year later, which recounted his life-changing experience of the psychedelic drug. He believed that there were many paths to enlightenment besides prayer and meditation, and that the drug might help break down ego-caused impediments to genuine mystical experience. He continued to experiment with various psychedelics and hallucinogenics, including LSD, for the rest of his life and became a major influence on the nascent hippie culture of the sixties. Psychedelics made possible a different kind of fuga mundi, in which the world of normal sensory experience was temporarily abandoned for, as the Beatles later put it, the "Magical Mystery Tour."

Thus, the complex of ten thermal sulphur springs with its combined flow of fifty gallons per minute became the center of a revolution in American spiritual practice. The New Age movement, alternative medicine, East-West religious dialogue, yoga, massage, mind-body interventions, Joseph Campbell's archetypes, and Fritz Perl's Gestalt therapy owe much of their widespread practice today to the impressive lineup of radical thinkers who passed through Esalen during the revolutionary sixties. Like the psychedelic revolution, the Esalen phenomenon was also prompted by a kind of fuga mundi. The message Esalen imparted during these early post-war years was, You are not stuck in the boring and mundane grind laid out for you in 1950s America. You do not have to wear a gray flannel suit; you can grow out your hair, go barefoot, float naked in the waters of a natural hot spring, as though you were back in the womb. And you will not be alone if you do. Countless others are feeling the same urge. Battlefield carnage and death camps and atomic bombs are only a decade and a half behind you, and the nightmares linger on.

Fuga mundi is a natural response to a world seemingly gone mad, and it strikes religious and non-religious people alike. It struck particularly hard on the wild and untamed Big Sur coast in the fifties and early sixties, at the very time Modotti was working out the tricky practicalities of his own flight from the world, eleven miles down the road from Esalen.

During the years that Henry Miller was learning to make a go of it under the primitive conditions of Partington Ridge, a young monk called Thomas Merton was struggling to answer the same question that had drawn Miller to Big Sur in the first place: How shall I live? Born in France to a painter father and a mother who died of liver cancer when he was still a child, Merton stayed for a while with his grandparents in New York, was enrolled in a boarding school in France at the age of eleven, then moved to London with his father, who subsequently died of brain cancer. In 1935, the same year that the Italian dictator Mussolini invaded Ethiopia in hopes of re-establishing the Roman Empire, Merton entered Columbia University as an English student. There, he joined a picket line in front of the campus Casa Italiana, which was accused of disseminating pro-Fascist literature.

The following year, he read Aldous Huxley's *Ends and Means,* which introduced him to the concept of mysticism, along with Etienne Gilson's *The Spirit of Medieval Philosophy,* which, to his own surprise, drew him toward Catholicism. But it was not until 1938, when he was introduced to a Hindu monk and academic called Mahanambrata Brahmachari that he received the advice that changed his life. Instead of discussing Hinduism, Brahmachari recommended that Merton reconnect with his own Western spiritual roots. For example, said Brahmachari, why not read *The Imitation of Christ* and *The Confessions of St. Augustine?* Merton did. A year later, he became Catholic.

But much as he loved this new immersion in ancient Catholic practice, parish church life did not satisfy his deepest spiritual longings. He first tried to become a Franciscan and was told he wouldn't suit. Crushed, and thinking he would soon be drafted into the looming war anyway, he decided to make an Easter retreat at the Trappist Abbey of Gethsemani near Louisville, Kentucky. In preparation for the retreat, he went to the library and read the *Catholic Encyclopedia* entry on the Trappists, where he discovered that they were

Cistercians, part of the same eleventh-century monastic reform movement that produced both the strictly enclosed Carthusians and the hermits of Camaldoli. He studied a large photograph of the Sacro Eremo where Modotti would become, within the decade, a hermit and recluse. And he was struck by his own overpowering urge toward fuga mundi.

Sacro Eremo, Camaldoli

"What I saw on those pages pierced my heart like a knife. What wonderful happiness there was, then, in the world! There were still men on this miserable, noisy, cruel earth, who tasted the marvelous joy of silence and solitude, who dwelt in forgotten mountain cells, in secluded monasteries, where the news and desires and appetites and conflicts of the world no longer reached them."[10] More, for those strong enough to cut their ties to the world, at the end of this flight lay the possibility of enlightenment: "They were free from the burden of flesh's tyranny, and their clear vision, clean of the world's smoke and of its bitter sting, were raised to heaven and penetrated into the deeps of heaven's infinite and healing light."[11] Merton made his Easter retreat, then months later, returned to Gethsemani. On December 13, 1941, four days after the Japanese attacked Pearl Harbor and two days after Nazi Germany declared war on the United States, Merton was accepted as a Trappist postulant. With the 1948 publication of his spiritual autobiography, *The Seven Storey Mountain*, he would go on to become the most famous Catholic monk in America.

What, exactly, was so compelling about this story of an idealistic young man leaving the world to become a contemplative monastic? That question puzzled Robert Giroux, Merton's editor at Harcourt Brace, for years. Though he was impressed by the manuscript when he first read it, he had no idea it would become an international best-seller. As he put it:

> When advance proofs arrived in the summer of 1948, I decided to send them to Evelyn Waugh, Clare Boothe Luce, Graham Greene and Bishop Fulton J. Sheen. To my delight they all responded in laudatory terms, and we used the quotations on the book jacket and in advertisements. At this point the first printing was increased from 5,000 to 12,500. By November, a month after publication, the book had sold 12,951 copies, but in December it shot up to 31,028. From mid-December to after New Year's Day is usually the slowest period for orders, because bookstores are so well stocked by then. This new pattern of sales was significant—the "Mountain" was a best seller! . . . Today, including paperback editions and translations, the total sale of *The Seven Storey Mountain* has reached the multiple millions, and it continues to sell year after year.[12]

Thanks to Merton's unusual spiritual autobiography and its clarion call toward fuga mundi, coming as it did in the aftermath of a brutal world war and just as the Cold War was beginning, Gethsemani Abbey and other Trappist monasteries became magnets for numerous other young seekers of the 1950s, who, legend has it, invariably arrived at the front gates with copies of *Seven Storey Mountain* tucked in their bags.

Meanwhile, though Merton had chosen to become a Trappist, he'd never forgotten about that photo of the Sacro Eremo at Camaldoli. And within four years of his rise to literary stardom, he was writing his first letter to Dom Anselmo Giabbani, prior general of the Camaldolese, wondering if he might become a hermit in the thousand-year-old Italian order.

3

You wouldn't think that a mountain-fast hermitage in the Apennines of Italy could remind you of the Big Sur coast. It is true there is no ocean. Or redwoods. But the famous sweet chestnut and coniferous forests of Camaldoli—today, close to four and a half million acres of them, planted and tended by the monks for more than eight hundred years—could easily fit on the coastal range of California. Wild boar root for mushrooms and stags bugle their mating calls in the spring. The storms are just as powerful, the lightning as violent, the wildflowers as sweet during their brief spring bloom.

If the year is 1023 and you have just arrived in this forest sanctuary east of Florence and north of Arezzo in the throes of your own *fuga mundi*, you'll have found exactly the sort of wilderness best suited to the life you are seeking. There is even a version of someday's California Highway 1 nearby, a pilgrim road from Ravenna on the Adriatic Sea that leads over the mountain pass and on to Rome.[1] A few kilometers down the mountain is a guesthouse for people who are making penances, people on pilgrimage: Fontebono, the "good spring," where travelers in these dangerous times can fill up their jugs with sweet, cold water, eat a good meal, sleep in safety for the night, and be blessed on their way by a monk and a handful of brothers.

But you are no pilgrim. You've made up your mind. You know what you want to do. The question is, can you do it? It is thus a relief to see that there really are others like yourself already living on this broad, grassy meadow ringed by beech trees: five hermits each in his own cell, clustered around a church and a lodge for common meals. Among them is the spiritual master, the monk called

Romuald, whose reputation for wisdom has drawn you, just as seekers will be drawn to Esalen a millennium later, out of your everyday life and into the compelling possibility of transformation. They say he is living proof that a person can become holy. People pull wool out of his sheepskin when he walks by, just in case they might get a miracle out of it.[2] Stories abound: that he once healed a madman by kissing him. That he cured another monk's vicious toothache by breathing on him. That he has the gift of tears, and that he often breaks into spontaneous weeping with compunction or joy when he is presiding over the Eucharist, or preaching, or traveling from one monastery to another. For a monk, he travels a lot.[3]

He is also reputed to be humble and gentle and cheerful, in spite of the rigorous spiritual disciplines he imposes on himself. He is proof that you can leave the world without losing your mind. Which, as you too well know, often happens to would-be hermits. Which is why you have chosen him, who is known as the "father of hermits who live according to right reason and follow the monastic Rule."[4] He may be kind, but he knows human nature.

Are you up to this? Can you really fast and recite the psalms from memory and pray the Divine Office—the bell is ringing, you can see the hermits making their way to the church in their goatskins and leather sandals and mantles—every single day for the rest of your life? Can you live on chickpeas and chestnut cakes and broad beans and unleavened bread and hardly any wine?[5] Or will you give it all up and return to the world? However you answer these questions, how can you possibly know, here in this simple encampment in this broad meadow in the Apennines, that if you do stay and become a disciple of the holy man, you'll be helping to build the oldest continuous religious community in the Western Church?[6]

Though Ugo Modotti was more than ten years older than Anselmo Giabbani when he entered the Sacro Eremo in 1950—he was fifty-three to Giabbani's forty-two—Giabbani had three decades of seniority on him. It was not unusual when, as a Tuscan boy in post–World War I Italy, Giabbani entered into Camaldolese life at age eleven; in the aftermath of that violent cataclysm, it was natural for survivors to seek marriage and babies, yet all too often, people did not have the resources to raise their children well. So it was common practice to send sons to monasteries and daughters to convents.[7] But there was no guarantee that these youngsters had a genuine call to the monastic life. Even if they stayed, they were not necessarily compelled by fuga mundi or personally committed to *conversatio morum*, the lifetime process of becoming holy. They were not seeking contemplation or the ability to pray without ceasing. They were there for more practical reasons, like regular meals and shelter they could count on.

To further complicate matters, all the monasteries in Italy had been officially suppressed twice within the previous one hundred and fifty years: first, by Napoleon in 1810, and second, by the newly unified Kingdom of Italy in 1866. Many ancient communities were permanently destroyed, and those that survived lost touch with their roots during the long years of banishment from their monasteries, now owned by the state. When the Camaldolese remnant was finally allowed to return home after working out a rental fee in 1873 for the use of their own buildings, they faced the most precarious of situations. Not only did they have to figure out a means of support, they had to recover monastic discipline and rebuild their relationships with one another. Unfortunately, the resources they had were pretty well confined to historical documents edited in the eighteenth century; these focused almost exclusively on the strictly eremitical, or hermit, lifestyle.[8]

Yet these documents presented only half the picture. Romuald founded both hermitages and monasteries, plus combinations of the two. Monks in hermitages live in individual cells, spend more time in solitude, and are called hermits. Monks in monasteries live in dormitory-style buildings, spend more time in community, and are referred to as "cenobites." Romuald believed that both lifestyles were necessary and that each fed the other—that it was the experience of community that prepared a man to live in solitude, and the wisdom that a man gained as a solitary that in turn fed the community. The Camaldolese "stemma," or coat of arms, an ancient symbol that predates the order, reflects the dual nature of the Romualdian monastic life: two doves (sometimes peacocks) drinking from the same chalice. Underneath the chalice are the words *Ego vobis, vos mihi*, which translate as "I am yours, you are mine."

Camaldoli, one of Romuald's last foundations, exemplified his ideal: high on the mountain and well off the pilgrim highway, the hermits of the Sacro Eremo devoted most of their hours to contemplative prayer, while three kilometers below at Fontebono, several cenobites and lay brothers ran the guesthouse, the hospital, and eventually a pharmacy in order to serve weary travelers. At some point, a cenobite would naturally crave more solitude and head up the mountain for a while. At another, a hermit would go down to Fontebono to help with the charitable work of the community. The underlying structure that allowed for this kind of dynamism was the Rule of St. Benedict, at that time already five hundred years old. As a young monk at the Benedictine monastery of Sant'Apollinare in Classe near Ravenna, Romuald himself had been formed by that Rule and even though he eventually left the great monastery to become an itinerant hermit, he never let go of the wisdom offered by his long-ago predecessor.[9]

But by the time young Anselmo Giabbani made his monastic profession at age seventeen, much of this broad and flexible Romualdian/Benedictine vision had been forgotten. The Camaldolese had split themselves into five branches more than three hundred years before. Of the three remaining, one branch was strictly eremitical (the Hermits of Monte Corona), one was strictly cenobitical (Camaldolese Cenobitic Congregation), and the third, headed by the Sacro Eremo and the monastery of Camaldoli, continued to struggle over the right relationship between the two (Hermits of Tuscany). The ancient symbol of the two doves drinking from the chalice no longer represented who they had become. More, the notion that being a monk could or should be a spiritual quest characterized by a deep interior journey did not compute. Instead, monks were judged by their strict devotional practices and how well they observed the many regulations that governed monastic life.

Giabbani's monastic call was genuine, however, and this inner assurance that he was meant to be a monk was combined with a brilliant, searching intellect. When the old guesthouse at Camaldoli was finally reopened in 1934, the isolated monks weren't quite sure how to handle an influx of visitors from the outside. However, it was not long before university students, led by prominent theologians and pastors including the future Pope Paul VI, Giovanni

Battista Montini, began gathering there for seminars and lectures and exciting discussions about the spiritual life.

The following year, in an attempt to reunite the separated Camaldolese congregations, the Holy See abruptly ordered the suppression of the entirely cenobitical Camaldolese house called St. Michael of Murano near Venice.[10] They were not living as hermits, after all, and the Camaldolese were supposed to be hermits, weren't they? The newly disenfranchised monks were given a difficult choice: you can begin a novitiate at the Sacro Eremo and learn how to become as hardy and tough-minded as the modern-day desert dwellers you will find there, you can leave the monastic life altogether and become a diocesan priest, or you can go to Fonte Avellana, another ancient, mountain-fast hermitage in the Marches near Umbria, where things might be a little different—perhaps more flexible—than they would be at the legendary eremo.

Giabbani, only twenty-seven at the time, was sent to Fonte Avellana as prior to take charge of this community now filled with the newly disenfranchised young cenobites from St. Michael's along with boys who had been recruited from the college of Buonsollazzo. There he began reading several of the "new theologians" who were causing such a stir at the Vatican. Pius XI believed that scholars like Henri de Lubac and Yves Congar and others were spreading the dangerous modernist philosophy condemned by his predecessor, Piux X, in his encyclical *Pascendi Dominici Gregis* of 1907.

What these banned theologians of the so-called ressourcement ("return to the sources") movement did for Giabbani, however, was life-changing. They reconnected him in a visceral way to the ancient interior spirituality of Christian monasticism—the Desert Fathers, plus Romuald himself, who had been consciously following in their footsteps. They reawakened him to Romuald's vision of the intertwined eremitical and cenobitical life: not strictly one, not strictly the other, but necessarily both. And as he read the foundational eleventh- and twelfth-century Camaldolese documents through this new lens, Giabbani rediscovered the beautiful three-part charism of the Romualdian way of life, known as the *Triplex Bonum*, or Three-Fold Good: community, solitude, and missionary-martyrdom.

The deeper he got, the more he began to realize what he was uncovering: the Camaldolese pearl of great price.

The monasteries were not the only losers after *Il Risorgimento*, or the Italian reunification effort. The church itself sustained major blows. Italy's many independent states had not been united under one umbrella since the fall of the Roman Empire fourteen hundred years before, which made them vulnerable to the political machinations of foreign powers and attack by one another. Reunification meant they would be stronger. However, the states in the middle of the Italian peninsula were in a different situation; for over a thousand years, they had been ruled by the popes, who reigned as both spiritual and temporal monarchs, including commanding their own armies. By 1870, all the Papal States, including Rome, had fallen into secular hands.

But this should have been no surprise; the political clout of the popes had been diminishing for years by then. The Protestant Reformation of the sixteenth century struck a major blow against Catholicism's claim to be the "One True Church." The great revolutions of the eighteenth century spelled the beginning of the end for most of Europe's monarchies, including the papacy as it had always been styled. A new wind was blowing; democracy was in the air, and with it came a mighty backlash against those who would stand in its way—especially the Catholic hierarchy.

From the perspective of the church, the overthrow of the Papal States was devastating, but the loss of Rome was unbearable. Italy's new leader, King Victor Emmanuel II, poured salt into this open wound by moving himself and his government officials into the Quirinil Palace, one of the papacy's traditional residences.[11] Rome became the official capital of the new nation of Italy. It didn't help that Victor Emmanuel had long since been ex-communicated. It didn't make any difference when the popes from 1870 on refused to legitimize the new nation or to recognize the right of the king and his successors to rule the land. It didn't change a thing when they forbade Catholics to run for office or vote. And when they dug in their heels and refused to venture out of the Vatican compound from 1870 until nearly 1930, even that did not resolve what had come to be known as the "Roman Question."

Meanwhile, an ambitious man who passionately hated popes and all they represented was working out a new ideology called fascism. Instead of worshipping the traditional God, people would worship the state. A onetime socialist known as a "priest-eater," because of his contempt for the Catholic clergy, ingeniously crafted a rise to national prominence after World War I that won him a seat in the Italian Chamber of Deputies in 1921. At roughly the same time the six-year-old child called Thomas Merton was losing his mother to liver cancer, the brilliant eleven-year-old called Anselmo Giabbani was arriving at Camaldoli, and the twenty-three-year-old Jesuit called Ugo Modotti was heading out to India, the inventor of fascism was completely engrossed in the task of consolidating his political power.

Soon enough, he made his move. Thirty-thousand armed *squadristi* wearing black shirts converged on Rome. Mostly discontented World War I soldiers, these ultra-nationalist Black Shirts posed as guardians of "law and order." Their real job was to terrorize and attack any group who opposed the ideology of their leader. They hunted down communists, socialists, union bosses—anyone who might impede the fascist juggernaut. They attacked and humiliated priests, often forcing them to drink castor oil in front of their students or congregation. The king's successor, King Victor Emmanuel III, not known for his courage or manliness, promptly handed over the reins of government to their leader. The former priest-eater from the radical north had overnight become the new prime minister of Italy.

But he had much bigger plans. He despised the mess his country had become. However, instead of succumbing to fuga mundi, fleeing to the wilderness in search of personal transformation and enlightenment, he vowed to take Italy by the neck and reshape it in his own image. He'd start by rebuilding the Roman Empire. The fascist ideology he'd been working out for the past ten years would give him the structure he needed to pull it off. Still humiliated by the defeats of World War I and especially the devastating loss to the Germans during the infamous Battle of Caporetto, Italians had lost their pride and sense of purpose. He would give it back to them. Yes, he would demand great sacrifices, but they would not mind; they would be working for something larger than themselves. He had only one true competitor for their loyalty—the church.

So Benito Mussolini began formulating a plan that would not only solve the Roman Question once and for all, but would prevent the newly elected Pope Pius XI from standing in his way.

4

If, on March 3, 1958, you happen to spot the current *Time* magazine at your local newsstand and decide you want to buy it, you'll need to come up with a quarter. But you can already tell that it will probably be worth it. On the cover, a wildly grinning, Norman Rockwell–ish rendition of Teddy Roosevelt beside a moose medal hanging from a blue silk ribbon. On the back, a beautiful redhead in an evening gown giving a handsome, tuxedoed devil with an Air Force tattoo on the back of his cigarette-holding hand what is clearly the eye: "Where there's a Man, there's a Marlboro," declares the ad, adding helpfully that this is "the cigarette designed for men that women like." Inside, you find, there are articles on the launch of the X-15, the wonder of gyroscopes, the murder trial of Leopold and Loeb, and the crime of Minnie Lee—a sweet-faced, bespectacled elementary school teacher in Lakeland, Georgia, who made the fatal mistake of allowing a nine-year-old white boy who had missed his ride to take the "Negro" bus instead, and was subsequently forced to resign her position.

In the Religion section, you'll come upon an unusual photo for this time and place in America: two monks—"hermits," the writer calls them—wearing cowled, white habits. The clean-shaven monk on the left is smaller and younger than the other, and though smiling bravely at the camera, looks nervous enough that you suspect he is entirely out of his comfort zone. His compatriot is a different story: tall and strong, his flashing grin above a substantial beard that does not include a mustache and starts at the edges of his chin—hermit-style, apparently— projects the self-confidence of the Marlboro man on the back cover. You can tell that this is a person with energy and enthusiasm to burn. These two are called Dom Aliprando Catani

21

and Dom Agostino Modotti, and they have come to Manhattan via the ocean liner *Constitution* from their Camaldolese monastery in the mountains of Italy. They are here, they say, to look over prospective sites in Nebraska, Arizona, New Mexico, Colorado, and California for a possible American foundation. And the amazing thing is that there are already more than twenty applicants hoping to become hermits too!

The smaller monk—Catani—is not quoted in the piece. The big monk—Modotti—has plenty to say, and some of it is funny: "We are so impressed with the eremetical tendencies we see here," he says. "In our hermitage, each monk lives alone in his hut, pursuing his own way or meditating in silence. But in Italy, community life is very communal. An Italian who gets on a train introduces himself to his fellow passengers and states his business. The others do the same. Then follows a discussion of each one's affairs.

"But in America, what do we see? Each traveler minds his own business. He sits alone, free and silent, reading and contemplating—if not Holy Scripture, then at least the New York *Times*. You are hermits at heart."

From left, Aliprando Catani, Agostino Modotti, and Fulton Sheen

The arrival of two Camaldolese monks in America was a long time coming. Not that there hadn't been attempts to make an overseas foundation before. Each of the separated branches had tried at least once. In 1898, for example, the hermits of the Sacro Eremo experienced a powerful moment of inspiration during their annual retreat. A visiting Italian bishop from the southernmost state of Brazil was asked to say a few words to the brothers during their chapter meeting. He told them that he was moved by the peacefulness of their contemplative lives and impressed by the humility of their worship. How he wished he had a group just like them living close by in Brazil![1]

Four monks promptly raised their hands—we'll go! The South American monastery they built included both hermits and cenobites, just as Romuald's had, and was by all accounts successful. But their departure left the Sacro Eremo short-handed during a particularly precarious time. Being a monk did not necessarily exempt a person from conscription or monasteries from being appropriated by the military, so World War I further disrupted communities still trying to recover from the suppressions of the nineteenth century. The cenobitic branch of the Camaldolese, for example, saw sixteen of its monks march off to war. And after the war came more political turmoil coupled with the rapid rise of the new dictator, Mussolini.

Nearly thirty years after the exodus to Brazil, the hermits of the Sacro Eremo decided that enough was enough and called their four monks home on the grounds that they were not living the strictly eremitical life. But this was 1927, the nine-hundredth anniversary of Romuald's death, and the separated branches of the Camaldolese, hermits and cenobites, found themselves working together on a celebration. The unexpected success of the collaboration convinced them that something had gone seriously wrong in the past that needed to be addressed—and that maybe those eighteenth-century documents they'd been studying so assiduously for so many years had not prepared them for the twentieth-century future they were now facing. Traditional monastic reform, which in the past had always meant trying to recover the primitive practices of the original foundation—in this case, life as it was lived in the Sacro Eremo of 1085 when the prior, Blessed Rudolph, wrote the first Camaldolese constitutions—did not seem adequate at this time in history. They needed a broader understanding of Romuald's vision in order to move forward, work that Anselmo Giabbani and several other monks from the eremo, Benedetto Calati and Bernardo Ignesti, took up with great determination at the newly reopened Venerable Hermitage of Fonte Avellana in 1935.[2]

The thought of an American foundation, however, still lingered. Was this a way the Camaldolese could more fully live out the third aspect of the Three-Fold Good? Would Romuald have crossed an ocean to bear gospel witness to a still brash, young America? Could contemplative monastic life take root in the land of the Marlboro Man? Or was this simply another urge toward fuga mundi—leaving the old, tired, war-weary Europe for a new frontier?

The famous young monk and writer Thomas Merton had been living at the Trappist Abbey of Gethsemani for ten years when he underwent a powerful resurgence of the yearning that had driven him to the monastery in the first place. He needed solitude, he was desperate for it, yet even in this strictest of monasteries, it seemed impossible to find. His only brother had died in World War II in a fighter plane over the English Channel a year after he became a novice: Could this account for his spiritual unease? Was his unexpected and unasked for literary fame a bigger burden than he realized? Or had monastic life as he was living it simply become sterile?

Once again he recalled the large photo he'd found in the *Catholic Encyclopedia* the week before making his first retreat at Gethsemani: the ancient, mountain-fast Sacro Eremo of Camaldoli, with its high walls backed by stately firs, its white-plastered huts and red-tiled roofs, its individual gardens. He'd thought of that image every so often during his years at Gethsemani, writing in his journal on January 7, 1947, that he'd had a series of "big, spurious lights about becoming a Camaldolese hermit," though in response, he'd gone to confession and "got straightened out."[3]

But push the thought away though he might, he could not deny that the first sight of the eremo had struck him in his very heart. As he later put it in *Seven Storey Mountain*, "I had to slam the book shut on the picture of Camaldoli and the bearded hermits standing in the stone street of cells, and I went out of the library, trying to stamp out the embers that had broken into flame, there, for an instant within me."[4] Now it appeared that those embers had never died out.

Even more significantly, given his current state of mind, one of those cells had belonged to Romuald himself, the holy man who, nearly one thousand years before, had put into words *exactly* what Merton was urgently longing for: "Sit in your cell as in a paradise. Put the whole world behind you and forget it. Watch your thoughts like a good fisherman watching for fish. . . ."

Merton wrote his first letter to recently elected Prior General Anselmo Giabbani on September 11, 1952. Giabbani replied almost immediately. Neither letter any longer exists but according to Merton's journal entry in October, Giabbani told him that he could come if he wished and start right out as a hermit—exactly what he wanted to hear. On December 25, 1952, Merton wrote back with an overflowing heart: "Oh my father, I have an immense need for that silence, for that *quies* in which the soul rests. . . . I am worn out by the intense activism of the life of a writer, of a spiritual director, of a cenobite subjected to the demands of a timetable full of movement and activity."[5] It appears that, along with encouraging his eremitical impulse, Giabbani may have also asked Merton for his opinion regarding a possible American foundation because Merton requests that Giabbani send him the Camaldolese constitutions and promises to write to him again about the American idea. "I believe it is *necessary*. We need you."

Just after Easter, Merton writes a long letter to Giabbani, full of advice about the best way to get started in the States. He points out that a lot would depend on the source of revenue and suggests that it would be "quite easy for a monastery of contemplatives to support itself here with a big retreat house" that could be staffed by people other than the monks and "would not interfere too much with the peace of the hermits." But, he adds, "There is a fervent minority in America seeking the very purest ideal of the contemplative life in all its simplicity and poverty—the true simplicity and humility of St. Benedict, which is actually so incompatible with the spirit of secular life in America." In other words, just a hermitage with no cenobites nearby. He warns Giabbani of the "noise and bustling business spirit of America" and suggests that fund-raising be handled extremely discreetly. While American publicity methods might attract interest, they could quickly lead to contamination of the pure contemplative ideal.[6]

Giabbani responds on January 21, 1954, that "Your eremitical vocation is very interesting, even if you never come to the *eremo.* You demonstrate, however, the growing need of cenobitic spirituality, which as it develops wants to flow over into solitude." And then he adds, "I believe that monasticism without eremitical solitude cannot and will not be complete."[7]

In these few words, and no doubt without Merton realizing it, Anselmo Giabbani is letting him know that all is not well at the Sacro Eremo. And the issue is the same one the Camaldolese have been grappling with for centuries by now, which is, Who is the true monk? By which they mean, who is the true Christian? The hermit or the cenobite? After years of plumbing the ancient Camaldolese documents through the lens provided by the ressourcement theologians, with the help of other scholar monks like Benedetto Calati and Bernardo Ignesti, Giabbani is about to offer his solution to the ancient dilemma. But his proposal, encapsulated in a new set of constitutions, will cause a major rift between the hermits and cenobites of Camaldoli, one that will eventually travel across the Atlantic, over the mountains and cornfields and wheat fields of the United States, all the way to rugged and remote Big Sur on the isolated coast of California.

Thomas Merton was not the only person urging the Camaldolese to come to the US. The prior general before Giabbani, Pierdamiano Buffadini, started receiving inquiries about an American foundation at the end of World War II. In 1950, a college student named Jim Cottrell, working on a research paper for a class at St. Mary's College in Michigan, found a reference to Romuald in Butler's *Lives of the Saints,* and then Camaldoli in the *Catholic Encyclopedia.* He wrote an enthusiastic letter to one of the hermits, Dom Ambrogio, at the Sacro Eremo; the reply was very likely written, at least in part, by a recent entry into the order, one Agostino Modotti, who was fluent in both English and Italian.[8] Cottrell kept the correspondence going after graduation, asking whether there were any plans for an American hermitage, and was told that maybe they would be interested in coming if there were property available.

This was all the encouragement Cottrell needed. Soon he had launched a new organization, "Friends of the Camaldolese," and gotten busy writing articles for Catholic publications. He researched potential donors in *Who's Who* and wrote letters appealing for help. The response was unexpectedly positive; he heard back from Peter Grace of Grace Ship Lines, Clare Booth Luce, the famous Thomas Merton, and Harry John, a major Catholic benefactor. In 1956, Cottrell visited the eremo in person and got permission to meet Modotti, who by now had been a recluse for three years. The two of them struck up a warm friendship.[9]

When he returned to the States, Cottrell formed a group of supporters to help him get the plan off the ground. Several of them were well-connected diocesan priests; others were laypeople. There was money to raise, land to be looked at, and a whole lineup of bishops to be approached. All the Americans agreed: what they wanted—and eventually demanded—was something totally missing in this hustle-bustle young country of theirs: a real hermitage of pure contemplatives, no cenobites allowed. But it was in part the enthusiastic proddings of this group, who romanticized fuga mundi, had never been Camaldolese themselves, and did not know about the Three-Fold Good, that turned the smoldering family crisis at the Sacro Eremo into a full-blown blaze—one that nearly destroyed the future Big Sur foundation in its earliest and most vulnerable stage.

5

The priest-eater from the province of Emilia-Romagna—right next door to Tuscany and over the mountain from Camaldoli—knew what he needed to do to consolidate his already considerable political power: cut a deal with Pope Pius XI and thus the entire Catholic Church. It proved to be not that difficult. In 1925, he declared himself the "Head of Government, No Longer Answerable to Parliament" and began styling himself as "Il Duce." He could do this because, in an incredibly short amount of time, he'd successfully built a police state, thanks to his army of trained thugs, the Black Shirts. People were afraid of him and tended to do his will.

But there were impediments to his plan, many of them directly tied to the church. Catholic Action, a lay-run social justice group, had been allowed to operate without too much oversight by the Holy See. The group earnestly tried to apply Catholic teachings to contemporary social problems. Worse, Catholic Action—and particularly its university division known as FUCI—was quite popular among young people, the very group Mussolini needed to recruit to the fascist cause.[1] Even worse, at least from the fledgling dictator's perspective, was the immensely influential political party that sprang up after the pope finally allowed Catholic participation in politics at the turn of the century. *Partito Popolare*, or the Popular Party of Italy (PPI), was led by a priest from Sicily called Luigi Sturzo who not only declared fascism incompatible with Catholicism but, as far as Mussolini could tell, harbored suspiciously leftist sympathies. Mussolini was in total agreement with the church on this issue: those sympathetic with leftist causes were sitting ducks for the communist propaganda that had been steadily seeping into

Italy from Russia after the Bolshevik Revolution. Worse, *Partito Popolare* was dangerously independent of the Vatican, which was strongly invested in appearing apolitical. This party would need to be curbed or disbanded if Mussolini were ever to establish a working relationship with the pope.

So Sturzo was forced out of his leadership role in the PPI and, after a fascist assassination attempt, escaped to London, where he continued to speak out strongly against any cooperation of Catholicism with Italy's new dictator. However, with the gadfly Sturzo out of the picture, the Vatican was free to disavow the *Partito Popolare* and open secret negotiations with Mussolini, who had let it be known he was interested in settling the Roman Question once and for all.[2] Would the church finally reclaim its status as a temporal, and not simply spiritual, independent state? Yes—though considerably smaller in actual geographical size than it was before *Il Risorgimento* in 1870. Vatican City, the tiniest sovereign state in the world, was comprised of just 121 walled acres and would always be a mere postage stamp in the middle of a map of sprawling Rome—but thanks to Mussolini, the reigning monarch in this theocracy would continue to rule, unimpeded by Italy's secular government, over seventeen percent of the world's entire population.

Would Catholicism once again be the official religion of Italy? Certainly—as long as Pius XI and Mussolini carefully preserved one another's public images. Would the church be in charge of education of the youth? Well—not exactly. It was too important that children be formed into good little fascists. But by law religion would once again be taught in both primary and secondary schools. Crucifixes could again be hung in the classrooms. Priests and nuns could teach—but heaven help any antifascists among them. Would the church, woefully short of money since *Il Risorgimento* had stripped it of its temporal powers, finally be compensated for the loss of the Papal States? Naturally—Mussolini was more than happy to release 750 million lire, plus one billion lire in Italian bonds, to the floundering, Vatican-owned Bank of Rome.[3]

And in return? The pope would make sure that influential Catholic newspapers and magazines did not criticize Il Duce. The pope would formally disband what was left of Sturzo's antifascist

Partito Popolare, thereby eliminating once and for all any political opposition to the rule of the Fascist Party and its leader, Mussolini. The pope would refrain from publicly disagreeing with fascist policies that did not directly contradict Catholic teachings. Mussolini, himself a notorious adulterer, believed that a powerful Italy required strict social mores and that Catholic morality, with its emphasis on the sanctity of marriage, family bonds, responsibility, hard work, self-sacrifice, and the practice of virtue, fit nicely within the fascist ideology. He would ban public swearing. He would urge women to remain homemakers rather than work. He would strive to make contraception and divorce unheard of in Italy. He would close bars and wine shops if he had to—all to show his Catholic constituency that he was one of them, at least in spirit. All he had to do was get the pope to agree and everyone would be happy.

These negotiations, which were quietly conducted by surrogates of Pius XI and Mussolini so as not to arouse public opinion before they were complete, culminated in the 1929 Lateran Treaties and Concordats. For the most part, they were gratefully accepted by Italian Catholics, especially as the pope seemingly approved of Mussolini. Really, what was not to like? Mussolini appeared to be doing a good job of rebuilding the war-shattered Italian economy. He was making Italians feel proud of themselves once again. And the church was in far better shape than it had been for fifty years.

All this, at least, on the purely practical level. In fact, Mussolini and Pope Pius XI were oddly compatible in at least one significant way: they both harbored totalitarian visions. Mussolini understood that fascism was a kind of religion, one in which "man was viewed in an immanent relationship with a superior law that elevated and made him a member of a spiritual society."[4] In order for that to happen, however, the individual would have to give way to a "defied state." But a religion needed a god, which Il Duce, given his natural charisma, was happy to provide. And he understood the mythic power of history, of the ideals, power, and imagery of the ancient Roman Empire. So he set out to style himself as the heir of Augustus, the most impressive of the Roman Emperors.[5]

Pius XI could, on some level, understand that impulse to recover lost magnificence and reclaim a world-shaping role. The church had been steadily losing ground for the past five hundred years, and those who were determined to destroy it were no longer afraid to risk everything in the process. Modernity had fractured humankind from within, and the crisis of civilization was becoming more desperate by the day. The Catholic vision, he firmly believed, was both unifying and organic and had the power to heal the world. This was no time for a lukewarm, apologetic Christianity; what was needed was a Catholic spirit of "conquest, dynamic, youthful, even aggressive at times." For Pius XI, "objective totalitarianism" meant "everything that was needed for the totality of the citizens, in their domestic lives, individual existence, spiritual and supernatural elements. In this sense, only the Catholic Church could claim to be truly totalitarian."[6]

Such self-assurance on competing sides did not bode well for continued cooperation between the duce and the pope. The mutual satisfaction felt at the beginning of their new relationship was soon replaced by irritation, frustration, and anger when one pushed the other too hard in their ongoing power struggle over the soul of Italy. Worse, little did Pius XI know that less than a decade after signing the treaties with one dictator, he would once again be negotiating with another. Hitler, six years younger than his idol, so admired Mussolini that he kept a bust of Il Duce in his office. And at first, Hitler seemed to be nothing but a more brutish imitation of his exemplar. But soon it became clear that, thanks in part to its accords with Mussolini, the church was now in a far more dangerous and delicate situation.

It was one thing to carve out an official detente with the Vatican and another to convince suspicious Catholics, some of whom remembered him as the socialist who referred to priests as "black germs," that Il Duce was now on the side of the church. So he took care to look pious. First, he had his three children baptized. Then his wife, Rachelle, while vacationing with the family near Camaldoli, became friends with the prior, Timoteo Chimenti, and asked him if he'd be willing to give her children some religious education. By all accounts, Chimenti was thrilled with the opportunity and prepared young Edda, Vittorio, and Bruno for their First Communion.

A few months later, according to the Camaldolese monk Bernardo Ignesti, "Chimenti succeeded in bringing the duce himself, who arrived at the hermitage preceded by the might of a powerful Alfa Romeo, in the late afternoon of August 25, 1924 and was welcomed by the Major, in . . . pectoral cross, with all the honors. Father Chimenti even solicited Mussolini's privilege to kiss his hand, that hand that had put the fixed cross back in the schools and the Courts."[7] Like many Catholics whose fervent nationalism made them easy to bedazzle, Chimenti thereafter "became a fascist of mind, heart, language."[8]

But he was certainly not the only monk or religious to fall for Mussolini's bigger-than-life personality. Cardinal Vannutelli, a long-time friend of the Camaldolese who regularly vacationed in one of their houses in Tuscany, the Musolea, wrote to the pope's secretary of state, Cardinal Gasparri, that he, in fact, had personally presided over the sacrament of confirmation for Mussolini's children after Chimenti had given them First Communion in the church of the Sacro Eremo. Everything, Vannutelli assured the Holy Father, was conducted with perfect propriety and could not have gone better. It is clear from his letter that Vannutelli considers this a major coup for the church.[9] A year earlier, Vannutelli, in his official role as dean of the College of Cardinals, had publicly praised Mussolini as the man "already acclaimed by all Italy as the rebuilder of the fate of the nation according to its religious and civil traditions."[10]

Another proud fascist was the general of the Jesuits, Polish count Wlodzimierz Ledochowski, whose reign (1915–1942) spanned two world wars and a global depression. Elected in 1915, the birth year of both Thomas Merton and Aliprando Catani (the somewhat nervous-looking monk standing beside Modotti in that *Time* article in 1958), Ledochowski was firmly convinced that the biggest threat to Catholicism, and thus the world, was godless communism. And clearly, the Jews who had masterminded the Bolshevik Revolution—Marx, Lenin, Engels, etc.—were to blame. As he put it to the pope in a handwritten letter addressed to his secretary of state, Eugenio Pacelli, "[T]he atheist propaganda from Moscow becomes ever more intense, nonetheless the world press in the hands of the Jews, hardly makes a reference."[11] In 1936, convinced that the church was in imminent danger thanks to the communists, the Jews, and the Free Masons (whose bizarre version of religion, he thought, was clearly, dangerously pagan), Ledochowski formed a "Special Secretariat on Atheism." That spring, he summoned to Rome Jesuits from all over the world in order to enlist them in his impassioned battle against communism.[12]

It is entirely possible that Ugo Modotti, known for being both a fervent, old-school Catholic and an ardent anticommunist, was present at this congress. After sixteen years in India, where Mussolini-style fascism was established in Bombay by 1922, he had just returned to Rome, where he was working as the procurator of the Jesuit Italian mission in the subcontinent.[13] And his great gifts were apparent. He was fluent in both Italian and English. He was a fine writer and an inspiring speaker. In fact, by the following year, he would be working for the Jesuit broadcasting company Vatican Radio. So it's hard to imagine he would not have been invited to this world-wide meeting intended to shape the global Catholic response to the Red Menace. Or that he wouldn't have been recruited for Ledochowski's anticommunist corps.

Meanwhile, everything was going quite smoothly for the would-be Augustus and rebuilder of the Roman Empire. A year before Ledochowski's gathering of Jesuits, Mussolini attacked Ethiopia, supposedly in retaliation for an attack by Ethiopian forces on a group of Italian soldiers who were where they shouldn't be—far inside the Ethiopian border. Naturally, this constituted a stain on Italy's national honor.[14] Wily politician that he was, Mussolini made sure his Italian faithful were given the chance to go all in. If they weren't themselves in the army, they could still make major sacrifices for the war effort. For example, they could donate their family heirlooms—a golden broach, inherited from a great-grandmother, a precious locket, their wedding rings—and turn them in to be melted down. In fact, along with the meticulous records being kept by OVRA (Organization for Vigilance and Repression of Anti-Fascism), which was in charge of surveilling the population and arresting anyone who dared criticize the fascist government, this was a perfect way to weed out dissidents and malcontents; a family who did not give up their gold was automatically suspect.

And the scheme was designed to be global; wherever Italian immigrants, many of them desiring to put as many miles between themselves and Mussolini as possible, had settled in the world, they were fair game—even, though it was hard to believe, as far away as distant Australia. Send those wedding rings, they were told. Il Duce needs them.

6

Like many otherwise unremarkable places, the city of Udine needed a famous writer to thrust it into the public eye. Udine is on the Austrian border in the northeastern region of Italy known as Friuli. The area around Udine is thought to have been populated since Neolithic times, but the name itself was first recorded in 983, five years after the holy man Romuald formed his initial community of hermits just down the road toward Ravenna. Over the centuries, Friuli has changed hands many times as warring armies invaded and reclaimed it. In 1917 it was the site of the Battle of Caporetto, the worst Italian defeat of World War I, when the Austrians, aided by Germans using poison gas, finally broke the Italian line and forced its army into a massive, days-long retreat back toward Udine in the soaking rain.

In his novel *A Farewell to Arms*, Ernest Hemingway—who worked as a Red Cross ambulance driver on the Italian front during World War I—describes the retreat from Caporetto toward Udine and what it is like to be suddenly fleeing an advancing army: "In the night, many peasants had joined the column from the roads of the country and in the column there were carts loaded with household goods; there were mirrors projecting up between mattresses, and chickens and ducks tied to carts. There was a sewing machine on the cart ahead of us in the rain. They had saved the most valuable things."[1] But the swaying column of army trucks and troops and ambulances filled with wounded soldiers keeps grinding to interminable halts: "No one knew where the Austrians were nor how things were going but I was certain that if the rain should stop and planes come over and get to work on that column that it would be all over.

All that was needed was for a few men to leave their truck or a few horses be killed to tie up completely the movement on the road."[2]

Ugo Modotti, two years Hemingway's senior, was born in Udine in 1897, which means he was twenty when the Battle of Caporetto took place on his home turf. Though a prime candidate for military conscription, he'd already entered the Jesuits and was busy studying philosophy at Gregorian University in Rome when Italy suffered its terrible defeat. Were his siblings and his parents still in Udine? Were they part of the long, halting column in the rain? It is impossible to say. What does seem possible is that coming to young adulthood in the midst of a world war, especially when the results were so humiliating for your nation, might permanently shape your attitude toward politics.

In 1920, just about the time Mussolini won his deputy seat and began his rapid ascent to power, the newly minted Jesuit Modotti was given his first assignment: exotic Malabar, on the west coast of India overlooking the Arabian Sea. There, he studied theology at Kurseong and was ordained to the priesthood at the age of twenty-six. For the next sixteen years, he served as director of St. Aloysius College house and hostel in Mangalore, and was the rector of St. Joseph's College in Callicut.[3] Characterized by their open air, multi-arched corridors and sweeping veranda-style rooflines and broad green lawns dotted with palm trees, these were both fine Jesuit-run Anglo-Indian schools, established in the nineteenth century when the sun never set on the British Empire. But the term "Anglo-Indian" reveals the strict social hierarchy that prevailed in British-run India. At the top of the system were the well-born Brits in high-level positions they would eventually retire from in order to return to England. Below them were the middle-class English ex-pats who kept the system running: post office officials, army sergeants, train conductors—bureaucrats who would never make enough money to leave the subcontinent. These were the Anglo-Indians, and this group also included Brits who married Indians. At the bottom of the pyramid were, of course, the Indians themselves—also divided into categories within the strict Hindu caste system.

But just before Modotti arrived, the established order had been dramatically shaken up. The young lawyer Mahatma Gandhi, in protest against recent legislation that stripped Indians of crucial civil rights, had organized his first peaceful demonstrations. Even worse in the eyes of his opponents, he was championing the cause of the "Sweepers," also known as the "Untouchables," the very lowest of the low in the elaborate social system. Gandhi's demonstrations terrified the British, who had long feared what might happen should the enormous, murmuring population of India finally decide it had had enough of the memsahibs. British anxiety at the sight of so many Indians united behind a common cause sparked the infamous Amritsar Massacre of 1919, when British rifles were turned on an unarmed, peaceful crowd of protesters, killing five hundred and injuring over a thousand—and thereby accelerating the growing clamor for Indian independence. Once again, Modotti had landed in the midst of a political maelstrom.[4]

As did the British writer E. M. Forster, who arrived shortly after Modotti did, and whose famous novel *A Passage to India* paints a vivid picture of the cruel colonial society in which the young Jesuit found himself. But Modotti would have soon discovered that there was more to India than the burgeoning struggle for freedom. India is the birthplace of the world's oldest religion, one that takes fuga mundi to a dizzyingly destabilizing degree for those not adequately trained. Advaita, samadhi, the Void—Forster describes the spiritual crisis precipitated in the very British Mrs. Moore after she enters an ancient cave and, for the first time in her conventionally Christian life, has an experience of Rudolph Otto's numinous: "What had spoken to her in that scoured-out cavity of granite? What dwelt in the first of the caves? Something very old and very small. Before time, it was before space also."[5] Mrs. Moore is never the same, and in fact, dies very soon after this experience.

How did Modotti respond to the spiritual challenges that India must have thrown across his path? We don't know, though it is interesting to speculate, given his eventual attraction to the contemplative Camaldolese. There is some evidence that he was involved in the Syro-Malankara Catholic Church in Kerala, a branch of the church legendarily established by St. Thomas in the first century, which means he may have learned to speak some Malayalam along with English, Italian, and Latin. If so, he preceded by several decades a fellow Camaldolese who also practiced the Syrian rite and struggled to learn Malayalam. In the 1950s, Bede Griffiths, a Benedictine monk from Prinknash Abbey in England, would spend ten years co-directing a Christian ashram in Kerala before moving on to take the reins at Shantivanam—"Forest of Peace"—in the neighboring province of Tamil Nadu in South India.[6]

In the late 1930s, Modotti returned to an Italy still under the thumb of its dictator and his grandiose imperial vision. Mussolini and Hitler had just formed the Rome/Berlin Axis. The quasi-fascist monarchist General Francisco Franco was now receiving massive support from the Italian government to crush pro-democracy revolutionaries in Spain. In the midst of all this drama, Modotti was sent on to his third continent (before he died, he would live in five of them). He was tapped for the mission by the father general of the Jesuits himself, Wlodzimierz Ledochowski, who had been asked by soon-to-become pope Eugenio Pacelli to find a good Jesuit to serve in Australia as a chaplain to its extensive Italian immigrant population. The request for help had come from the most powerful prelate in Australia, Archbishop Daniel Mannix of Melbourne, a towering, majestic, outspoken Irishman who lived to be ninety-nine and bore a deep resentment toward the British Empire and all its works and all its ways. The Australian Church had traditionally been run by Irish priests and bishops, but Mannix, despite his fierce Irish patriotism, believed the future lay in developing a truly Australian Catholicism.

This meant that the Italian Catholics, whose religious style was completely different from that of the Irish (Italians tended to be more Franciscan, more connected to the earth, more likely to be emotionally moved by their faith than the more nationalistic, virtue-centered, no-nonsense Irish), needed to stop congregating solely within their own ethnic group and start assimilating.[7] A major impediment to this plan was that many did not speak English well, if at all. Another was the racism of the English and Irish Australians, who openly mocked and denigrated the often uneducated and unsophisticated peasant farmers from Italy. A third was the ominous presence of Mussolini's octopus-like global surveillance system. Who in the Italian community could even be trusted? The reality was, however, that though some immigrants had fled Italy because they themselves were antifascists (the origin of today's term Antifa), and some had left because they were socialists, communists, or anarchists and had suffered mightily at the hands of the Black Shirts, the vast bulk of them were simply looking for a better shake—and were ready to welcome a priest who spoke their language.

Modotti's arrival was heralded with enthusiasm by all the Catholic papers in Melbourne. The *Advocate* raved, "Venice, India, Australia: Brilliant Jesuit comes among Us," adding that even though Modotti's mission was "approved by the Duce," it was "purely religious and has no political significance whatever."[8] Yet the Italian consular officials, well-known as Mussolini's fascist henchmen abroad, were clearly filled with delighted anticipation at his coming. The Italian Consulate in Melbourne wrote to the Italian Minister of Foreign Affairs that Modotti was a "fascist and an Italian and has had the honor of being received by the Duce in Rome." They immediately set to work to use him for their own purposes, going so far as to collect money to buy him a Fiat, though others, including Mannix, contributed also.[9]

But Modotti seemed intent on carving out his own path. Soon after his arrival, he ordered Catholic men to stop wearing their black shirts to religious festivals and meetings. He started a new Catholic women's group, *Gruppo Cattolico Femminile,* even though a fascist women's group (which included many Catholics) already existed.[10] He set up English classes and encouraged immigrants who had been attending the Italian language classes offered by the highly political Club Cavour in Melbourne to start coming.[11] And he launched a new periodical—*L'Angelo della Famiglia* (The Angel of the Family)—that he promised would be strictly religious. On a personal level, he maintained cordial relationships with people of all political stripes.

However, several Italian Australian scholars are convinced to this day that he was indeed working within the church as an agent of Mussolini.[12] They point to his columns in *L'Angelo* describing antifascists as atheist traitors to their fatherland, and accusing them of having "abandoned" Italy. They describe his habit of branding all antifascists as communists, a common reactionary slur. They quote lines from speeches and essays that appear to bolster their thesis, this one in particular from the quarterly *Vade Mecum*: "[H]istory—impartial judge—will show how far-sighted and wise was Benito Mussolini's domestic policy that in understanding the value of religion has wanted to return to the homeland as a better guarantee of that renewal and of that grandeur that has made Italy the mother of the people."[13]

Yet despite these damning accusations against him, much evidence exists that Modotti was not an undercover fascist agent posing as a chaplain to the Italian immigrant community, but instead a traditional Catholic priest of his day—a man who was at times openly grateful for the ways that Mussolini had improved the lot of the church, but whose true loyalty was unshakably to Catholicism. In the eight years he spent in Australia, he worked tirelessly to further the aims of Archbishop Mannix, which was to create a truly Australian (not Irish, not Roman) Catholic church. Countless letters in the Jesuit archives in Melbourne attest to his unflagging concern for the immigrant parishioners in his care. He was clearly much loved by those he served. And he was bold and creative in his efforts to pull together a community that had become divided and despairing because of the political strife in the homeland.

He was the driving force behind a welfare program for the Italians after World War II broke out. His most lasting material legacy was no doubt the Lourdes Grotto he conceived and built on the grounds of St. George's parish church in Carlton. Italian construction companies and tile workers volunteered their labor to build this sanctuary out of 120 tons of stone and cement. Several well-known communists and anarchists were part of the crew. The grotto celebrated its grand opening in August 1941, and thousands came to marvel.[14] But Modotti had not yet run out of creative ideas. Toward the end of his time in Australia, he envisioned a Jesuit house where several priests might live to serve the community and figured out a way to purchase a residence in Manressa.

Meanwhile, back in Italy, Mussolini had finally gone too far. On June 10, 1940, emboldened by his "Pact of Steel" with Hitler and not bothering to first get approval from his Grand Fascist Council, he declared war on both Britain and France. Repercussions for the Italian community in Australia as part of the British Commonwealth were swift. The government ordered the immediate internment of all "enemy aliens" and "potential saboteurs," which meant that even some naturalized British subjects were rounded up as potential threats. Modotti, too, was targeted. His arrest warrant, stating that "detention is considered necessary or expedient in the interest of public safety," was signed by the lieutenant general of the Southern Command himself. Two plainclothes officers pulled up at the Jesuit House in Manressa the following day. One of them opened the door of the unmarked vehicle and gestured for Modotti to get in, but he slammed it in their faces, jumped in his own car, and sped off toward Mannix's house, Raheen in Kew, with the officers in chase behind him. Mannix immediately called the minister for the Army to lodge a protest, and was promised that no further action against Modotti would ensue.[15]

But Military Intelligence was not completely satisfied. Modotti was placed on travel restrictions and continued to be surveilled by the Security Service. From September 1940 on, in addition to the Italian residents already imprisoned, Australia took on 18,500 Italian POWs sent by Britain. The logic was that they would have a harder time escaping and making their way home if they were housed on a whole other continent.[16] Modotti was not only heavily involved with the Italian migrant internees, visiting them in the camps, carrying letters from their loved ones, pressing for their release, but he also visited the Italian POWs.

Then a POW named Simoni escaped, remaining at large for ten months and driving the authorities crazy. The Commonwealth Investigation Bureau was sure that Modotti was aiding and abetting him. The bureau decided to set a trap by hiring a secret agent, code-named "Colletti," from the American Armed Forces, who would approach Modotti in the confessional, pretend to be an American deserter, and beg him for help. What they didn't realize was that the politically savvy Mannix—no doubt hoping to shield Modotti from exactly this kind of dangerous and delicate situation—did not allow him to hear confessions.

When he was finally captured, Simoni was indeed carrying an identity card forged from Modotti's, but it turned out that he had stolen it and this, plus the vigorous defense mounted by Mannix and other influential friends, finally convinced the authorities that Modotti was not a danger to the security of Australia.[17]

Yet his troubles were not over. The worst was yet to come. Soon he would find himself embroiled in a church-related political controversy that would force him to leave his beloved Australia for good. And the sorrow that overtook him at this point led him to a place that—Jesuit-trained as he was, good soldier in the army of the pope—he may well have never reached without the incentive of despair at the state of the world: true fuga mundi.

During the mid-1870s, roughly the same years that the Camaldolese were figuring out how to survive the monastic suppressions of *Il Risorgimento*, the first Big Sur homesteaders were engaged in their own quest for survival. The wild coast had for several thousand years provided a home for the Esselens and Salinans, whose presence was noted by Spanish explorers. Though the first white settlers were often mountain men or wagon train guides, they did not have centuries of accumulated knowledge about what it took to live in the remote and challenging coastal environment of Big Sur. Unfortunately, by the time they began arriving after arduous treks over the precipitous Santa Lucia Mountains, the tribes were gone, their culture and acquired wisdom and any advice they might have offered long since wiped out by European diseases and the unforeseen effects of the Spanish mission system. Only a handful of Indigenous people remained, and they were soon assimilated through marriage or employment.

One would-be settler—himself a former scout and ox-team driver—was Gabriel Dani, a Vermonter of French Canadian heritage who had met his English wife, Elizabeth, on the westward trail. Once they arrived in Southern California, the young couple booked passage north to San Francisco, sailing past the spectacular cliffs and peaks of Big Sur during the voyage. The savage beauty of the coast took their breath away. Could they make a life in this daunting wilderness? By 1876 they had been ranching in an interior valley east of the coastal range for several years and had five children but had not forgotten about the coast. This, it seemed, was the time. They set off with a friend who had offered to carry the baby over the mountains, their other four kids trailing behind on horseback.

At one point, little Mary's saddle began slipping and Gabriel lifted her off to tighten the cinch, but the mountainside was so steep that her feet, numb from riding, slid out from under her. Down the mountain she rolled, not stopping until she hit a tree. The family Newfoundland, named "Watch," raced down and held her in place until Gabriel could rescue her.[1]

Like other homesteaders, the Danis scraped by. Gabriel got a job working for Tom Slate, owner of what would someday become Henry Miller's much-beloved hot springs. Slate paid him in dried peas and corn, which he carried home on his back to his wife, who ground them into flour for bread. A year later, the Danis finally moved onto their own homestead, which was situated just a little south of the ancient border between Salinan territory and Esselen land to the north, and began raising goats, hogs, cows, and the crops to feed them. The round of work was endless and had to be supplemented by Gabriel's periodically leaving his family on their own in order to find farmwork in the inland valleys. During one of these forays, he lost an arm in a threshing machine.

The poet Robinson Jeffers first set eyes on the Big Sur coast in the early 1900s, not so many years after the Danis' arrival, and as the Danis had, as so many others have since, immediately succumbed to its compelling beauty. By 1914, he was living with his wife, Una, in Carmel, fifty-one miles north of the Dani homestead. The two of them ended up making, as Una put it, "a thousand pilgrimages" south down the coast and into the backcountry, where "with books and maps and local gossip we have tried to piece together a fairly complete picture of this region, its treasures of natural beauty and vivid human life."[2] Jeffers had a darker soul than his cheerful wife. In his poem "The Coast Road," about the building of Highway 1 (in his eyes a disaster that would destroy the wilderness), he asks:

> Where is our consolation? Beautiful beyond belief,
> the heights glimmer in the sliding cloud, the great bronze gorge-
>   cut sides of
> the mountains tower up invincibly
> Not the least hurt by this ribbon of road carved on their
>   sea-foot.[3]

Jeffers was convinced, and Henry Miller would concur three decades later, that the daunting landscape had the power to transform the psyches of those who tried to live there. But Jeffers would have disagreed with Miller's belief that the sheer magnificence of the natural environment made for nobler people. In contrast, he saw in the dazzling juxtaposition of sea, cliffs, and mountains something close to Rudolph Otto's *mysterium tremendum*—a force so overwhelmingly magnificent that, in its face, humans become insignificant. As he put it, "It is not possible to be quite sane here."[4]

This attitude may explain why his famous poem cycles about the pioneers of Big Sur, often compared to the tragic epic poems of the ancient Greeks, are filled with destructive fires, massive floods, shipwrecks, violent death, incest, rape, murder, and suicide. The bleakness of his poetry shocked the literary world of his day, but as he pointed out, he was basing his poems on actual stories told to him and Una during their extensive explorations of the coast.

Arguably, the saddest of these tales involved the Dani clan. Alvin Dani, one of the four kids on horseback who watched in amazement as their little sister rolled down the mountainside, married a girl from another family of Big Sur pioneers in 1895. But Mary Ellen Pfeiffer, who had been raped while alone in the Pfeiffer ranch house nine years before, was not well. In fact, she'd been committed to an asylum in Stockton following the attack. Though she would never reveal the name of the father, or even whether he was a stranger or a local man, she had gone on to bear and raise her rapist's son. Despite now being married to Alvin, Mary Ellen Dani was a haunted woman; a year after her third child was born, she killed herself with strychnine.[5] Her grave, standing within its own small picket fence, lies on NoName Ridge, on a grassy knoll overlooking the Pacific.[6]

Fifty-eight years after Mary Ellen Dani's suicide, the onetime Jesuit Fr. Ugo Modotti, formerly of India and Australia, arrived at the site of the old Dani homestead with real estate agent in tow. At sixty-one, he wondered if he were up to the task that lay ahead.[7] It had been a long, difficult journey. Though that time of sorrow now lay behind him, part of his heart would always remain in Australia.[8] The political tightrope he'd had to walk during the war years, including the surveillance and attempted arrests by the Security

Service, had been challenging though not surprising or even disillusioning. It was only when a powerful churchman leveled a false accusation that went all the way to the pope that he experienced momentary despair.[9]

Apostolic delegate Giovanni Panico had been assigned to Australia for a couple of years by the time Modotti arrived. An apostolic delegate is in a peculiar position: he is sent to a country that has no diplomatic relations with the Holy See, and to make things more challenging, he has no official power to deal with the civil government. His job is to make sure the national church hierarchy is in tune with Vatican policy—however, if he is savvy enough, he can surreptitiously wield significant political influence in the country in which he serves. Modotti would certainly have understood this; his own cousin from Udine, Ildebrando Antoniutti, had been the apostolic delegate to Lisbon and Albania for the past few years and was now serving, one step up, as the charge d'affaires in civil war–torn Spain.

Panico's goal was twofold: to change the traditional Australian practice of appointing Irish priests as bishops and to gain control over the religious formation of the Italian immigrant population on behalf of Rome. His immediate challenger was the most powerful prelate in Australia, the fiercely patriotic Irishman Archbishop Daniel Mannix. Long expected to be declared a cardinal, Mannix had his own ideas and was not about to have them thwarted by a Roman delegate. Instead of complying with Panico's wishes, Mannix chose Modotti to spearhead the Italian immigrant religious formation project.[10]

Panico then set out to undermine the Irish archbishop's status in the Australian Church by surreptitiously attacking Mannix's right-hand man. He informed the provincial of the Jesuits in Melbourne—Modotti's immediate superior—that Modotti was considered a security risk by the Australian authorities and was thus no longer permitted to receive or transmit messages from immigrants to their relatives in Italy via the Vatican. He sought to block Modotti's application for Australian naturalization. He tried to interfere with Mannix and Modotti's plan to build the Jesuit center in Melbourne by inviting another order, the Capuchins, to come to Australia instead. And finally, when through Panico's influence Mannix was bypassed for the cardinal's hat (it was given to a much younger and less experienced bishop), Panico was unexpectedly presented with his perfect chance to get rid of Modotti once and for all. The influential federal minister Arthur Calwell, a friend and defender of both Mannix and Modotti, issued a sharp public criticism of the choice of cardinal, pinning the blame firmly on the apostolic delegate and suggesting he be fired: "I hope that Archbishop Panico's influence in Australian church politics, and in Australian affairs generally, will cease with his early return to Rome."[11]

Panico immediately informed the interim father general of the Jesuits, Norbert de Boynes, that Modotti had encouraged the federal minister to make this embarrassing statement—one that created a delicate situation for the Holy See. In a country that had no formal diplomatic relations with the Vatican, a government official was not only criticizing the crowning of a new cardinal but publicly attacking a Vatican-appointed delegate. And this was not the only official complaint Panico had made about Modotti; given his well-documented request for information on the Jesuit priest from the head of the Australian Security Service, it is certainly conceivable that these questionable "facts" were included in his letter to Rome. De Boynes sent Panico's complaint about Modotti directly to the Vatican secretary of state—which meant directly to Pope Pius XII.[12]

Meanwhile, Modotti—unaware of what was going on at higher levels, but inexplicably uneasy nevertheless—sailed for Italy, where he was charged with finding a group of Jesuits willing to come live in the new center at Manressa and serve as chaplains to the Italian immigrants. It didn't take long after arriving in Rome for him to realize that something was very amiss—and it soon became clear that he would not be allowed to return to the country he'd grown to love. He was crushed, writing to the priest who'd been charged with forwarding his mail that he had been strangely "moody and disheartened" even before leaving Melbourne, intuiting at some level that troubles lay ahead—but "still, never would I have believed what I heard had been reported here." He felt abandoned by those who should have some to his defense. He summed up his state of mind, saying simply: "I have not yet recovered from the blow and I do not know if I ever will."[13]

Banned from ever seeing his beloved *Opera Religiosa Italiana* come to life in the house at Manressa, he was once again assigned a desk at Vatican Radio, where, in an event perhaps arranged by his cousin from Udine, Ildebrando Antoniutti, he interviewed General Francisco Franco in 1949. And then he made a retreat with the Trappists at the ancient monastery of Tre-Fontane near Rome. And then in 1950, no longer a Jesuit, he arrived at the door of the thousand-year-old Sacro Eremo of Camaldoli and asked to become a hermit. He made his profession in December of 1951, the very year that Dom Anselmo Giabbani—a Camaldolese for more than thirty years by now—was elected prior general of the order.

If Mussolini's decision to declare war on Britain eleven years before had thrust the Italian immigrants of Australia into a painful situation not of their own making, his fall from power on July 25, 1943—thanks to two separate and intricate plots—had thrown Italy itself into complete chaos. But first, ecstatic joy. Paolo Monelli, writer and journalist, describes what happened in the capital: "The silence of the summer night is broken by songs, screams, clamors. . . . 'Citizens, wake up, they arrested Mussolini, Mussolini to death, down with Fascism!' It sounded like the scream of a mute who gets his voice back after twenty years."[14]

Yet the fascists didn't simply melt away. And Hitler was not about to accept the loss of his Axis partner. It didn't take long for the Nazis to free Mussolini and set him up as a puppet leader in northern Italy. What they didn't factor in was fierceness of the resistance—the antifascist partisans who were hiding in the hills all over the northwest. The ensuing bloody civil war lasted for well over a year and, because of the brutal German policy of taking ten lives for every one lost on their side, resulted in several horrific massacres.

One of the worst was not even an official reprisal but instead the work of a drunken lieutenant and sergeant who seem to have committed this war crime for the sheer pleasure it gave them. Camaldolese Prior General Antonio Buffadini recorded in his war diary what happened to the village of Moggiona. On September 11, 1944, a traumatized nine-year-old boy appeared at the Sacro Eremo and "with difficulty, through sobs and tears . . . managed to ask for help for his poor mother who had been seriously wounded in the breast and one thigh and who was still lying in the cellar in the midst of the nineteen corpses of people who had been killed four days earlier." Little Aurelio Ceccherini said it was only when they couldn't bear the stink of the dead and their own ravishing hunger that his mother, "trusting me to the care and protection of the Madonna," allowed him to go for help to Camaldoli. A week later, the monastery underwent a bombardment that killed a young girl, Alessandra Acuti, who had been brought there by her mother in hopes of finding safety. Some months later, the bodies of two murdered partisans were found in shallow graves among the stately firs ringing the hermitage.[15]

Mussolini died soon after. When the Allies got close to the German defenses in northern Italy, he tried to escape but was captured by partisans. On April 28, 1945, two days before Hitler's suicide, Mussolini's twenty-one-year dictatorship was ended by an executioner's bullet. But what happened next could have come straight out of one of Robinson Jeffers's Big Sur epics. Il Duce's body and that of his mistress were flung down in the Piazzale Loreto in Milan and left to the mercy of an angry crowd. Their corpses were beaten, hit with hammers, and shot at—and then hung upside down from a steel girder above a service station, as though somehow, this act of public retribution could bring back everything that had been lost.

All of this, only five years before Modotti arrived at the Sacro Eremo in hopes of becoming a hermit. And now, here he was, starting over once again on the edge of a new continent in the grip of a new fuga mundi. Seeking that which Jeffers, enslaved to his own dark vision, occasionally managed to find in spite of himself:

> The ocean has not been so quiet for a long while; five
>   nightherons
> Fly shorelong voiceless in the hush of the air
> Over the calm of an ebb that almost mirrors their wings.
> The sun has gone down, and the water has gone down
> From the weed-clad rock, but the distant cloud-wall rises. The
>   ebb whispers.
> Great cloud-shadows float in the opal water.
>   (from "Evening Ebb")[16]

8

As Henry Miller had discovered on Partington Ridge, the spiritual challenges of living on the coast could at times be overwhelming, but the day-to-day practicalities were what could really wipe you out. How about your water source, for example? Did you have a good spring? And if not, a nearby creek? And fuel—where did a person get that? Could you really grow food on such steep slopes? Yes, those hardy enough to survive the homesteading era had done all right for themselves, but they were a whole different breed, weren't they? And even they couldn't keep the earth from shifting beneath their feet during quakes and landslides. So how did you, a twentieth-century modern person, keep your house from rolling down the mountain like little Mary Dani?

The best answer was, unsurprisingly, money. If you had access to unlimited funds, you could beat the odds against making it on the coast. Which meant that Robinson Jeffers's dark prophecy came true in the high-rolling Roaring Twenties, when the monied began buying up one of the most beautiful coastlines in the world. Media baron William Randolph Hearst led the way by purchasing 240,000 acres of prime land north of Cambria and south of Ragged Point as a site for his dream castle.[1] The wealthy buyers who followed in his wake were not merely looking for profitable real estate investments. They, too, were enchanted by the coast. But the fuga mundi they were seeking was different from the one sought by the penniless young artists who tracked down Henry Miller two decades later. The typical Big Sur investor was not looking for a nitty-gritty coastal life, but instead a private sanctuary, well-protected from prying eyes—a retreat when the hurly-burly of the business world got to be too much.

In the late 1920s, the entire Big Creek area north of Lucia was purchased by a team of developers, Horton, Marble, and Gorrell, who planned to turn it into a resort for wealthy outdoorsmen seeking a spectacular setting for horseback riding, hunting, fishing, and soaking one's troubles away in a natural hot spring. George Harlan, whose family had ranched next door to the Danis since pioneer days, was more than happy to earn extra money by constructing roadways, installing water pipes, and splitting logs for fencing.[2] In the very early 1930s, the two-story hewed timber building known today as "the ranch house" was built as part of this project.

At roughly the same time, a real estate broker named Marian Hollins, working on behalf of an investor named Edward S. Moore, was busily buying up as many of the old homesteader ranches as she could get her hands on, including the Dani property. Despite the looming Depression, the Harlans firmly refused to sell. After the Big Creek investor team defaulted, Hollins was able to add their acreage to the holdings of her Santa Lucia Corporation. In 1931, all of it—nearly ten thousand acres—became the property of her wealthy backer, Edward S. Moore, who named his acquisition the Circle M Ranch.

Moore offered Harlan, who only had three hundred acres of usable cattle land, a six-thousand-acre grazing contract in exchange for one quarter of his annual net profits. In addition, Harlan was to supply Moore with a butchered nine-hundred-pound steer every two weeks, a tricky operation given that the butchering had to be done under a tree using a winch.[3] Moore was allegedly preparing the ranch as a haven if the Depression got too serious. After Highway 1 was completed later that decade, Moore built a gigantic mansion on Point 16, the large bluff below the highway that noses out over the sea. He was not able to spend much time there; thanks to the unstable ground beneath it, each winter the house invariably began to list and had to be jacked up and re-leveled. In 1944, finally defeated, he sold eight thousand acres of the Circle M to a man known as "The Golden Voice of Radio."[4]

John Nesbitt, host of the popular nationally broadcast radio show *The Passing Parade*, did not live on-site either but maintained the grazing contract with George Harlan, minus the butchered steer every two weeks. He hired Harlan to cut a road up to the ranch buildings, increase dairy production, maintain the local gardens and orchards, and dig a swimming pool. Near the end of World War II, Nesbitt asked the Harlans to move onto the Circle M where Esther Harlan became ranch cook. He himself lived in Carmel but used the ranch as a retreat from the busy world of radio broadcasting. With the advent of TV, he lost his contract with MGM and found himself in financial trouble. In 1955 he sold the Circle M to two ranchers from King City, who soon put it back on the market, this time in parcels.[5] And when the parcel made up of Section 9 and much of Section 16 was shown to the real estate agent working on behalf of Fr. Joseph Klinglesmith, he immediately got in touch with his client.

Klinglesmith, as a member of the Friends of Camaldoli committee formed by Jim Cottrell, had been looking for potential hermitage sites for several years by now. Both Klinglesmith and Cottrell had visited Old Camaldoli and were hoping to become hermits themselves, so Klinglesmith had a personal stake in where the Camaldolese finally wound up. His excitement fairly quivered off the page in the letter he wrote to Modotti: "To me the view is [i]ncomparable to anything I have ever seen. The setting is Camaldoli with the sea added."[6] Modotti himself was temporarily ensconced at the Monastery of the Angels in Hollywood, where he could more easily fundraise among the celebrities who lived there. Perhaps because the rich and famous had long since discovered Big Sur, this proved easier than he'd anticipated, especially when fellow Jesuit and consummate fund-raiser Pedro Rebello arrived from India in September of 1958.

Rebello made contact with Bob Hope, whose wife was a devout Catholic; not only was she willing to donate to the cause, she suggested he talk to fellow Catholic Bing Crosby. Rebello found out when Bing was going to be in his office, walked in, and bluntly told him that for the salvation of his soul, he needed to help support the hermitage. Bing promised one Saturday's take at Lick Pier in Long Beach when Lawrence Welk was wielding the baton.[7] Even the legendary Cecil B. DeMille got involved. DeMille's personal assistant, a writer and former priest named Donald Hayne who was remarkably well-informed about the Camaldolese, agreed to write a recruitment booklet for the new foundation.

But celebrities outside Hollywood were also intrigued by the project. Several years before, Merton had told Giabbani, "We need you here," and the famous television personality Bishop Fulton Sheen certainly seemed to agree. Modotti had met him in New York soon after disembarking from his transatlantic voyage, and Sheen had continued to send him short, witty, encouraging letters in his beautiful cursive handwriting. Really, the only discouraging words had come from Thomas Merton's superior, Abbott James Fox, who diplomatically but firmly told Modotti and Catani not to bother stopping in at Gethsemani on their way across the country (by then, the question of Merton's becoming Camaldolese had been firmly answered, and it was a no). But even Fox had nothing but praise for the idea of an American foundation.[8]

The real challenge, now that the perfect site had been found—and it did sound perfect, what with its two-story main house and second even larger house, not to mention the swimming pool (a swimming pool? what did monks need with a swimming pool?), in addition to four cottages and a well-built barn, several work sheds, and an unfinished steel-framed building—the real challenge, beyond paying for the six-hundred-acre parcel (the asking price was $100,000! how would they come up with *that*?) was to get the bishop of Monterey/Fresno on board. This cenobitical setup would get the monks through a couple of years, but at some point—they were hermits, after all!—they'd have to start building individual cells. And that would take a lot of muscle and a lot of money. Would Bishop Willinger agree the project was worthwhile?[9]

He would, with several stern stipulations. No funds would come from the diocese. The monks would have to be self-supporting. And this hermitage must be a *real* hermitage, which in his mind (a view of things strongly encouraged by Modotti) meant hermits only, no cenobites allowed, and certainly no large guesthouse like the one at the motherhouse.

Letters flew back and forth between California and Italy. Giabbani told Modotti he had already written to the pope for permission to send five hermits to America. Modotti told Giabbani they had obtained the full purchase price of the property, now bargained down to $75,000, thanks to a group of American donors in Milwaukee who were eager to support contemplative foundations in the States.[10] Another major Catholic donor named Harry John, the heir to the Miller Beer fortune, had written out a check for building costs. And by July 28, 1958, Bishop Willinger had given his canonical approval for the new foundation and the Congregation of Religious in Rome had officially said yes. The project was off and running.

But for Dom Agostino Modotti, who really did appear to be some kind of human lightning rod, trouble once again lay ahead.

The end of World War I left Italy in a deeply divided state. The question was, Whose ideals for the nation would now prevail? Mussolini, determined to rebuild the Roman Empire, had tried to resurrect the ancient warrior ethic. Average, everyday Italians were suddenly to become legendarily loyal, epically valorous, impeccably self-disciplined, stunningly fit: in short, battle-ready citizen-soldiers, fully prepared to die for the duce and the nation. The church, which for the past 150 years had seen itself as a mighty fortress under siege, was on somewhat the same page, perfectly at home with the term "Church Militant" and the image of Catholics as stalwart foot soldiers, charged with defending the faith against heretical secular modernists.

Monks were also moved by this moral call to arms, which had its parallels in desert spirituality. The Christian hermits of the third and fourth centuries were viewed as spiritual warriors sent into the wilderness to fight the demons on behalf of a sleeping world. The severe ascetical disciplines that so appalled the British historian Edward Gibbon were not only in service of purifying the heart and clarifying the vision but were part and parcel of the monastic warrior ethos, which gave pride of place to the hermit.

The Camaldolese reflected this thinking in their Book of the Eremitical Rule, written in 1085 by Blessed Rudolph, fourth prior of the Sacro Eremo. "Who," Rudolph asks, "could adequately commend the ancient fathers who lived in the deserts of Egypt, the Thebaid, and Nitria . . . ? These are they who went around covered in sheepskins and goatskins, poor, distressed, and afflicted. . . . They wandered through the deserts, on the mountains, in caves, and in grottoes. They crucified their flesh with its vices and concupiscences."[11] But this harsh, self-sacrificial existence was worth it, for "this is the life that conquers the world, represses the flesh, vanquishes demons, cancels sins, holds vices in check, and exhausts the carnal desires that fight against the soul."[12] The Rule enumerates the practices considered essential for a healthy solitary life: along with continual prayer, recitation of the psalms, frequent confession, and practice of the virtues, the hermits were expected to engage in self-flagellation, periods of strict fasting, regular abstinence from many common foods, occasional bloodletting, sleep deprivation, silencing of the tongue, and—though optional, always admirable— the wearing of a hair shirt.

The rewards of the hermit life, however, were beyond compare, which is why the first Camaldolese constitutions, decided upon after much discussion and written down by Blessed Rudolph, gave absolute and perpetual primacy to the Sacro Eremo. The hermits would always be in authority over the brothers down below at the Fontebono hospice. The eremo would never, under any circumstances, become a cenobium, and to ensure that it would not, the prior of the Sacro Eremo would hold authority over any foundations that might become attached to Camaldoli in the future. And to make absolutely, totally, and *completely* sure, Rudolph added the following: "If a prior of this Hermitage, or someone else of a diabolical nature, murderous and sacrilegious, should dare to transform this glorious Hermitage into a monastery of cenobites and uproot the customs of this place and holy practices . . . . we curse, excommunicate, and anathematize him forever, with many lit candles. Amen."[13]

These dire words would come back to haunt the twentieth-century Camaldolese. Anselmo Giabbani, who along with Benedetto Calati and Bernardo Ignesti had been studying the ancient sources, would have surely known the curse by heart. Yet a thousand years after Blessed Rudolph uttered it, the Camaldolese situation had changed. By now there were centuries of major accomplishments in philosophy, science, and the arts, many of these pursued in cenobitical houses, that seemed to contradict the notion that the strictly eremitical life produced the better fruit.

Cardinal and theologian Peter Damian, in spite of remaining a hermit, was far more famous for his active life as a reformer of the church; he is valorized in Canto 21 of Dante's *Divine Comedy* and was declared a Doctor of the Church in 1872.[14] The Florentine cenobium called Holy Mary of the Angels was known for producing painters on the level of Lorenzo Monaco and influential thinkers like the philosopher Ambrogio Traversari. The cenobium of Fontebono at Camaldoli became a college and a center for intellectual humanism. The cenobitical St. Michael of Murano produced Mauro the Cosmographer. And in the early nineteenth century, a Camaldolese cenobite reigned as Pope Gregory XVI.

Yet, the same old question still lingered in the air: who were the real monks, the hermits or the cenobites? Giabbani and his fellow scholars were more and more convinced that the question was moot. Despite the sudden brutal suppression of the Camaldolese Cenobites in 1935, the ancient Camaldolese symbol of the two doves drinking from the same chalice seemed to point the way toward the future. The three-part charism did the same. It was time for new constitutions.

Giabbani presented a draft to the hermits of the Sacro Eremo in 1954, the year after Modotti became a recluse. The understanding was that everyone, including the recluses, would have an opportunity to offer a full-throated response and that this response would be carefully considered by the whole order before the document was finalized and sent on to the pope for approval. But three years later, Giabbani's version achieved official status and a full-blown hermit rebellion ensued.

The issue was twofold. First, the hermits took Rudolph seriously; their way of life was meant, in perpetuity, to hold the place of primacy within the order, a foundational truth they believed was being cast aside in this new version of the constitutions. Second, at least some of them were still driven by the ancient monastic warrior ethic, and cenobites, by definition, did not qualify under this set of standards. They did not live in the wilderness, like the austere and self-sacrificing hermits of the Sacro Eremo, but instead tended to gravitate toward high-culture cities like Florence and Venice. They were too involved in the intellectual life of the world. They were effete city mice as opposed to stalwart country mice.

The hermit rebellion, though fierce, was bogged down by procedural rules, and so they turned to the man most qualified to do battle for their side, the brilliant former Jesuit who spoke both fluent Italian and fluent English, the recluse who had lived so many lives before he came to them, the man with a powerful cardinal for a cousin. The controversy grew more bitter as Modotti—formed as a Jesuit to object to decisions he disagreed with—refused to back down in the standoff with Giabbani. Inevitably, the conflict made its way to Rome, mortifying the order and causing deep wounds within the community.

In the midst of all this, the pressure from America continued unabated via the Friends of Camaldoli committee established by Jim Cottrell. It's time to cross the ocean! It's time to found a hermitage in the States! And who, the thought came, would be a better choice to spearhead such an operation than the rebel in the Sacro Eremo, a man who clearly knew how to operate in the world, who knew how to negotiate with people in power, who spoke perfect English—and, given his role as translator for Giabbani, had also been in touch with this very committee for quite some time?

Who else indeed?

Modotti, 1958

9

In the winter of 1959, a Pomona College senior named Robert Hale was overtaken, like so many other young men during this era, by an intense longing for fuga mundi. And as usual, Thomas Merton was to blame. Hale, a straight-A philosophy student destined for grad school, had read Merton's latest book, *The Silent Life,* at exactly the wrong moment—only months before his final exams. The book concludes with words that riveted him: "One of the most venerable and ancient shoots of the primitive Benedictine stock is the Order of Camaldoli. This Order explicitly takes upon itself the task of providing a refuge for the pure contemplative life in solitude."[1] And now, he'd heard, the Camaldolese had made a foundation on the Big Sur coast. There was nothing for it but to go.

The friend who drove him up the precarious dirt road carved by George Harlan for the Circle M Ranch thought Hale was making an Easter Week retreat. But Hale had already made up his mind: if he truly had a vocation, he would soon know it, and if he *did* know it—if he felt the conviction reverberating in the very core of his being—why, then, he would simply stay on until somebody either threw him out or welcomed him into the community. It was that simple. Plus, he'd learned from one of the books he'd been reading that this is how you did things in the world of monks.

His friend parked the car, caked with road dust, in what appeared to be a dirt parking lot, and the two of them got out to look around. Hale soon spotted a wiry monk in full white habit plying a shovel in a little garden below some wooden ranch buildings. He introduced himself, explaining that he was the college student who had written the prior and been told to come. The monk, who didn't appear to understand what he'd said, rushed off to find someone who did. Soon, Fr. Modotti—for this large man with the gloriously long beard had to be him, didn't he?— came smiling toward him. Like the other monk (and despite all the dirt), Modotti wore the white habit of the Camaldolese. He welcomed Hale warmly in perfect, pleasantly accented English, then took him to his guest room in the hewn timber ranch house built nearly thirty years before by three would-be dude ranch owners from Wyoming.

Modotti's cell, ranch house, 1958

The following day, Modotti called Hale into the little shack that served as his cell. The other two Italian monks were already there waiting. What are your impressions so far? Modotti asked him. What are your plans? Hale told them that he hoped to begin monastic life immediately, not even returning to Pomona to take his finals and go through graduation exercises. A long pause, then—but do you think that is the most reasonable choice? Wouldn't it be more prudent to return and graduate, then come to the hermitage afterward? Of course it would, Hale thought but did not say. Yet there were good reasons for doing it his way. He explained that he'd already been offered a Wilson and other scholarships to continue studies at the graduate level and felt a lot of peer pressure to stay on the academic track. If he returned and announced he was going to become a hermit, everyone would try to dissuade him from taking such a curious side road.

The three monks pondered, then came to a decision. He was assigned the job of librarian, organizing the books that were pouring in as gifts from supportive parishes and seminaries. Given that his mother had been a librarian and he himself a library page, this suited him just fine. But there were rough shoals still ahead, the first being that it was time to inform his advisor, Frederick Sontag, that he would not be coming back to school. Horrified, Sontag consulted the only Catholic professor on the faculty to see if he could find out more about these hermits. The professor confirmed Sontag's worst fears: the Camaldolese were a minor, ultra-austere eremitical order, nothing to take seriously. Sontag jumped in his car and made the five-hour drive to Big Sur to talk his prize student off the ledge.

Modotti met Sontag when he arrived, had a friendly conversation, and then, "with a kind of insightful shrewdness and already aware of [Hale's] stubborn determination," told the professor he could talk with his protege as long as he wanted.[2] Sontag did, bluntly conjecturing that Hale was simply "freaking out" from fear of the upcoming finals and that he should just stir up his courage, go home, and get the job done. Hale responded with youthful indignation; he had no fear of the finals, he declared, but also no intention of leaving the hermitage. So Sontag presented him with a challenge: would he be willing to take his finals on-site? He would, if Fr. Prior Modotti agreed.

But first he got a lesson in monastic obedience. He'd brought many of his philosophy and religion books with him, thinking he would donate them to the nascent hermitage library. As it turned out, he would not—or at least, not all of them. Sartre, it appeared, was unsuitable for hermits, as were Kierkegaard, Niebuhr, and Tillich. Teilhard's *Phenomenon of Man*, a gift from the physics professor at Pomona, turned out to be okay despite the *monitum* (a warning rather than an outright condemnation) leveled by the Holy Office of the Doctrine of the Faith against it.

Meanwhile, he was getting to know the fledgling community. There were the three from Italy: Fr. Modotti, the nervous Fr. Andrea Agnoletti, who'd so precipitously fled when Hale first greeted him, and Fr. Adalbert Paulmichel, who was from the South Tyrol area of northern Italy and spoke with a gentle German accent. The new foundation had already attracted several American postulants besides. None, as far as Hale could tell, were what you'd call "ordinary men," and he was immediately struck by an important insight: the Camaldolese seemed to attract a remarkable diversity of types. The question was, how did you get such different personalities to come together in community?

One of the Americans, Francis Gannon, was a swaggering Texan who could never pass up the opportunity for a good argument; in the coming days, he and Hale began to form a relationship characterized by frequent, fierce, but friendly philosophical and theological debates. Another would-be novice, Philip Klee, had been a conscientious objector in World War II and was already fifty-two when he arrived. He not only took diligent care of the cow, he slept in the barn in his rarely washed white habit. A third, Michael Burke, was already ordained. And a fourth, Marino, was a short, rotund man with a full beard and a cherubic smile. Hale, a lifetime Episcopalian, was a bit shocked at the number of hours Marino spent conversing with the three-foot-high statue of the Infant of Prague that stood in the back of the chapel.

The flow of potential novices remained steady. A day after Hale's arrival, Bruno Barnhart drove in from the east. A Navy man with a degree in chemical engineering, he had lost an eye in a laboratory experiment. Right behind him came John Coulson, formerly of the British secret service, who spoke fluent Italian. And a few months later, Jim Cottrell, whose Friends of Camaldoli committee had been so instrumental in kicking off the American foundation project, finally made it to the hermitage he'd helped fund.

Although the official novitiate had not yet been opened, the group of postulants began formation under Modotti's tutelage. For his first conferences, Modotti focused on the Rule of St. Benedict, which he insisted should be considered *the* Holy Rule, as it had been the primary rule for Western monasticism since medieval times. He also introduced his students to Blessed Rudolph's Book of the Eremitical Rule, pointing out, without mentioning the still-smoldering family crisis at the Sacro Eremo, the emphatic emphasis on the primacy of the hermitage. Finally, he lectured them on a subject close to his heart: the mystagogical interpretation of the psalms. *Mystagogy,* Hale discovered, meant "interpretation of mystery" and was concerned with initiation into the sacramental mysteries of the Catholic Church. Modotti had begun writing a mystagogical manuscript called *Jesus in the Psalms and Liturgy* while he was still in Italy.

Hale was an enthusiastic learner, though he found that Modotti's reflections could sometimes be a bit off-putting. "He had a large clock on the wall of his wooden shack, and the tick-tock was quite pronounced. He said he often meditated on just that—on the passage of time, on impermanence, on the deeper present moment we should endeavor to dwell in, open to eternity."[3] Modotti's devotion to Mary helped soften the starkness of his tick-tock view of things. He told his postulants that he had worn a Mary medal since childhood in Udine, primarily because his mother had insisted that going out without his medal would be like going out naked.

But he could be challenging for eager young postulants. There was the matter of the discipline, for one thing. Just as described in the Book of the Eremitical Rule, they too would take the discipline—self-flagellation with a small scourge while reciting the *Miserere* (Psalm 50)—every Friday alone in their often extremely chilly rooms in the old bunkhouse. Gannon the Texan was so zealous that the others could clearly hear the dramatic sounds of the little whip connecting with his flesh. As Hale recalls, "There was even blood on his wall!"[4]

Modotti could also be quite blunt. "Later in 1959," says Hale, "I had accumulated a series of grievances (or were they murmurings?) and took them to his cell and resolutely presented them to him. He . . . replied firmly at a certain point, 'Well, this isn't a prison! If you want to leave, you always can!' That sobered me up and helped me put my laments in perspective. I assured him I was committed to New Camaldoli all the way. One of his exhortations: beware of 'ad oculos,' doing things to be seen and admired by others. It was a temptation for young monks."[5]

Robert Hale and Bruno Barnhart, 1959

From the moment Modotti took up residence on the newly acquired Big Sur property in the summer of 1958, he had been in close touch with Prior General Giabbani and other monks in Italy. He wrote voluminous letters, full of details about the donations that were pouring in, both monetary and material, including goats, cows, pews—and, thanks to the generous Italian American farmers of the Salinas Valley, quantities of good food. He described the would-be postulants he was hearing from, his interactions with the bishop, the daily Office schedule, the religious items he would need for the chapel. He answered Giabbani's questions about the recruitment pamphlet they had published, written under the pseudonym "Michael Bede," and the fact that it was actually composed by the personal secretary of Cecil B. DeMille of *Ten Commandments* fame. He enumerated the spiritual needs of the tiny community and urged Giabbani to send five monks soon.[6]

Giabbani, writing in Italian in tiny square typescript on ancient-looking Sacro Eremo letterhead, addressed Modotti with apparent affection and expressed gratitude for all that was transpiring in the new American foundation. He approved of the speed and efficiency of Modotti's handling of this truly difficult project and assured him of his ongoing help. He promised to send the five monks as soon as he got permission from the pope and to ship the "religious goods" needed for the chapel when he could. He mused out loud about why everyone seemed to be sporting beards and whether Americans might find this monkish custom off-putting (Modotti assured him that all the American postulants—for what reason, he could not explain—wanted to grow beards immediately, so the prior general shouldn't worry). Despite Modotti's leadership role in the hermit rebellion, both men seemed determined to put the bitter family feud behind them and move on.

But underneath the apparent good cheer, a new conflict—firmly rooted in the old—was building. The only reason Modotti had been able to fund the purchase of the property, he believed, was that he had assured the Friends of Camaldoli committee and other donors that the new foundation would be strictly eremitical. The only reason he'd been able to convince Bishop Willinger to give canonical approval for a new foundation in his diocese was because he, Modotti, had guaranteed that New Camaldoli would be made up solely of hermits. The only reason he was hearing from so many young inquirers, including the ones who had already arrived, was that they believed New Camaldoli would be a true, old-fashioned hermitage. And until he was absolutely and completely assured by Giabbani that this is what they would have—that there would be no nearby cenobium or, even worse, large guesthouse as at Camaldoli—then he could not in good conscience accept postulants into the novitiate.

Giabbani, in turn, reiterated that New Camaldoli *would* be a *sui iuris* hermitage and hermitage alone, over which Modotti would act as superior. *Sui iuris* is a legal term meaning "the right to manage one's own affairs," as opposed to being a dependent house, which is managed by a superior somewhere else. As soon as Willinger set his final seal of approval on New Camaldoli, the new hermitage would be self-sustaining—it would not be run by the diocese. Nor would it be run by Old Camaldoli. It would, however, be regularly visited by the Camaldolese superiors from Italy, and it would have to accept the ultimate authority of the prior general, in this case, Giabbani. But—and this was critical to what happened next—the constitutions of the order *had* to be translated into English, and the community *had* to abide by them. In fact, they had to be translated before the official novitiate could even open. And anybody who spoke against them would be punished.

Herein lay the sticking point. It was these controversial 1957 constitutions that had triggered the hermit uprising in the first place, thereby fracturing the community at Camaldoli. What was so offensive about them? First, in the eyes of the hermits, they violated Blessed Rudolph's thousand-year-old insistence that the Sacro Eremo would always retain authority over all other houses, especially cenobitical houses. The hermits felt that the new constitutions were giving the cenobites the upper hand. Second, the hermits felt they had been shut out of the discussions—that indeed Giabbani had written most of the new constitutions himself. Third, they were deeply offended that the Holy See had given its approval before the Camaldolese had even come to an agreement among themselves. And to bolster their position, they sent a formal letter of objection to Pope Pius XII—which was no doubt written by their spokesman and leader, Modotti.[7]

Ironically, it was this very controversy that had opened the door for Modotti to go to America. But had he been sent only for the purpose of getting the project off the ground? Would he be called back to Italy as soon as he had things up and running? And would Giabbani ultimately send an Italian to take his place as superior—an Italian who would promptly build a guesthouse and cenobium and run things according to those ill-founded new constitutions?

To some degree, he was not simply the victim of an overactive imagination. He knew there were those who believed he'd been sent into exile so he couldn't cause more trouble at home. He knew that some monks at the motherhouse jokingly or not so jokingly referred to him as "il ducetto," the "little duce"—not funny, after being shadowed by the security police in Australia. And he'd been told by several people he trusted that Giabbani was planning to replace him soon. So even as he worked day and night to create a new monastic community, he was growing increasingly suspicious.

The arrival of the two hermits from Italy in the fall of 1958, Agnoletti and Paulmichel, only made things worse. They confided to Modotti that they had come not of their own free will but under duress. They told him they had both asked for the "transitus," a document that would allow them to leave the order, but instead had been sent to America under threat of ecclesiastical censure if they disobeyed. And they confirmed Modotti's suspicions that he would soon be replaced.

Then, as though reflecting the dangerous level of tension in the air, a fire broke out in the most valuable building on the property, the villa built by radio announcer John Nesbitt. Several days before the blaze, two of the postulants had found a painting in the house: a pink elephant on its hind legs, wearing an apron and carrying a tray of drinks. At the time, they speculated that it was a symbolic representation of the debauched parties that must have taken place on the property. Now, as the small community battled late into the night of December 4 against the inferno, they wondered if this was a divinely ordered purification taking place—maybe even a sin offering for any moral excesses that may have occurred on what was meant to be a holy site. Especially since despite their best efforts, the building was a total loss.[8]

Modotti immediately sent word to Giabbani and also to Dr. Francis McGinley, a member of the Friends of Camaldoli fundraising committee. The miracle was, as he put it, that "while in the few days past we had had plenty of wind, it was now perfectly still, and the flames went straight up to heaven as in a holocaust, barely scorching the trees all around. . . . It was finally 1 o'clock before the fire was completely subdued, and we could somehow take some rest and feel relieved of the fear of a conflagration which would have been a terrible disaster, not only for us but for the surrounding countryside as well."[9]

For Modotti, however, the worst was yet to come.

10

On Christmas Eve 1958, Modotti wrote two letters, both of them long. One was to Prior General Anselmo Giabbani. In it, he complained bitterly about the news he had learned from Agnoletti and Paulmichel. They should have never been forced to go to America, he said, and he himself should have never been misled by his Camaldolese superiors about their true intentions. He could not in good faith accept new postulants nor open an official novitiate until he knew for sure what was going to happen next.

The second, at Bishop Willinger's behest, was to Pope John XXIII. He explained the seriousness of the situation in Big Sur: "As long as the present Constitutions are in force, there will always be the immediate danger that the scandal and tragedy of Italy will be repeated in America." He asked that the Vatican intervene to make sure that the new American foundation would proceed as planned. But then he added a paragraph that was guaranteed to backfire on him: "We are also anxious to remain united to our Motherhouse at Camaldoli, but if this is not possible on account of the circumstances enumerated above, rather than compromise with our eremetical profession, we beg of Your Holiness to grant the recommendation of our Bishop, the Most Reverend Aloysius Joseph Willinger." And what was the bishop's recommendation? That if Modotti and Giabbani could not reach an iron-clad agreement about the strictly eremetical nature of the foundation, then Modotti should break with the Camaldolese entirely and attach the hermitage to the diocese of Fresno.[1]

Thanks in part to Klinglesmith, who was in Italy when much of this story was unfolding, concerns about whether or not New Camaldoli would ever become a true hermitage or instead be appropriated by the Camaldolese superiors for cenobitical purposes quickly leaked out in the fledgling Big Sur community. Rumors began circulating in the American monastic world as well, particularly among the Trappists, and some hermitage postulants wondered out loud whether Modotti was indeed the right leader for the new foundation. Modotti remained in close touch with Willinger, who asked him to specify the problems with the new constitutions, which he did in another long letter written on January 20, 1959.[2]

When Willinger made an informal visit to New Camaldoli in March of 1959 to see for himself what was going on, he was immediately approached by one of these postulants, who poured out his worries that the hermitage he dreamed of would never come to fruition. Afterward, Willinger severely chastised Modotti for allowing the group to become so fractured. In his letter of March 12, 1959, he wrote: "The impression I carried away was that all was not well at Camaldoli, that instead of a spirit of contemplation and spiritual happiness I found an atmosphere of division and dissatisfaction. It was most dis-edifying and left my soul disconsolate. It seemed that my approbation and patronage of the Order had come to naught and the blessing of God had not rested upon the effort. My one response and hope are that the Holy See will recognize our petition and approve the setup as determined by the original agreement regarding the Foundation in the diocese."[3]

On March 23, the Sacred Congregation of Religious responded to separate letters from Modotti and Giabbani. Given that the situation was so "delicate," Cardinal Valeri urged Giabbani to go to New Camaldoli himself in order to "meet with the persons concerned," in an attempt at "clearing the queries that have arisen."[4] Giabbani, who would be accompanied by official visitors Catani and Dom Placito Menchini, began planning his trip to America.

He made his visit in early June. While he was still in the States, he spoke by phone to Willinger, apparently reaching an amicable understanding and declaring himself moved by the bishop's obvious care for and concern about the new foundation. On June 20, now back in Italy, Giabbani sent Modotti the order's official response to his persistent queries, a formal document from the Camaldolese General Council: 1) the new foundation would be, as promised both orally and in writing, strictly eremetical, with an eremetical novitiate, and its "own traditions adapted to local needs," but 2) the novitiate could not open until the new constitutions were translated into English, and 3) there would be no more appeals to higher authorities, and no more false interpretations of the constitutions or the orders of superiors, or there would be "serious and painful measures" taken. Meanwhile, "we heartily bless your efforts and pray to the Holy Spirit that he may be generous with light and wisdom, particularly in the choice and formation of novices."[5]

The constitutions again! They could not seem to get past those dratted constitutions. And as long as he was forced to keep them at the forefront of his mind, Modotti could not relax. Worse, rumors continued to fly. It became more and more obvious that the original controversy at the Sacro Eremo had neither been resolved nor the resulting wounds healed. Perhaps because of his terrible disillusionment in Australia and his sense of being abandoned and betrayed by those he thought should have come to his defense, Modotti seemed incapable of backing off now. If so many passages in the new constitutions were not ever going to apply to New Camaldoli, then why did he have to translate them for his would-be novices? Wouldn't they only confuse them? Worse, wouldn't these flawed constitutions sow doubt that the new foundation would always remain strictly eremitical?

Once again he turned to Bishop Willinger, who, on July 7, 1959, took matters into his own hands. His letter to Cardinal Valeri of the Sacred Congregation of Religious lay down his requirements for continued diocesan approval of the new Camaldolese foundation in America. It would be for hermits only. It would be in no way subject to or dependent on any other houses in the order. It was to have its own novitiate. No monks could be transferred anywhere except to a strictly eremitical foundation. No cenobites were allowed. The novitiate needed to open immediately. And if the property was not used strictly as a hermitage, it would automatically revert to the Diocese of Monterey-Fresno.[6]

Given Willinger's somewhat high-handed tone and apparent lack of knowledge regarding Camaldolese history and tradition, Rome's reply on August 12 was a masterwork of diplomacy. Though Rome thought that the two parties were essentially in agreement, it was necessary for Willinger to modify two of his conditions. "First of all, though the foundation is to be *sui iuris,* it must nevertheless be directly subject to the Abbot General [a.k.a. Giabbani] of the Camaldolese Order. . . . [A]ny other arrangement would do violence to the essential unity of the Order, and would be equivalent to establishing a new Institute." The same applied to any disposition of personnel. Somewhat surprisingly, given his previous forcefulness, Willinger seemed to accept that there was nothing further to be done at this point. He sent a copy of the official response to Modotti, with a handwritten note at the bottom of the page: "The reply may or may not clarify the situation completely, but I think that for the present it could be made workable."[7]

Meanwhile, there was increasing worry at Old Camaldoli that Modotti was simply not going to work out—that, in fact, he was incapable of leading this new foundation without once again becoming a major thorn in the side of the order. An Extraordinary Diet (special formal deliberative assembly) met on August 5, 1959, to discuss the situation, and the consensus was that Modotti was becoming a big enough problem that something had to be done. One of the monks wrote an extremely negative assessment of the original decision to send Modotti to America at all, given his combativeness while he was supposed to be in reclusion at the eremo. The foundation had been launched in bad faith and was thus doomed and would not survive, the letter writer dourly predicted, just as had happened in Brazil forty years before.[8] Information about the secret Diet made its way to Modotti via Agnoletti and Paulmichel: the council had "decided to replace [Modotti] as soon as possible." Worse, they were "substituting him with" Catani, who came from the suppressed cenobitical congregation of St. Michael of Murano, had not lived the eremitical life, and did not even speak English.[9]

Modotti was furious and responded to the news with two more voluminous letters of complaint, one of them directed to the customer service department for monks, the Sacred Congregation of Religious, and the other, as usual, to Giabbani. In both, he protested vehemently against the secret Diet and its conclusions. In so many words, he accused his superiors of betraying him. On September 1, he and Agnoletti and Paulmichel wrote a second big letter, this time to Monsignor Romoli of the Holy Office (the familiar name for the Holy Office for the Doctrine of the Faith, historically known as the Inquisition). By drawing the Holy Office into the fray, Modotti was subtly suggesting that his superiors were not only guilty of betraying him but of heresy besides.[10]

On September 25, Aliprando Catani, Prior General Giabbani's first assistant and the very monk who'd sailed across the Atlantic with Modotti when the mission to America was first launched, made a not-entirely-surprising visit to New Camaldoli. Though Modotti immediately assumed the worst, he was there, Catani insisted, to help. He assured Modotti that he would push for the long-delayed opening of the novitiate. And he would also make clear to Giabbani that Modotti had no intention of breaking away from the order. But by now, the pot had reached the boiling point. When Willinger was informed that Catani had arrived, presumably to take over Modotti's job as superior, he ordered his chancellor-secretary to write him a scathing letter. Whether he was there at the behest of his Italian superiors or acting on his own, Catani was in error. Big Sur was not yet a canonical community, and wouldn't be until the Sacred Congregation of Religious formally approved.[11]

How did a new house qualify for canonical approval? The superior named in the constitutions of the religious institute concerned (in this case, the prior general of the Camaldolese, Anselmo Giabbani) could only establish the house after obtaining in writing the consent of the bishop of the diocese (in this case, the bishop of the Monterey/Fresno diocese, Joseph Willinger). Once he had obtained this consent, the religious community had the right to 1) exercise in accordance with canon law the works proper to the institute (for the Camaldolese, this meant living by their official charism, the *Triplex Bonum*, or Three-Fold Good) while at the same time observing any conditions that the bishop had attached to his granting of consent (several of which had already been dismissed by the Sacred Congregation of the Religious), and 2) to lead a life that accorded with the character and proper purposes of the institute (which for a thousand years of Camaldolese history had meant the uneasy but fruitful tension between eremitical and cenobitical life). As far as

Giabbani and the council were concerned, these canonical strictures clearly implied accordance with the constitutions of 1957.

But thanks in large part to Modotti and his many promises to the fund-raising Friends of Camaldoli in America, not to mention his interviews in numerous American periodicals and his appeals to prospective donors who were enthralled with Thomas Merton and his intense focus on fuga mundi, Americans were convinced that New Camaldoli must be strictly eremitical, no cenobites allowed, or the new foundation would become a cancer in the soul of the Camaldolese. Modotti's passionately held position, though perhaps understandable given his fraught personal history, was clearly wrong. The Camaldolese had always been far more nuanced, complex, and open-minded than a strict reading of the thousand-year-old Book of the Eremitical Rule, written by Blessed Rudolph, could ever imply. Giabbani, as a pioneer of ressourcement ("returning to the sources") and *aggiornamento* ("bringing up to date") within the order, understood the subtleties of Camaldolese spirituality and was ready to lead his monks into a whole new era. Willinger, on the other hand, was taking his cues from an implacable traditionalist, Modotti.

The stern letter from the chancellor-secretary to Catani went downhill from there. The diocese was officially refusing to extend him its hospitality. Catani had entered the United States "fraudulently" by coming in to the country on a tourist visa, and the only ecclesiastical authority that could bring him in permanently was Willinger. Thus, Catani was forbidden to say Mass beyond the next three days and forbidden to use any of the faculties of the diocese besides. More, there were "many other aspects of the case that we do not like. The present representative of the General [Modotti] speaks English very well. He has the good will of the Bishop, the clergy of the diocese and of the Foundation that purchased the land and which is contemplating further purchases."[12] All of these parties and others, too, would be offended by Modotti's removal. Therefore, Catani must return at once to Italy while everyone awaited the decision of the case before the Sacred Congregation of Religious, which had just been vastly complicated by Giabbani's attempted coup.

Willinger followed up the Catani letter with a direct appeal to Rome, while Modotti, Agnoletti, and Paulmichel wrote their own letter to Monsignor Romoli of the Holy See, telling him Catani had said the new foundation was about to be closed, though they had no idea why. By December 1, 1959, it was clear that Willinger had had it in regard to waiting for a decision. In a ferocious letter to Modotti, he wrote, "This whole thing has become disgusting and unworthy of any institution with such noble ideals. I have been clear about my desires. I desire that you return to Italy, Fr. Modotti, take with you whom you desire, see the Holy Father or whomever he wishes you to see and obtain from the competent authority the necessary documents to establish the hermitage."

Modotti wrote this note at the bottom of Willinger's letter: "The Bishop told me to go, send a telegram to Fr. General [Giabbani] from LA when leaving; the Bishop wrote to Romoli informing him he was sending me and Dom Andrea [Agnoletti] to speak directly with the Holy Father."[13] What happened next is not entirely clear. Some years later, Jim Cottrell—who had started the Friends of Camaldoli committee that helped kickstart the American foundation and was a loyal ally of Modotti—composed a long, dramatic handwritten account of what he remembered Modotti telling him about the fiasco in Rome. All of this is secondhand, however, and at the present time, not verifiable through other sources, so what follows is a necessarily truncated version of the story.

Cottrell writes that once arrived in Rome, Modotti was ordered to go, under obedience, straight to a Camaldolese hermitage. There, he was locked in a cell like St. John of the Cross, where he languished for some weeks. He was forbidden to wear his habit or say Mass. He was in fact undergoing the strictest form of monastic excommunication possible, aside from being drummed out of the order, and it is ironic that this eerily medieval punishment was imposed on him by a superior he deemed insufficiently traditional.[14]

But perhaps Giabbani's decision was prompted by more than the anger of a prior toward an insubordinate monk. Long ago, shortly after Modotti entered reclusion, he and Giabbani had exchanged several long letters about what it was like to become an "inmate" of the hermitage. The issue had come up over Modotti's desire to hear confessions coupled with Giabbani's concern that, as a recluse, he could easily become overly involved with people, which would not help him maintain the solitude and silence to which he believed himself called. Modotti was miffed about Giabbani's restrictions—yet after he was finally allowed to become a confessor, it was he who knew best what was going on in the hearts of the hermits who joined the rebellion, which may be why they chose him as their leader. And this, of course, is where his troubles with the order began. Perhaps Giabbani was really acting out of a particularly tough kind of love. Perhaps he knew that Modotti had never really lived the life of a recluse, and that this was partly his own fault for sending him under obedience to America. Perhaps he was giving him another chance at the solitude and silence he'd never truly experienced.

In any event, Modotti was not freed until he got a letter to Pope John XXIII via his Jesuit confessor. The pope sent a telegram to Giabbani ordering his release and advised Modotti to seek a dispensation from his Camaldolese vows. This he did—after first going to his powerful cousin, Cardinal Antoniutti, and describing the whole mess in detail. If it was indeed Antoniutti who launched the subsequent investigation into the Camaldolese Order, then it took nearly three years for Giabbani to pay the penalty for imprisoning the cardinal's cousin.

11

Within a few weeks of his Easter arrival, Robert Hale knew he had made the right decision. By coming to New Camaldoli, he had truly come home. Not that life at the hermitage was easy. But hermit life was not meant for the faint of heart. The fact that it took toughness and guts, along with a level of humility he did not yet possess, was in part why he had to do it. Raised Episcopalian, he'd converted to Catholicism relatively recently. Monastic practice was not only helping him dive deeper into the Catholic perspective on his Christian faith, he was learning about himself in a way that may have never happened in academia—though he had not abandoned that path either. With Modotti as his proctor, he'd taken and passed his Pomona College finals and was already thinking of graduate school, this time, of course, as a Camaldolese monk.

Perhaps even more importantly, he'd discovered that you didn't have to be a natural-born academic in order to live with intellectual rigor in this wilderness hermitage. Everyone, future priest or not, was expected to feed his mind with nourishing food. He was thrilled, for example, by the first official retreat presented to the postulants. Fr. Raphael Vincerelli, founder of St. Andrew's Abbey at Valyermo, offered "substantial conferences," all based on the work of the brilliant young theologian Fr. Cyprian Vagaggini, who would one day become Camaldolese himself. Hale found these talks on Vagaggini's *Theological Dimensions of the Liturgy* intellectually stimulating, thoroughly monastic, and richly contemplative, and he credited this retreat with helping the community move forward "solidly" during this first phase of its existence.[1]

Sadly, this inspiring retreat took place shortly before Aliprando Catani, first assistant to Prior General Anselmo Giabbani, was unceremoniously thrown out of the diocese by Bishop Willinger. Did Hale know anything about the cataclysmic events occurring just beneath the surface? It appears that he did not, which says much about Modotti's ability to hold things together for the young men in his care despite the stress he was surely undergoing.

A month or so later, on the feast of the Guardian Angels and at Modotti's behest, Hale wrote a long, glowing letter to a religious writer and prospective postulant who had asked for information on the Big Sur hermitage. After giving him a synopsis of Camaldolese history and a list of prominent artists, scientists, and thinkers produced by the order, Hale added, with a forgivable soupçon of idealistic naïveté, that the most influential monks of all were of course the "countless holy hermits, who sought hiddenness in Christ and are known only to the inner Mind of the Church."[2]

Though he was obviously familiar with the unique two-part nature of Romuald's famous foundation of Camaldoli, he also understood that its American daughter house did not quite fit into that picture: "The foundation in America is strictly eremetical, so that perhaps the unique inter-relations and character that this dual-structured house gave rise to . . . won't be relevant to an article that would have New Camaldoli as its referent."[3] But at least the strictly eremitical nature of the hermitage allowed for an appropriate austerity, as proven by the rigorous daily horarium:

2:30	Rise
2:45	Matins and Lauds
5:30	Meditation
6:00	Prime, private Masses, community breakfast
8:00	Terce, conventual High Mass
9:00	Work
12:00	Sext, None
12:30	Dinner and visit to Blessed Sacrament

2:15   Spiritual reading

2:30   Vespers, novice conference, duties

5:15   Meditation

5:45   Supper, free time

6:45   Spiritual reading and Compline

7:30   Lights out

Though the rules were strict, "a beard, of whatever length, density and form the individual feels most suited to his physical and spiritual being" was included as an option, even for postulants. And the Camaldolese were unique in other ways: all the hours were "recited in common, at a high monotone pitch, and at a markedly slower pace than the usual Benedictine." But for Hale, it was the land itself, the spectacular Big Sur coastline, that really set the community apart. "As one hermit has put it, God has forced us to put our back to the whole inhabited continent, hidden from us by His mountains, and we must consider only our own pilgrimage-rest, and the vast contemplative waters that mark it."[4]

Hale was clearly in love with the pioneer spirit of the place: "The present buildings are actually done-over farm buildings—I'm sitting in the barn, the chapel was a large garage, Dom Micheal is in the tool shed, and the proposed rooms for Rev. Father were lately occupied by brother hog."[5] The good news, however, was that the new foundation was receiving a lot of publicity, most recently from *Life Magazine* and also the December 1958 edition of *Jubilee,* the Catholic monthly founded and edited by Thomas Merton's Columbia friend and godfather, Edward Rice. And those had helped prompt donations toward the major building project that lay ahead. So if anyone asks, quipped Hale, "we can make an $80,000 donation suffice—just make your check out to the Camaldolese Hermits of America."[6]

On October 9, 1958, the nearly twenty-year reign of the wartime pope, Pius XII, ended with his death via ischemia in the Castel Gandolfo in Rome. Between them, the closely allied Pius XI and Pius

XII had ruled the Catholic world for most of the first half of the twentieth century. Each of them had been forced to negotiate with the most powerful and destructive totalitarian regimes in modern times. Each had faced almost unimaginable moral choices that had ramifications for millions of human beings. Each had done his best to defend the church against its perceived enemies. Thanks in great part to the French Revolution, both popes believed that one of the most fearful of these was democracy, which was strongly associated with anti-clericalism, atheism, and the many heresies of modernism.

But on Christmas Eve of 1944, just as World War II was winding down, Pius XII gave a remarkable and game-changing global address: "Taught by bitter experience, people today more and more oppose monopolies of power that are dictatorial, accountable to no one, and impossible to reject. They want a system of government more compatible with the dignity and the liberty due to citizens." And in case his message was not perfectly clear, he added, "the future belongs to democracy."[7]

Young Catholics around the world took the pope's Christmas message as implicit permission to get openly involved in politics. And as war-hammered Western nations struggled to rebuild their devastated countries in the aftermath of Mussolini and Hitler, Catholics became a significant force in the creation of new parliamentary governments. By the time of Pius's death in the fall of 1958, a whole generation of Catholics had experienced democracy, and it was inevitable that this experience would begin to affect their view of the church itself—especially in light of the three encyclicals that had appeared between 1943 and 1950. In the first, *Divino Afflante Spiritu*, Pius XII gave strong approval to the literary, historical, and philological methods of biblical exegesis that had been condemned as modernist by his predecessor, Pius X, who reigned in the years leading up to World War I. The second, *Mystici Corporis,* spoke of the church as the Body of Christ and insisted that a balance be maintained between satisfying the needs of the institution and staying alert to the sometimes disruptive manifestation of the Holy Spirit in the midst of business as usual. The third, *Mediator Dei,* gave official approval to the liturgical movement and thus opened the door to changing or recovering lost aspects of the liturgy.

All three encyclicals pointed subtly toward aggiornamento, or "bringing up to date," while at the same time echoing, however faintly, the work of ressourcement, or "return to the sources," that had been ongoing for most of the century—including within the Camaldolese order, thanks to Giabbani, Ignesti, and Calati. Given that new perspectives were automatically viewed with suspicion by a number of old-school prelates, however, these three papal documents were not universally welcomed, which may be why Pius XII seemed to reverse course toward the end of his life. His last major work was *Humani Generis*, published in 1950. As opposed to the more hopeful tenor of the first three, the tone here was negative and accusatory. In it, the pope condemned "false opinions" and "novelties" that threatened to undermine the integrity of official church teachings.[8]

One of the results was an immediate clampdown on the major ressourcement theologians—Henri de Lubac, Yves Congar, Marie-Dominique Chenu—whose work had so inspired Giabbani, Ignesti, and Calati. Theologian Karl Rahner was censored for certain writings. Jacques Maritain was strongly attacked for his views on church-state relations, and the great Jesuit paleontologist Teilhard de Chardin was forbidden to publish any of his books during his own lifetime. According to one historian of the Second Vatican Council, by the end of the fifties, the Supreme Congregation of the Holy Office had "screwed the lid on tight."[9]

But in its attempt to stem the tide of new thinking about ancient truths, the Holy Office created deep divisions within the church body. Theologians and bishops lined up on one side or the other. More, the Holy Office's aggressively authoritarian tone at a time when more and more Catholics were finally enjoying life in real democracies after decades of dictatorship was bitterly resented. The ideological battle between Modotti's hermit party and their Camaldolese superiors was in some ways a microcosm of what was happening in the church at large: "In the 1950s . . . behind the placid facade that Catholicism presented to the world, a clash of epic proportions was waiting to happen."[10]

The days of absolute papal authority over the lives of individual Catholics were clearly coming to an end—and this shift revealed itself in the way that parishioners now saw themselves: as citizens of nations that deserved the loyalty and commitment they had once bestowed solely on the church: "They now identified themselves not with monarchy but with the liberty, fraternity, and equality of the democratic ethos. In this context, the [still remaining] right-wing, staunchly Catholic dictatorships under Francisco Franco in Spain and Salazar in Portugal seemed like embarrassing anachronisms."[11]

Yet even as the church adjusted itself to the new democratic spirit, it remained on high alert regarding what it held to be its most formidable foe, communism. Unlike Mussolini, who had been more than willing to form a transactional relationship with the church he hated in order to consolidate his power in Italy, the brutal Russian dictator Stalin saw Christianity as a competing religion that could never coexist with communism. The Soviets seized the great Orthodox cathedrals of Russia and turned them into state-owned property. What they couldn't make use of, they destroyed. Widespread persecutions of Christians occurred periodically during the thirties, resulting in the murder, torture, or imprisonment of more than 100,000 bishops and priests in one two-year period alone.

Though Stalin eventually reversed course, the church did not forget. Its deep-seated hostility toward communism culminated in a 1949 Holy Office decree declaring that the two philosophies of life could never be reconciled and any Catholic who joined the Communist Party—which was strong in both France and Italy—was thereby excommunicated.[12] Since the church had cooperated with fascism for decades, the message seemed clear: we can work with the right, never the left. The decree intensified the rift between the new theologians and the old-school traditionalists. Those in the first camp tended to be open to change in the liturgy, collegiality over hierarchy, ecumenism, and—most dangerously, from the perspective of the conservatives—dialogue with everyone, including communists. Those in the second tended to be highly protective of the status quo and suspicious of those who strayed too far from orthodoxy.

Where did the Camaldolese fall on this spectrum? Shortly after the motherhouse was reopened in 1935, it became a retreat center for the Laureati, an organization of young Catholic graduate students led by Giovanni Battista Montini, the future Pope Paul VI and no friend of fascism. The Laureati were deeply interested in the question of how faith and society could most fruitfully intersect. Many of them went on to become key figures in the building of the Christian Democratic Party after the fall of Mussolini. Some attended a special study session in 1943 that produced the *Codice of Camaldoli*, a plan for creating a just democratic society based on Christian principles. And some of the Laureati who had studied at Camaldoli served on the commission for the constitution of the Italian democracy.[13]

Giabbani got to know Montini through the Laureati retreats and they developed a good relationship that came into play later, during the early days of the American foundation, when Montini provided a lovely epigram for New Camaldoli's recruiting pamphlet entitled *Growth of a Hermitage*: "You are the peak of the religious life. The Church sees in contemplative souls those who embrace her program in the most sublime way."[14] Giabbani was also friends with the new Italian prime minister, a man who believed that Catholics and communists should be able to work together for the good of the people. Though Giabbani never wanted to be in any way identified with the left, he did have a connection to the progressive side of Catholic politics through the Laureati and the party they helped build. Giabbani's friend and longtime collaborator in the Camaldolese ressourcement project, Benedetto Calati—eventually elected prior general himself—absolutely refused to give up his longtime friendships with several high-profile Catholic communists who were excommunicated by the 1949 decree. The result? The Camaldolese were seen as a bit left of center. Or as one monk quipped, "We were pinkos."[15] But in the long run, according to the same monk, it was democracy that best served the order. Not Mussolini's fascism, not communism, but a democracy that respected the dignity of the individual human person.

Like the other novices at New Camaldoli, Hale was shocked to hear that Modotti would never be returning to Big Sur. The word was that he'd been monastically excommunicated, but no details were forthcoming. Bishop Willinger and the major benefactors were equally stunned. Hale wondered how the situation, whatever it had been, had come to this. Were the Camaldolese not all brothers in Christ? Could the differences, however serious they were, not have been worked out by Christian dialogue? If love was the source and way and end of Christianity, what was to be thought of all this?

Clearly, Modotti's excommunication dealt a blow to Hale's idealism. But the questions it raised were to become central to his developing philosophy of monasticism. Fuga mundi could never be an end in itself, and neither could the eremitical lifestyle. The Camaldolese had in fact never taught this. The goal was much deeper and more difficult, and it was beautifully summed up in the first of the Three-Fold Goods: the Primacy of Love.

Meanwhile, life went on in the new foundation. Shortly before Christmas of 1959, Dom Clemente Roggi arrived from the Sacro Eremo to take Modotti's place as prior. Like so many other Italian monks born shortly before the first World War, he had entered Camaldoli at the age of eleven and made his simple vows six years later, at seventeen; by the time he was twenty-three, he was an ordained priest. Though not a member of Modotti's rebellious hermit party, he had deeply loved his hermit life at the Sacro Eremo. But now he was ready to take on the job of healing the badly shaken group of novices at Big Sur. First, however, he had to learn English.

Thus, the "clerics" (novices on track for priesthood studies and ordination) took their classes with Fr. Joseph Diemer, on loan from Holy Cross Abbey in Colorado. It was required that their philosophy textbooks be in Latin, so everyone, including the teacher, struggled just to translate the words into English. And the Latin made already difficult subjects even harder. For example, when they got to the tricky question of how God's omnipotence and omniscience could be reconciled with human freedom, Diemer finally had to throw up his hands and say, "Don't think too hard about it, boys, just believe!"

But when it came to the contemplative life, their new teacher could not have been more inspiring. Some of them already knew Br. Lawrence's *Practice of the Presence of God* and the Orthodox Jesus Prayer from *The Way of a Pilgrim*. Diemer encouraged them to continue with these and *The Philokalia*, John of the Cross, and Teresa of Avila besides. They talked about the value of the cell and the spiritual disciplines of solitude, silence, measured asceticism, mindfulness, and *lectio divina* (meditative reading of Scripture), all these practices held together through the Benedictine stress on liturgy. Like so many men before him, Hale had originally been driven by a romantic view of the hermit as solitary hero. Now he began to understand monastic life in a new way: as a both/and rather than an either/or enterprise. Not solitude against community, or contemplation in the cell versus liturgy in the church, but an ongoing back-and-forth movement between these poles, like breathing in and breathing out.

This insight, like the one about the primacy of love, was destined to stay with him and become a shaping force in his life.

12

Thomas Matus, about to leave for his freshman year at Occidental College, was perusing the stacks of the San Bernardino Public Library on a late August afternoon in 1957 when his "good angel" directed him to turn left and look up at the latest releases. On the top shelf was a book with a compelling title down the spine—*The Silent Life,* by Thomas Merton. To a young man of intense intellectual curiosity who had been practicing yoga meditation for a while, this sounded interesting enough to check out. Within its pages, he discovered something new: there were actually Catholic monks in America.

Not that he knew a lot about Catholicism. He had been born in Hollywood in 1940 to a Baptist mother and a Polish Catholic father, so the connection with Catholicism had at best been distant and ancestral rather than spiritual. But when he was eleven, he saw the movie *Quo Vadis* and decided, on his own, to be baptized. This was fine with his non-practicing mother—baptism was a good thing, wasn't it?—so she took him to church the next Easter Sunday and he went through the ceremony. Deep down, however, she preferred that this new spiritual path of his encompass more than the Baptists could likely provide, so when he was fourteen, she gave him a copy of Yogananda's *Autobiography of a Yogi.* Here, he learned that religion involved more than ideas; if you were going to develop and grow, you needed to adopt actual practices. Eventually, he was initiated into Kriya Yoga by two of Yogananda's disciples.

But *The Silent Life* was opening up something new for him: "There's something about Merton . . . even when he's saying things he doesn't quite believe in, he convinces you to read him and think about these things. This was a great book. I immediately connected with it. He said that monks were fighting about what was the best form of monastic observance. He said that this was not helpful if you were trying to achieve mystical union. He quoted St. Bernard, saying that monks who argue about these things are heading down a slippery slope to hell—this is not something they are called to do, they are called to live their vocation but not argue about it. Good! I was inoculated!" By this, he meant that if and when he ever checked out monasticism, he would know better than to enter into any ideological battles over practice and process. He would simply do his best to live the life.[1]

When the *Time* magazine issue sporting a grinning Teddy Roosevelt on the front cover and the Marlboro man on the back came out on March 3, 1958, Thomas Matus was halfway through his freshman year. The photo of Modotti and Catani, just off the boat from Italy and seeking land in America on which to build a hermitage, immediately set bells to ringing: *this* is what he'd been reading about in Merton's *The Silent Life*. However, he did not succumb immediately to the allure of fuga mundi: he was comfortable with his "Hollywood Hinduism," and before he could seriously consider monasticism, he had to decide about Catholicism.

By 1961, he'd made his choice and asked to be received into the church. Later that same year, after Mass in the Cathedral of Honolulu, he spotted an issue of *Jubilee* magazine, published by Merton and his friends, in the rack at the back of the narthex. And there was a photo of the new Camaldolese hermitage in California, along with a picture of a novice—someone who could be *him*, if only he stopped fantasizing about the silent life and started actively pursuing it. As he recalls, "I looked at those pictures and I knew I had to check it out. I was aware of my weakness. I was a fresh convert. I didn't entirely trust God's grace. I was too smart to accept easy explanations of the doctrine of the Catholic church. I'd asked questions that I couldn't answer but others couldn't either. You come in from the lovely self-realization fellowship—it's all sweetness and light—and you come into the Catholic Church, and wham. These archetypes! Everything hits you at the deepest level of your consciousness."[2]

He visited New Camaldoli as soon as he could, where he was welcomed by Prior Clemente Roggi, now speaking English quite well considering how recently he'd come to America. Roggi gave him a copy of the tract pseudonymously published under the name Michael Bede. The author was clearly so knowledgeable and the pamphlet so well written that for decades, many who didn't know the real story assumed the secret author was Merton himself. Not so: the writer was the former priest named Donald Hayne—the writer Modotti had bragged about to Giabbani—who for many years served as Cecil B. DeMille's personal assistant. Hayne had at one point thought about becoming a monk himself and so understood the draw toward fuga mundi and the mystique of the hermit's cell, and more importantly, how to convey all this enticingly to prospective postulants.

Matus found Hayne's tract utterly riveting, and so the quest began. Would he stick with academic life—for, like Hale, he was an outstanding student with a promising future—or would he become an anonymous monk in a wilderness hermitage on the wild, wild Big Sur coast that had inspired so many and proved too much for so many others?

Meanwhile, life in the infant hermitage went on. With Modotti gone, most of the fund-raising duties fell to Pedro Rebello, the Jesuit from Modotti's India days who'd arrived at the hermitage in the fall of 1958. Rebello was indefatigable and had no qualms about asking potential donors for money—after all, the monks with their life of continual prayer were doing the world an incredible service, weren't they? In this spirit, one of the more aggressive fund-raising leaflets during this time featured two side-by-side photos: the first of a kneeling, intently praying monk, and the other of a portly man asleep in his easy chair. The text read, "We pray while you sleep!"[3]

A support committee was organized in Salinas, a major agricultural center that included many Italian American farmers. Prior Roggi had already become quite popular with the Italian Catholic Federation branches in Monterey and Salinas, and they were eager to help out. Michael Murphy, a laymen in residence at the hermitage, made regular trips to Monterey, Salinas, and even south to San Luis Obispo, driving the twisty roads of the Big Sur coast in an ancient truck, begging and buying food and other essentials. Rebello, sometimes with Roggi, visited parishes and Italian Catholic groups, including individual donors like Alex Madonna of the iconic Madonna Inn in San Luis Obispo, one of the eighteenth-century mission towns founded by Junipero Serra. Rebello seemed willing to address any group, regardless of whether he had the permission of the bishop ahead of time—a practice that occasionally got him into hot water. But he was not to be dissuaded and continued his travels up and down the state, speaking on a variety of topics to a number of different audiences: one week, for example, to the Military Council of Catholic Women at Fort Ord, and the next, to a group in Los Angeles on the difference between beatniks and hermits.

Aliprando Catani, who had somehow quietly avoided Bishop Willinger's demand that he vacate the diocese, gave all the support he could to Roggi. A true man of the soil, he went to Madera to extract olive oil for the hermitage. Then Roggi made him the construction boss. Numerous retaining walls were required to level the property before the long-awaited individual cells could be started, and Catani was in charge of all of this. In June 1960, two bulldozers went to work on the mountainside that had once been part of Nesbitt's Circle M Ranch, and before that, the Danis' pioneer homestead, and long before that, the Salinan people's tribal home. In a twentieth-century replay of the eleventh-century enterprise launched by the holy man Romuald in the Apennines of Italy, the two dozers chugged back and forth through the billowing dust and dirt and slanting sunlight, preparing the land for hermits.

Andrea Agnoletti and Aliprando Catani pressing olives, 1960

By August 13, 1960, the cornerstone of the first cell was laid and blessed. Much of the brick-laying was handled by the crew of unskilled, sweating novices, including Hale and Barnhart. By November three more cells were done, and so was the first class of novices. That week, the ex-Jesuit and fund-raiser Pedro Rebello, the Pomona College philosophy major Robert Hale, the chemist and ex-Navy man Bruno Barnhart, the conscientious objector Philip Klee, the Friends of Camaldoli founder Jim Cottrell, and the argumentative Texan Francis Gannon made their first profession, along with several others who would not stay.

Perhaps as a kind of graduation gift or perhaps not, shortly thereafter six real masons arrived to speed up the building project. Within the following year, a whole crew of local carpenters, "cat skinners" (Caterpillar operators), plumbers, and unskilled laborers from "Skid Row," provided by the St. Vincent de Paul Society of San Francisco, would complete more cells and several other essential buildings. The construction men lived in some of the completed cells and ate in the old ranch house refectory with the monks, absorbing Latin with their meals.[4]

Building crew eating with the monks (sketch by Bruce Ariss, Monterey Peninsula Herald)

Meanwhile, the word was out: after the struggles of the first year and a half, the Big Sur hermitage was actually under construction. Visitors began to arrive, including the Benedictine archabbot of St. Meinrad Abbey, the Trappist abbot of Vina, a Carmelite novice master with six novices trailing behind, a group of fourteen Boy Scouts who camped above the water reservoir, and two officers from Fort Ord, who landed in a helicopter just to see if it could be done. On April 9, 1961, the apostolic delegate to the United States, Archbishop Egidio Vagnozzi, came to dedicate and bless the first fifteen cells, the guesthouse, and the retreat house, while a long procession of monks and guests trailed up the hill behind the very Italian archbishop and the equally Italian Roggi chatting happily away in their native language.

Though there is no record of Willinger being present at this event, the auxiliary bishop of his diocese, Harry Clinch, did indeed appear, writing in the large brown guest book that "above all things we are committed to the 'Salus Animarum,' " or spiritual health of souls. A few weeks later, the young community hosted its first open house, inviting seventy-six guests: Franciscans from San Miguel Mission, Sisters of the Poor from Oakland, and a number of lay friends committed to the growth and development of the new foundation. Later that year, the young American hermitage celebrated the 950th anniversary of the Camaldolese Order. The building site for the church was blessed. As part of a fund-raiser, a Lincoln Continental was raffled. Much to the delight of the monks, the winner immediately donated it back to them, and up for sale it went.

The hermitage continued to attract new vocations. Like Modotti, Roggi had no problem accepting older postulants. One of these was a sixty-year-old former officer in the British secret service who'd once been caught behind the lines with a suitcase full of money. A gentleman to the core, Bede Janvrin had been awarded the OBE (Order of British Empire medal) when he left the service. Afterward, he studied at the Beda in Rome in a program for delayed vocations. His first assignment as a priest took him to a Canadian diocese, but when he read about the austerity of the Camaldolese and the fact that they allowed reclusion, he made his way to Big Sur. He soon befriended young Hale, graciously bestowing upon him a set of Tanquery, a summary of the neoscholastic systematic theology beloved of the traditionalists. Neoscholasticism was based on the philosophy of Thomas Aquinas and sought to restore—in the face of the modernist scourge—the fundamental faith doctrines of the thirteenth century. Janvrin assured Hale that this was all he would ever need to know about theology. Given that Vatican II was right around the corner, this was like being handed a pair of hobnail boots and a knee-length woolen coat and told to get out there on the back-packing trail. But Hale, being Hale, thanked him profusely anyway.

Besides, he and the other students were soon headed to Rome. The Camaldolese superiors, including Giabbani and Catani, wanted them to get a proper theological training (presumably, minus Tanquery) at the International Benedictine College of Sant'Anselmo. They would stay at the Camaldolese monastery of San Gregorio, right in the heart of the ancient city, and while they were in Italy, they would also get to experience, firsthand, the motherhouse, the Sacro Eremo, and the Italian Camaldolese themselves. In the summer of 1962, four brothers, including Hale, Barnhart, and Gannon, sailed for Italy on the Holland American Line (the tickets had been donated). A major storm hit along the way, and the ship pitched and tossed, causing at least one of them to pray for a swift and painless death.

Sant'Anselmo employed a typically European style of teaching. The professor would enter, read his lecture in Latin, then exit. The students were to memorize the material for the fifteen-minute oral test at the end of the semester, on which their grade totally depended. One teacher, a bit less rigid, did allow for questions in class. As usual, the argumentative Texan, Francis Gannon, loved to challenge him. One time Professor Gunther was attempting to justify the widespread practice of abbots opening both the incoming and the outgoing mail of their monks. The Benedictine vow of obedience they had all taken, he assured them, made this seemingly harsh practice a reasonable one. Gannon's hand shot in the air. "But my mother didn't take a vow of obedience, so a superior has no right to read her letters!" Yet truth was, he'd already given in; back home, the young monks were only allowed to send and receive mail twice a year.

Some of the Italian students at Sant'Anselmo, though a generation younger than Giabbani, Calati, and Roggi, had been formed in the same old-fashioned way: they'd entered Camaldoli as children of nine, ten, or eleven, and spent their entire youth surrounded by monks. They were delighted by the presence of these strange Americani in their midst, and teased them incessantly. One of them told Hale he thought the American flag looked like a pair of pajamas because of its red stripes. Another tormented Gannon until Gannon asked permission to dump him in the fish pond (permission denied). What was unfolding, however, was something impossible to make out while it was happening. After the intense tug-of-war between the rich, complex worldview of the Italian Camaldolese and the stubborn, competitive spirit of the Americans, egged on by Modotti, the first glimmer appeared of something new forming within the order. Though the Camaldolese did not know it yet, the Third Good of their three-part charism, amplified by these international friendships they were making in Rome, would in coming years lead them to establish foundations in places as far-flung as Germany, Tanzania, India, and Brazil.

But meanwhile, the Italian experience was not so easy. After a day filled with intensive note-taking in Latin, the young Americans had to return to the monastery, where they were expected to speak nothing but Italian. When several years later their studies were finally complete and it was time to go home, they realized they had all been changed. Hale had seemingly flourished in the cosmopolitan swirl of the venerable old city, as though he had found his true self. Barnhart, on the other hand, felt the opposite, as though he'd lost himself and needed to figure out what came next. Gannon didn't say much, but apparently emerged with an even stronger urge toward an even stricter form of eremitical life.

These individual shifts of perspective were not entirely due to time spent among the Italian Camaldolese, however. The young American students were present for one of the most significant events in the history of the church. At 8:30 a.m. on October 11, 1962, in Vatican Square, "some 2,500 council fathers, fully vested in flowing white garments with white miters atop their heads descended the great staircase of the palace next to the church and seemed to flow from it through the piazza into St. Peter's. The Swiss Guards, the Noble Guards, the Palatine Guards, the bishops and patriarchs from the

Eastern Catholic churches in their exotic vestments and crowns . . . [and then, at] the very end of the procession, which took more than an hour to complete, came Pope John XXIII, carried on the *sedia gestatoria*, the famous chair borne on the shoulders of attendants."[5]

The Second Vatican Council, called into session by Pope John XXIII, had begun, and the "long nineteenth century" that started with the French Revolution and extended all the way to the death of Pius XII in 1958 was finally, irreversibly over.

13

Another issue of *Time* magazine, this time April 13, 1962. Soviet poet Evgeny Yevtushenko broods in front of a bleak Russian snowfield beneath an ominous sky, a bright, singing bird on the bare winter branch above him. The article inside, called "Russia," sums up his view of life: there is no absolute truth in Russia because there is "no faith and faith means love, and there is no love." The young poet was born in the wilds of Siberia, where his banished Ukrainian great-grandfather was heading in 1881 when he died in the middle of the 3,500-mile trek. Another grandfather was murdered during Stalin's 1938 Red army purge. Yevtushenko was ten when the charismatic Stalin, hater of Christianity and butcher of millions, finally died after a twenty-five-year cult-of-personality-driven dictatorship.

Thomas Matus, flipping through this very issue in his Occidental dorm room, would certainly have spotted this article about a dissident poet trying to create beauty in the wasteland of a totalitarian regime. Maybe he even read it. What riveted him, however, was a much smaller piece about a Camaldolese recluse called Sr. Nazarena, accompanied by a blurred photo of the tall American nun in full white habit. Said *Time*, "In a coarse sackcloth robe worn over a hairshirt, she sits alone in her stone-floored cell. Her food is bread, water, an occasional cooked vegetable. Through a small grilled window she may look into a chapel, and down a narrow passageway there is another barred window where she takes her daily communion. In the cell is a straight chair, a table, a board that serves as her bed, and a small washroom with a cold shower. Not since she closed the door behind her 16 years ago has she ever left this confined area."[1]

Nazarena was by this time fifty-four. She would spend a total of forty-five years as a recluse, or in the old terminology, an "anchoress." Her cell was in the Camaldolese women's monastery of Sant'Antonio in Rome, not so far from San Gregorio, where Hale, Gannon, and Barnhart would soon be taking up residence while they completed their theological studies at Sant'Anselmo. Nazarena's spiritual director was none other than the prior general of the Camaldolese, Dom Anselmo Giabbani. When asked about why he had agreed to take on this difficult role with a woman who had such an unusual vocation, he said, "You know what convinced me? The joy she radiated. Many times, she said, 'Father, I am never alone. Jesus told me he would never leave me alone, and he has kept his promise.' "[2]

Matus was so struck by the notion of a modern-day anchoress that he decided to pray to her for advice. Should he, or shouldn't he, become a Camaldolese hermit? Apparently, it did not take long for her to answer. A little over a year after he read the *Time* article and fifteen days after the death of Pope John XXIII, he began his novitiate at New Camaldoli, along with two other postulants, one of them the young artist and charismatic, Gabriel Kirby.

Though Prior Roggi certainly didn't mention it to the novices, shortly before their ceremony, he had gotten some alarming news: the Camaldolese general chapter, which took place every six years and which determined the course of the congregation for the six to follow, had been inexplicably postponed until August 1. And contrary to longtime tradition, Msgr. Romoli, OP, of the Holy Office would be presiding. But prior generals *always* presided over the general chapter, didn't they? Why wasn't Giabbani in charge? What was going on, and what might it mean for New Camaldoli? Especially with the wounds of the Modotti-Giabbani controversy still not fully healed?

Meanwhile, an old friend of Camaldoli, Cardinal Giovanni Battista Montini, was elected Pope Paul VI on June 21, 1963, thereby taking on the unenviable task of shepherding Vatican II, launched only months before by his predecessor, through to its final session. This would require three more ten-week fall gatherings at St. Peter's over the next three years—not including hours and hours of labor on the part of 2,200 bishops and *periti* (Latin for experts) during the "intersessions" between official meetings.[3]

By its close in 1965, Pope Paul VI and the council had produced sixteen major documents. The most important were the four "constitutions": *Sacrosanctum Concilium* (On the Sacred Liturgy), *Lumen Gentium* (On the Church), *Dei Verbum* (On Divine Revelation), and *Guadium et Spes* (On the Church in the Modern World). These constitutions were accompanied by nine decrees on different subjects, including the renewal of religious life, the apostolate of the laity, the role of bishops and priests, and the relationship between Roman Catholicism and the Eastern Catholic churches. Finally, there were three additional declarations, several of which would become key to Catholic thought over the next sixty years: *Gravissimum Educationis* on Christian education, *Nostra Aetate* on non-Christian religions, and *Dignitatis Humanae* on religious liberty.[4]

The council went deep, touching—and often painfully disturbing—the very roots of Catholic culture and tradition. As bishops and *periti* (theological advisors to councils of the Catholic Church) engaged in intense and sometimes fierce debates over the wording of documents, they were forced to finally grapple with the church-state issue, for example. When Constantine legalized Christianity in the early fourth century—in fact, flew the cross on his war banners—the Roman Empire began looking to the church as its moral and spiritual center, with all the attendant perks that came with political status. Those days, concluded the council, were now over. As for the sixteenth-century Protestant Reformation that had triggered so many dramatic counterattacks by the church, that battle was over too: you could not read the decree On Ecumenism or the constitution On Divine Revelation and miss that message. Finally, the terrible scourge of modernity, resisted so strenuously from the French Revolution through the end of Pius XII's reign in 1958, was now put on the table, studied carefully, debated, and absorbed into Catholic thought.

But the council was not only interested in its own ecclesial culture. After the carnage of World War II, the genocide carried out in the Nazi death camps, and the nuclear annihilation of Hiroshima and Nagasaki, it was clear that the church could no longer float majestically above the fray. But if it were to begin deliberately engaging with the world, how should it go about doing so? A shocking reminder of how closely intertwined the fate of the church and the world really were came just a few days after the opening of the first session of the council in 1962. Suddenly, the two great nuclear powers of the United States and the Soviet Union were engaged in a standoff called the Cuban Missile Crisis, which had the potential to wipe out every living thing on the planet.[5]

Not all council participants were on board with these dramatic changes in the church's long-held positions. Some—perhaps ten to fifteen percent—felt they were watching the annihilation of the church from within. The opposing party formed early and remained firm in its resistance to all these disruptive new ideas. How could the church adopt teachings that seemed to contradict what it had always taught? Or as one Vatican II historian put it, how was the church to deal with the "problem of change in an institution that draws its lifeblood from a belief in the transcendent validity of the message it received from the past"?[6]

The twentieth-century struggle of the Camaldolese can in some ways serve as a microcosm of the great tug-of-war that was Vatican II. The Modotti-led hermit rebellion, brandishing the eleventh-century Book of the Eremitical Rule as its primary weapon, met the ressourcement theology of Prior General Anselmo Giabbani and his scholar-monk brothers who had also read and studied the original fonts of the order—and interpreted them in a different way. Ressourcement for monks, according to Giabbani and the others, meant a greater focus on Desert Father and patristic spirituality, along with a deeper understanding of their own rich Camaldolese charism. Giabbani did not want to give way to an ideology about hermit life. He believed that everyone had received the Holy Spirit, and if you realized that and knew the Spirit had been infused into your soul, you should follow what the Spirit prompted you to do without needing to argue about it.[7] As Thomas Matus had already figured out by reading Merton's *The Silent Life*, the primary job of a monk was to *live* the monastic life, not fight about theories of monasticism.

But there is another way the struggles of the Camaldolese might serve as a microcosm for the struggles of Vatican II. Like the church at large, the monks could not help but be affected by their years of living under Mussolini. And just as there were prelates who became proud fascists, there were at least some Camaldolese who fell under the spell of the charismatic dictator, notably Timoteo Chimenti, who with so much fawning had baptized the children of Il Duce at the Sacro Eremo in the 1920s. In the eyes of an American monk who spent years living in Italy, "[Fascism] was a political/cultural contamination that affected people's mindset. If they entered the Camaldolese they would do so like joining the fascist troops. This was a pollution of the general spirit of the order. It's not to say that the Camaldolese are innately liberal—this is a slippery term and means different things in Europe and America. We cannot reduce the breadth and flexibility to some form of liberal category—it can't be done that way. In fact, the categories are often mixed in the same person. But it wasn't good for the Camaldolese to have Mussolini. Democracy was very good for them."[8]

In the same way the Camaldolese had to come to terms with the effects of fascism on their community—and the Modotti-Giabbani deadlock may well have been exacerbated by Modotti's reputation as a fascist when he was stationed in Australia—Vatican II forced a reckoning with the fascistic contamination suffered by many in the church at large, and forced a recognition that its aftereffects still lingered on, though in new disguises.

Back at New Camaldoli, it had become clear that the community could not rely on grocery runs to distant towns to keep itself supplied with food. After severe winter storms, Highway 1 was shut down in both directions, and Michael Murphy had to arrange with the Red Cross for three U.S. Army helicopters from Fort Ord to bring supplies while the monks were cut off. It seemed critical that in the future, the hermitage be as self-sustaining as possible, so Aliprando Catani, as hardworking as ever, planted olive trees and grapevines. A benefactor, impressed by his dedication, donated 375 trees of different varieties by way of thanks. But it was clear that simply growing the food would not be enough; they also needed a way to preserve it. They had to have a reliable source of electricity if they were going to keep a walk-in refrigerator going 24/7, so a new generator was installed by a truck crane.

Military bringing food after landslides, early 1960s

There was also the problem of income. How best to support themselves on this precarious mountainside overlooking the Pacific? Some generous nuns had given them nine sheep and a goat, but it didn't take long to realize this was not the route to a reliable income stream; the whole flock, plus goat, was transported to Monterey and auctioned off. Despite Philip Klee's dedication to the cows, not to mention a new barn that would keep them from free-ranging around the hermitage, the plain fact was that the bovine experiment was not working out so well either.

In time it became clear that the most realistic source of income for the future would likely be a strong retreat ministry that included a bookstore. If part of the store was set aside for gifts, the monks could sell homemade items—perhaps paintings, carvings, icons, ceramics, and the like. Maybe even fruit and date nut cakes! But first they would need to complete the sprawling building project, particularly the new, larger church. The holes for the foundation had in fact been bored. Different opinions were already being floated, however. Shouldn't there be *two* churches instead? One for the hermits and one for the guests and workers? It only seemed right and proper that hermits should remain as separate as possible from everyone else.

Then came more shocking news from Italy. Prior General Anselmo Giabbani would not continue as general. Instead, Aliprando Catani, planter of grapevines and olive trees, the priest who had been thrown out of the diocese by Bishop Willinger and who had only recently bid the monks of New Camaldoli farewell and returned to the motherhouse for the general chapter, would be taking Giabbani's place. Giabbani, in turn, would be taking Catani's as first assistant to the general; in essence, they would be switching roles. Clemente Roggi, who had been serving as acting prior of New Camaldoli since Modotti's departure, was now deemed official. And the hermitage would remain a hermitage forever—certainly with a significant guest ministry, but with no cenobium or large guesthouse attached. Modotti's burning question—would they, or wouldn't they, be able to guarantee prospective postulants that New Camaldoli was a hermitage and a hermitage alone?—had finally been definitively answered. But healing did not automatically follow, as it appeared to many that it was Modotti's final complaint to Vatican higher-ups—specifically, his cousin, Cardinal Antoniutti of the Sacred Congregation of Religious—that lay behind Giabbani's removal from office.

When a Camaldolese prior general's six-year term is up, the assumption is that he will be reelected by the congregation unless he himself says no, he would like to step down. The votes that are cast by the monks are thus essentially symbolic statements that, yes, they trust in his leadership and want him to continue. In this case, Giabbani was almost certainly reelected by the community, but the Vatican visitator took the unopened ballot box to the Vatican, saying the ballots were to be counted there. The announcement then came that Giabbani had *not* been reelected, which caused great consternation among the majority of the congregation. Giabbani's longtime monastic brother and scholarly colleague, Benedetto

Calati, was asked by the Vatican to take Giabbani's place, but Calati was appalled at the manipulation of the election and refused. So Aliprando Catani was pressured to take the role, agreeing only reluctantly and only on the condition that Giabbani would become his closest advisor.

The young Big Sur community had been asked to absorb a lot on faith, for they were almost certainly not privy to the story behind these abrupt and troubling changes in leadership—first Modotti and then Giabbani. But at least the status of New Camaldoli was now perfectly clear, so the monks, however shaken, moved ahead with their church-building plans. At the next chapter meeting, which took place only a few days after Roggi's return from the historic general chapter in Italy, the monks unanimously voted to designate the new church, whenever it got built, as "hermits only" and to use the existing guesthouse as a "Chapel for the people."⁹ The idea was that, as hermits, their solitude needed to be protected. They also voted that the solemnly professed priests among them would stand during services while everyone else in the community would kneel—a clear nod to the traditional hierarchical ranking that was currently under siege at the ongoing Vatican II Council.

An additional indication that monks of New Camaldoli were determined to conduct their lives in as strict and austere a manner as the legendary hermits of the Sacro Eremo: the chapter voted that parents were not allowed to visit their novice sons and that any letters from them would be withheld to be saved for special occasions.

The new prior general, Aliprando Catani, soon weighed in from Italy on the separate churches plan. The answer was simple: no. And in case there was any doubt about what he meant, he added, "Permission denied to build a separate chapel for the public." This was one of his first decisions as prior general, and he knew, from his lengthy stays at New Camaldoli, that it would not be a popular one. But he seemingly had a better sense of what was happening in the church at large than did the isolated, idealistic Big Sur community—and he knew that they and all Catholics around the world needed to prepare themselves for the far bigger changes that were coming very soon.¹⁰

Building church, 1964

14

Catani's attempts to sell the community on the middle way did not succeed. Now that the Vatican had finally and irrevocably weighed in—New Camaldoli was to be *strictly* a hermitage with no cenobium attached—the community doubled down on its hermit ethos. The rules were correspondingly strict. Letters could be written and received four times a year only, on Easter, August 15, November 1, and Christmas. Parents were permitted to visit once a year. And even on that long-awaited visit, they were not allowed to share a meal with their son. Novices could not go home under any circumstances, even if a parent was dying or had died. The point was clear: all family relationships, no matter how close—or perhaps, *especially* those that were close—from now on took second place to one's monastic calling.[1]

Postulants and novices were also separated from the rest of the monastic community. They could not have visitors, not even a fellow novice dropping by their cell for a brief chat. The monthly recreation day, looked forward to by all, must not include music, which all too often led to happy socializing. As for picnics, infamous for encouraging overeating and idle chitchat, they were verboten. The only time a novice might interact with the rest of the community outside the daily Office was while doing shared tasks. Postulants and novices were to wash dishes and serve tables just like the priests, and were also eligible to be readers at meals or Compline or for the epistle during the Liturgy of the Word.[2]

On December 25, 1964, Prior Roggi offered the first Mass in the new church. After a year of construction, the final touch had been made on the new building: the large cross had been placed on top of the cupola by block and tackle after a hovering helicopter tried and failed to pull off the job. The floor plan was highly symbolic: the monks stood behind plywood stalls in the high-ceilinged rotunda, and the tabernacle was placed in the center of this large open space. A curtain hid the monks from their guests, who sat in the nave and participated vicariously. It was not the best of solutions to the distraction problem (guests didn't *mean* to be distracting in spite of how distracting they actually *were)* but this was the only idea they could come up with after Catani forbade them to build separate chapels.

Besides the completion of the church, it had been an all-around big year, especially in regard to new vocations. Both Robert Hale and Bruno Barnhart had taken their solemn vows. Thomas Matus had made his simple vows, along with four other novices, including Gabriel Kirby. Philip Klee—the tender of the cows—and Bede Janvrin were on their way to solemn profession. And Bernard Massicotte, a French Canadian priest from northern Quebec, had arrived to begin his novitiate. These seven—Klee, Hale, Barnhart, Matus, Kirby, Janvrin, and Massicotte—along with two transfers from Holy Cross Abbey in Colorado, Joseph Diemer and Emmanuel Wasinger, would stay, persevere, and form the core of the New Camaldoli community for decades to come.

A few weeks after Christmas, the master fund-raiser Rebello scored another coup for the hermitage. He met with the ranchers who still owned part of the old Circle M Ranch, and talked them into selling an additional three hundred acres for the community. This gave the monks nine hundred acres of uninterrupted wilderness, from Highway 1 on the sea-cliffs all the way to the top of the mountain, including a peaceful lake in a meadow near the summit.[3] Though the new acreage was too steep and wooded to be worked for crops, their agrarian enterprises were going well enough at this point that after Matus and four other novices spent a week picking olives at Mission San Jose, Rebello paid $500 for an olive press. He also wangled a crusher from a donor, assuming that someday the hermitage would be harvesting its own crop.

In May of 1966, three monks arrived from Italy for an official visitation. The lives of two of them—Catani and Giabbani—had been permanently altered by their involvement with the founding

Recreation day, early 60s

of the American hermitage. Since the sad end of the Modotti affair, both men had also attended the Vatican Council, experiencing firsthand the mighty wind that was blowing through the church. Giabbani went to the initial session, and Catani attended sessions thereafter, even making written contributions to the discussions.[4]

Both men seemed at peace with the past. They stayed a week, talking with postulants, novices, and monks, visiting individual cells, and generally taking the temperature of the community. Given Rebello's new press, Catani almost certainly paid a visit to the olive trees and grapevines he had planted three years before. On Pentecost, Catani received the solemn profession of the decorated British secret service agent, Bede Janvrin. Catani asked the two men who were currently in reclusion to be present for both the ceremony and the dinner afterward—another hint that, for the Camaldolese, strong community relationships were just as important as solitude. An additional nudge toward the new Vatican II paradigm came at the last chapter meeting before the Italians departed: there would be no more group rosaries said on Fridays, and no more devotionals after Compline. In both cases, these could be recited privately instead.[5]

Why were devotionals being edged out of common life? In part, because for the past fifty years, the development of Italian Benedictine monasticism in general and the Italian Camaldolese in particular had been toward something new: an actual *renewal* of religious life, not simply an increase in personal piety. More and more, the life of a monk was seen as an interior journey leading toward an increased capacity for love—both for fellow community members and for the world at large. It was meant to be "evangelically free in scrutinizing and recognizing the mysterious presence of the Spirit in the ambivalent events of the Church and society."[6] Too great an allegiance to particular private devotionals could lead monks in the opposite direction: toward rote ritual instead of this "deeply innovative path, rooted in the word of God and in the living tradition of the Fathers."[7] The rosary and other devotionals, used in a spiritually healthy way, were of course fine as a method of extending prayer throughout the day, but the liturgy had to take pride of place; mingling the two only led to confusion.[8]

The Americans, however, were not yet fully on board with this and other Vatican II changes. The strict rules governing New Camaldoli—the tight boundaries around family relationships, the severe separation of novices from the rest of the community, the weekly use of the discipline, the curtain between the monks and their guests during services—were clearly more in tune with Blessed Rudolph of 1080 than with the Vatican Council of the 1960s. Though Modotti had been gone for six years by now, his vision of the eremitical life still dominated at the hermitage. Fuga mundi prompted many young men like Hale and Matus to make their way to the Big Sur wilderness, but—primarily because New Camaldoli did not yet have a solid formation program—most of these hopefuls did not last long. And the disillusionment could be deadly. One young man spent a year trying to live up to his vision of eremitical heroism before giving up, shortly thereafter ending his life by jumping from the Golden Gate Bridge.[9] As St. Benedict had figured out 1,500 years before, a monk has to be carefully formed before he can safely become a solitary.

Meanwhile, not all were pleased by the relegation of devotionals to the private sphere. If the Vatican Council was going to generate more changes like *this*, why then things could get a lot worse, couldn't they? Next thing you knew, they'd be telling you to pray in English. Even talk to Protestants! Several of the monks were more than just nervous; they were *irritably* nervous.

Especially the traditional and devout Klee.

The first batch of young monks were done with their theological studies in Rome. They had learned a lot, particularly about their own strengths and weaknesses. Certainly, they now understood the Italian Camaldolese and their own history as an order much better than they had when their perspective was limited to Big Sur. Barnhart was more than ready to return to the wilderness and went directly back to the hermitage. Hale, whose intellectual fires had been lit by this fascinating interlude in the Eternal City, headed straight for St. John's University in Minnesota, where he occupied a room in one of the largest Benedictine abbeys in the Western Hemisphere—nothing remotely like the wilderness hermitage to which he belonged—while studying for his master's degree in spirituality. Like Barnhart, Gannon the Texan also returned to Big Sur, only to find that New Camaldoli was still too busy and noisy—still more of a construction site than a real hermitage—so, after finishing his theology studies with the Santa Barbara Franciscans and being ordained with his original Camaldolese brothers, left for a hermit hut in Canada where he lived out the rest of his days.

Vocations were being sorted out and people were discovering where they fit in to the larger picture. Matus, for example, was realizing that even though he clearly had an eremitical call, he was a square peg in a round hole at New Camaldoli. He was neither skilled nor efficient nor highly motivated when he was assigned to work at the dusty and seemingly permanent building site. He was certainly the last person you would ask to push a wheelbarrow full of concrete. Neither was he a natural-born tender of livestock, like Klee, nor—in spite of his moderately enjoyable week of picking olives—an agrarian at heart. He was an *intellectual,* right? And he gravitated like any self-respecting intellectual toward his cell and his books as soon as the opportunity arose. Was he simply being lazy? This thought bothered him, and he wondered if he were dragging down the rest of the group.

Then came the visit of Catani and Giabbani. When Matus's name came up at a meeting of the fully professed members of the community—should he or shouldn't he be allowed to solemnly profess?—Catani told them in the most diplomatic way possible that Matus was clearly weak, a sensitive artist rather than a worker, and perhaps (shrugging with Italian resignation) they should send him away altogether. Catani then went to Matus and gave him a faithful report of what he'd said. But he smiled as he told the story, knowing full well that even though the creative young man was virtually worthless on the construction site, he was far too valuable a candidate for the Camaldolese to lose. For Matus, Catani's assessment was much-needed confirmation that he *did* have a real vocation and that he *wasn't* simply lazy but sensitive and artistic. If that's who he was, why then he would be part of a long line of sensitive and artistic Camaldolese monks!

It was down-to-earth Diemer, however, who had once told Hale's little cohort of novices to "not think too much about it, boys, just believe!" who gave Matus the "word" that stayed with him for the rest of his life. "Before you can be a good hermit," Diemer said, "you have to learn to be a good cenobite." For this longtime Benedictine, the cenobitic life was the active life—the life of the Third Good. It meant teaching and presiding over Masses and other kinds of outreach. But all this activity did not in any way preclude solitude. "It's a great set-up here," Diemer reminded Matus. "It gives us plenty of time for contemplation and silence."[10] In other words, the Camaldolese monk could have the best of both worlds—cenobitic and eremitical—if he could only figure out how to balance the two.

Matus would soon be given an opportunity to fit this philosophy into a larger picture. The Vatican II decree called *Perfectae Caritatis*, which was a further development of the major constitution *Lumen Gentium*, directed religious orders to embrace aggiornamento—an adaptation to modern conditions—while at the same time, remaining faithful to their "purpose, particular spirit, and healthy traditions."[11] In both documents, religious life was to be reoriented from "primarily a way of individual sanctification to a means for the sanctification of the church."[12]

In the spirit of ressourcement, monastic congregations were to re-see their own original fonts through the lens of the modern world—exactly what Giabbani, Calati, and Ignesti had been urging upon the order for several decades by now. But this time around, the Camaldolese would avoid the bitter strife that arose during the debacle of the 1957 constitutions because this time the process would require "the cooperation of all the members of the institute."[13] In other words, no more top-down, imposed changes in the thousand-year-old tradition; everyone would have to agree ahead of time.

Lumen Gentium and *Perfectae Caritatis* were two of the clearest indications that the old, familiar church—the only church known by generation upon generation of Catholics—was undergoing a significant transition. Laypeople were now part of the "priesthood of all believers." The concept of the "Church Militant," so beloved by a certain kind of Catholic, was giving way to a new and more ambiguous (and hence, for many, troubling) notion of the visible Catholic Church as a "pilgrim Church on earth" that would only someday be fully united with the invisible church in heaven. There were understandable concerns. For example, how would this new and far humbler pilgrim church deal with societal right and wrong if it couldn't simply call out sin with its old authoritarian self-confidence? There was a way, but not one with which Catholics were very familiar. Pope John XXIII understood the potential for unease and met it head-on. In his opening address at the first session of the council, he gave his answer: "by making use of the medicine of mercy rather than of severity . . . [and by] demonstrating the validity of her teaching rather than by condemnations."[14]

This new way of being church would have a major effect on the way that religious orders saw themselves, and certainly on an ancient eremitical order like the Camaldolese. The concept of hermit as spiritual warrior of the desert in continual mano a mano combat with Satan and his minions did not fit into this new, humbler paradigm as naturally as it fit into, say, the worldview of the holy man Romuald or Blessed Rudolph. The desert was no longer simply a remote physical place providing sanctuary from the distracting world but had become an intimate interior space: it was the "existential dimension" that characterized the monk "as a human person." This existential center was what determined a monk's way of "being and existing in relationship." It served as a "life-changing nerve-centre of personal and community life." In contrast to traditional fuga mundi, there was a new call "to integrate into the cultural context" in which the monastic community lived.[15]

For New Camaldoli, this meant the context of Big Sur in 1960s America, already a magnet for romantics hoping to escape an increasingly anxiety-ridden society but now a major draw for idealistic cultural revolutionaries besides. The wild beauty of the coast would always exert a strong pull on the public, which meant there would always be visitors, many of them having no clue about monastic life or even about Catholicism. This was a situation that required charitable but prudent practical responses from the monks. How should the spiritual progeny of the holy man Romuald handle the unfolding hippie invasion, for example? Or even just the ninety-four Lithuanian Girl and Boy Scouts, camped happily nearby, who flooded the new church for Mass one September morning?

Meanwhile, the process of creating new constitutions and declarations officially began. A drafting committee sent out its work to every Camaldolese house, where each draft was discussed by every professed monk and then returned with objections and suggestions. For the hermitage community, the first of these discussions took place in July of 1966. These revisory sessions would literally go on for years.

But this didn't stop significant changes from taking place almost immediately. By August of 1967, the lessons were being read in English, which Hale, home for the summer between semesters at St. John's, found to be a "great relief," given the lack of proficiency in Latin that characterized the Americans at New Camaldoli. And the very month that Latin quietly gave way to English, four more young monks headed off to Rome for studies, one of them Thomas Matus. This time, instead of making the long ocean voyage across the Atlantic, they flew World Airways.

Though Matus did not know it yet, his real gifts were about to be revealed. More, his years of study in Rome would change the trajectory of his life for years to come.

15

Shortly after the latest crop of Big Sur monks flew off to Rome, the hermitage found itself in yet another crisis. A different version of the old question was once again on the table: what was the best way to live the monastic life? More specifically, how large should New Camaldoli be? Would a smaller and more intimate community better protect the contemplative nature of the foundation? Or should the campus be expanded now, while the population was still relatively small, in anticipation of a future influx of new postulants? The

conflict came to a head on September 11, 1967, when—after nearly eight years of ongoing construction—the indefatigable Rebello ordered work to begin on six additional cells and an infirmary. Pushback came swiftly. In two separate chapter meetings the following week, Rebello's newest building project was unanimously blocked. No one wanted a larger hermitage than the one they already had.[1] The community needed to focus on the novices who were already there. Work on the new cells ground to a stop.

Gabriel Kirby delivering food to cells, 1967

110

Like his Jesuit brother Modotti, Rebello thought big, and he was frustrated at this eleventh-hour vetoing of his expansion plans. Why couldn't the community see that these additional cells would surely be needed? Rebello was so upset by this refusal to focus on the future that he began pondering other ways he could channel his energy—ways that might take him away from Big Sur entirely. For example, what about making a Camaldolese foundation in India?

This was not a new idea. He had been thinking about it for some time, possibly as long ago as 1963 when he went into six months of reclusion in the most remote cell at the hermitage. India had a history of honoring contemplation that extended back several millennia. In some ways, ancient India was more suited to the Camaldolese life than brash America. And India was his natal home. His deep roots there were obvious in the pages of his private spiritual journal, handwritten in exquisite blue Malayalam script. Before, he'd served as an Indian Jesuit in a rigidly hierarchical society structured for the benefit of its British colonizers. If he returned, it would be as a contemplative Camaldolese monk, an Indian among Indians.

Within six months of the vote to halt work on the new cells, he left for Italy for a year of reclusion at the Sacro Eremo. There in the fir-ringed hermitage in the Apennines built by the holy man Romuald, he continued to ponder and pray before heading off to Mangalore and the exotically beautiful west coast of Karnataka where he'd first met Modotti. What might he accomplish for the order by coming to this place? Would India take to Christian contemplation as naturally as he suspected it would?

Meanwhile, another monk was testing the same theory: that India was a naturally contemplative culture, a society that literally breathed prayer, and that a Christian prayer ashram could flourish in this soil. But so far, the Benedictine Bede Griffiths from Prinknash Abbey in England had not had much success. He had already spent ten disappointing years trying to make a go of it in Kerala, just south of Modotti's Karnataka Jesuit base.[2] But in 1968, a year before Rebello left Rome for India, Griffiths was asked to take up the reins at Shantivanam, an already established but primitive Christian house of prayer on the banks of the sacred river Cavery in the neighboring state of Tamil Nadu.

Griffiths immediately fell in love with the two wild and over-grown acres that comprised the ashram, for like much of India, the environment was enchantingly beautiful: "[It] was the patterns of the trees against the sky that delighted him, the setting sun, the gathering darkness, the broad spreading leaves of the young banana trees, the singing and the flight of the birds: kingfishers, crows, green parrots, golden orioles, the pariah kite, so called after its habit of living off garbage, the Brahminy Kite, known as the holy bird, for it is found only in places believed to be sacred."[3] Griffith's goal was the same as it had been for the past ten years: to establish the Christian contemplative tradition in the context of Hindu culture. And more, to learn as much as he could from that ancient Hindu tradition while at the same time sharing what Christian monks from the Desert Fathers to present times had gleaned by way of contemplative wisdom. Not, under any circumstances, to impose a Western version of Christianity on the "native population," as had traditionally been the case with Christian missionaries from Europe.

In service of this goal, Griffiths grew a beard, wore a dhoti, went barefoot, slept on the floor, ate with his hands. He was living among people whose customs and traditions had not changed much in the past 2,000 years, and what was the point of standing out among them as the foreigner? On the other hand, the ashram had to support itself by growing crops, so how could he entirely reject modern technology? Should he be ashamed of owning an oil engine to water the coconut trees, for instance?[4] However, this nagging question ultimately had to take second place to a larger one: why couldn't he "keep people together?" he mourned in a letter to a British friend. Young men would come, stay for a bit, and then leave.[5]

The issue was the same one that monks everywhere, including the monks at New Camaldoli, had been facing since time eternal: community, and how community was best formed. However unorthodox he might appear to many in the Catholic world, Griffiths was still a Benedictine and he had the ancient Rule of St. Benedict to help guide him. But he was a British Catholic living as a Hindu sannyasi in a society that had only twenty years before shrugged off British colonial rule. Many Indian Catholics, formed by traditional Western Jesuits like Modotti, were appalled at his experiment, believing that he was degrading the holy symbols and customs of the church. Some

Hindus, on the other hand, were suspicious of this British monk who seemed to be appropriating *their* sacred rites for his own purposes. It would take special people to fully commit to Griffith's audacious project, and it was several years before these men began to appear.

Meanwhile, Thomas Matus—formed as an adolescent in the milieu of "Hollywood Hinduism" and introduced to meditation by Yogananda—was ready to begin his studies in ecumenical theology at Sant'Anselmo. After an intense five years as a simply professed monk—and perhaps thanks to Catani's insight into his "sensitive, artistic" nature—he had gone ahead with his final vows before leaving Big Sur. But when he arrived in Italy on August 9, 1967, he did not head straight to Rome but instead took the train from France, through the Swiss Alps, and over the Simplon Pass all the way to Florence. There, he called the Sacro Eremo and asked to be picked up at the station. He waited for his ride in a parking lot across the street from the Gothic church of Santa Maria Novella.

Once at Camaldoli, he was driven straight up the mountain to the eremo. "The impression was overwhelming," he recalls. "I had spent the last few months at New Camaldoli preparing for this trip, studying Italian and looking at photographs of our monasteries in Italy. Now it was as if one of those black-and-white photos had suddenly taken on color and depth, and I was walking into it as through the magical picture-frame in a C.S. Lewis fantasy."[6] In one of those mysterious connections between monks that transcend time and space, it was Thomas Merton's *The Silent Life* that had introduced Matus to this holy place. Yet twenty years before, Merton himself had discovered the eremo through one of these very photos.

Matus stayed for two months. During this long retreat, he had time to think through his experience at New Camaldoli and exactly why it was he'd felt so out of place. He concluded two things: that his original call had indeed been to the infant hermitage in Big Sur, a call he could never deny or abandon, but also that God had now set him down in Italy for a reason and he needed to find out what that was.

In Rome, he lived at San Gregorio, where Hale and Barnhart had resided a few years before. Before the new Camaldolese constitutions went into effect, which stated that whichever house a monk was living in would determine his stability, Matus went to both Catani and Giabbani to ask for their advice. He loved Italy, he was already fluent in the language, and he knew he would do well in either the cenobio at Old Camaldoli or at San Gregorio in Rome. But he was counting on them to guide him in whatever work he was meant to do on behalf of New Camaldoli, which was still the home of his heart. Giabbani told him that one of the best ways he could serve the American foundation was to start translating the sources of Camaldolese history and spirituality from Latin and Italian into English.

Meanwhile, in spite of the many who came and left, the Big Sur community was slowly growing. In 1967, the Camaldolese became a congregation within the worldwide Benedictine Confederation, which subtly altered the strongly eremitical orientation of the group, opening it up to the more communal dimension of the charism. By 1968, there were eighteen religious in choir—eight priests and ten non-priests—plus two recluses, two priests, and two brothers on leave of absence, not to mention four students studying in Rome, Matus being one of them.[7] The rotunda was full, visitors came often and steadily, and the changes instigated by Vatican II made monastic life surprisingly exciting. In August, the community began to recite the Office of Lauds in English. More, they were now allowed to chant in an inflected voice (as opposed to *recto tono,* or a drone-like monotone). Next came concelebration of the Conventual Mass. This meant that all ordained priests now shared the presider's role, as had been common practice in the church until several centuries before. Then they began singing Vespers in English, using Gregorian melodies. And finally, they adopted the new practice of saying the prayer of the faithful daily, along with public petitions at the commemoration of the living and the dead.

Non-liturgical traditions were shifting too. Just as the community was getting used to the ease and comfort of English, the Conventual Chapter tackled two ancient monastic symbols. The beard—and some of these beards were impressively long and full—was no longer mandatory. And neither was the corona. The corona was a medieval monkish haircut that required most of the head to be shaved while leaving a circle of longer hair, like a crown, encircling the bald pate. The realization was that the beard and corona, coupled with the distinctive

From left, in black,
Bernard Massicotte,
Anselmo Giabbani,
Aliprando Catani,
Clemente Roggi,
early 1960s

white Camaldolese habit, attracted too much attention. Were these monks part of a cult? A kind of Catholic Hare Krishna community?

Possibly the most thrilling change of all, however, was the decision on the part of Prior Roggi, along with the Domestic Council, that picnics were now okay on the monthly recreation days. Picnics! Perhaps, went the reasoning, it would be good to strive for less rigidity and coldness. It might even be healthy for the monks to get to know individual community members as fellow human beings. Other monks should not be viewed as threats to one's own recollection. At the same time, of course, everyone had a duty to preserve and protect what was most precious about eremitical life: its beautiful silence.

Another welcome change: with the completion of the library and kitchen buildings, the bulk of the construction project was finally over. The monks were now free to turn their attention to the land itself. They'd necessarily been farmers from the beginning, and given their isolated location, that wasn't changing any time soon. The good news was that they were getting better at it. This year's garden, for example, boasted 150 yards by 150 yards of beans, corn, beets, salsify, onions, rutabaga, okra, beets, and squash. And as Roggi recorded in the Hermitage Chronicle in his slightly whimsical English, the sow had produced "11 piglings!"[8]

However, most of the hermitage's nine hundred acres were not farmland, but mixed forest. Old Camaldoli was famous for its well-tended, healthy forests, and the community was determined to adopt that proud heritage in Big Sur. One day, 7,500 Bishop pine starts were brought from Davis and the monks began planting them the next morning. Unfortunately, at the same time they were putting tree seedlings in the ground, their magnificent Redwood stands were being decimated. Loggers and hunters had in the past been allowed on the grounds in exchange for a contribution, and now when they were asked to stop, they refused to do so. New Camaldoli's neighbors were upset that the monks couldn't seem to halt the logging, and that bothered the community too. But the final straw was a full-page story, plus photos, in the *Monterey Peninsula Herald*. The monks, it said, were allowing their beautiful old trees to be destroyed. The community was extremely embarrassed—and further appalled when they went to the logging site. "A half-naked forest," one of them sighed, "is not a beautiful sight."[9] The diminutive French Canadian monk Bernard Massicotte was charged with negotiating with the loggers. A charmer in a black beret, he succeeded in arranging for a temporary cessation of the destruction until the issue could be resolved.

But his forest problems were not over. A group of hippies wanted to use the hermitage road to drive back and forth to their mining claim. Some of the monks were concerned—hippies after all!—but Massicotte thought the very best policy would be to allow them to do what they wanted and treat them with respect as long as they promised not to disturb the community. As he pointed out in a chapter meeting, some of them had religious practices that resonated with contemplative Catholicism and some were even Christians, so why not try to help? However, not many weeks later, during their hike on recreation day, the monks spotted an illegal camp on their property—naturally, the hippies. Given the extremely high chance of destructive wildfires on the coast, a camp that couldn't be seen or monitored from the hermitage presented a serious threat. Again, Massicotte tried his best to walk the line between Benedictine hospitality and good common sense and was able to work out at least a temporary compromise.

His kind French heart and willingness to help, combined with his past experience of caring for street people with alcohol and drug addiction in a big-city rehab center, earned him the trust of the hippies. Walking the hermitage road one night, he came upon a woman from the group who had ingested something that had clearly made her very sick. Not sure what the prior would say if he knew what Massicotte was about to do, the 5'2" monk half carried her to his cell, put her in his own bed, and slept beside her on the floor. Shortly before dawn, she bolted upright in bed, looked wildly around the room, then vomited all over him. A tad disoriented in his own right, he still managed to mop her up and get her back to her friends before anybody spotted him.[10] Like both Hale and Matus, Massicotte was discovering his particular vocation: pastoral care of those in spiritual or emotional pain, particularly those who had suffered abuse.

Joseph Diemer had been on a similar search for what he was meant to do with his life, given the spectacular wilderness setting in which God had placed him. He who had given Matus such a good word about the necessary connection between the cenobitic and eremitical life had been pondering for some time the more austere option allowed by the Camaldolese: reclusion. He knew that Modotti had once been a recluse and that there had been other modern-day recluses at the Sacro Eremo besides. And he knew that Nazarena, the Camaldolese anchoress in Rome, was still, after decades, living in total reclusion at the convent. On June 26, Diemer finally acted on his overwhelming desire for greater solitude by going into reclusion for an "indefinite period." Five years later, in 1973, his status as a monastic "inmate"—another term for anchorite or recluse—became permanent.

A state of unvarying *fuga mundi*.

As the sixties unfolded, Thomas Merton got tugged eastward too. Like Pedro Rebello, like Bede Griffiths, like a myriad of disillusioned young westerners, Merton became convinced that contemplation was universal and that the ancient traditions of Asia had a lot to teach serious spiritual seekers who'd been turned off by the church. And though he was a Trappist monk, he was perfectly within his canonical rights to begin an in-depth exploration of Eastern religion and philosophy. One of the more controversial declarations

of Vatican II had opened the door for him, and he was one of the
first religious pioneers to take seriously the earth-shaking statement known as the Declaration on the Church's Relation to Non-
Christian Religions:

> The catholic church rejects nothing of those things which are
> true and holy in these religions. . . . It therefore calls upon
> its sons and daughters with prudence and charity, through
> dialogues and cooperations with the followers of other reli-
> gions, bearing witness to the christian faith and way of life,
> to recognize, preserve and promote those spiritual and moral
> good things as well as the socio-cultural values which are to
> be found among them.[11]

In fact, even before Vatican II, Merton had begun his quest to
understand the spiritual traditions of Asia. In 1959, he began a
dialogue with D. T. Suzuki, a famous Zen Buddhist teacher, on the
possible correlations between contemplative Christianity and Zen.
In 1962, he published *New Seeds of Contemplation*, conjecturing
on the universals of mysticism. He continued to study Buddhism,
Confucianism, Taoism, Hinduism, Sikhism, Jainism, and Sufism, all
while living in his hermitage on the Gethsemani Abbey grounds.
And in late October of 1968, with the permission of his abbot, he
took off for a long speaking tour in Asia.

But in early December, not so long after he embarked on this
journey in search of spiritual friendship and understanding between
practitioners of the great religious traditions, he died at a Red Cross
retreat center in Thailand. His presentation was in the morning;
that afternoon he was found lying on his back in his cottage with
a short-circuited floor fan draped over him. Though there was no
autopsy, the assumption was that he'd been electrocuted, then gone
into cardiac arrest. He who had so strongly encouraged Anselmo
Giabbani to make a Camaldolese foundation in America, who had
led so many young people to monastic life, including Robert Hale
and Thomas Matus, was dead at fifty-three.

16

Several years before he arrived at New Camaldoli in the spring of 1959, Bruno Barnhart had an experience few people ever have: the "Prayer of Union" described by Teresa of Avila in her famous sixteenth-century manual about the stages of mystical prayer, known as *The Interior Castle*.[1] In what she labels the "fifth stage," the soul seems to withdraw from both body and mind, which then fall into a state of unconsciousness; all faculties are suspended. During this usually very brief experience, the soul is completely united to God. Teresa explains the Prayer of Union thus:

> God implants Himself in the interior of that soul in such a way that, when it returns to itself, it cannot possibly doubt that God has been in it and it has been in God; so firmly does this truth remain within it that, although for years God may never grant it that favor again, it can never forget it or doubt that it has received it. This certainty of the soul is very material.[2]

Barnhart, who up to this point had been a typical dutiful Long Island Catholic, could not forget or doubt it either. At the time the experience occurred, he was a young scientist in the Navy with a master's degree in chemistry from Dartmouth; during the preceding two years, he had been a biochemical lab tech at Bethesda Naval Hospital, where he met the biophysicist Manuel Morales. When Morales moved to the Dartmouth lab to continue his research on muscle contraction, Barnhart went with him. One day, something went wrong during a chemical procedure and young Barnhart lost his eye. It was during his long recovery that he experienced an extraordinarily lengthy full half hour of the Prayer of Union—a mystical event that normally only happens to people who've spent years in ascetical practice and contemplative prayer. According to Teresa, however, it occasionally, if rarely, happens at the very beginning of a spiritual journey.[3]

In this case, it prompted Barnhart, who after his recovery was hired at the Brookhaven National Laboratory to explore the peaceful applications of atomic energy, to begin a concurrent exploration of the contemplative monastic life. The following year, he visited the Trappists of Spencer, Massachusetts, and Genesee, New York, along with the Carthusians of Skyfarm, Vermont, before calling Modotti at the brand-new hermitage in Big Sur.

Barnhart's penetrating mind, spiritual insight, and wickedly dry wit, coupled with his lanky height and shy, almost bashful courtesy, soon made him a beloved and respected member of the community. In 1967, when the commission for updating the constitutions was formed in Italy, he was elected to represent New Camaldoli, for he was "much trusted by the Italians, even held in awe."[4] The new position meant he would be flying back and forth to participate in the discussions for some years to come. Despite his deep connections within the European Camaldolese community, however, his spiritual home and official stability remained with the hermitage in Big Sur.

Robert Hale spent two years completing his master's degree at St. John's University in Minnesota. It was at St. John's that his own particular vocation within the congregation began to constellate, and it was politics that showed him the way. The sixties profoundly tested the principles of American democracy, beginning with the civil rights movement, moving through the earth-shaking feminist revolution, and culminating with the massive antiwar protests of the Vietnam era. Along the way, the nation was set reeling by the assassinations of a president, a world-famous civil rights leader, and a presidential candidate. Hale became convinced that a genuine Christian faith cannot ignore injustice—and that contemplative prayer leads naturally to peace-making. While still in Minnesota, he started taking part in antiwar protests, along with St. John's monks and some of the sisters from nearby St. Benedict's, and when he began his doctoral studies at Fordham in New York, he kept marching for peace, this time with thousands of other protesters.

In January of 1969, and much to Thomas Matus's surprised consternation, Hale asked to be transferred to Old Camaldoli in order to teach at Sant'Anselmo in Rome while he finished up his doctoral thesis on Teilhard de Chardin's "cosmic Christology." Even though Matus was also thinking of transferring, he was worried about Hale's decision. Wasn't Hale the natural choice for prior of New Camaldoli someday? And if he moved permanently to Italy, then who would lead the young American community? Hale, however, seemed serene about his choice and went on to receive his PhD from Fordham in 1972, continuing to teach philosophy and spirituality at Sant'Anselmo while participating in the huge demonstrations in Rome. On several occasions, he went with Andrew Colnaghi, a Camaldolese monk he'd met at the Sacro Eremo a few years before. At times, the demonstrations became tumultuous, with the police having to intervene; once, in a tightly packed crowd, a young man with a covered face ran right past the two of them, brandishing a pistol.[5]

Thomas Matus made his announcement in January of 1969: like Hale, he wanted to transfer to Old Camaldoli. His request was granted. During his ensuing years at Sant'Anselmo, he spent a lot of time with both Giabbani, who was now the prior at San Gregorio in Rome and thus his superior, and Catani, who had become his confessor. It was Giabbani who pointed out to him that a genuine monastic vocation involves being called "repeatedly." As long as he was on a true monastic journey, the call would come again and again.[6] This was extremely helpful for Matus, who tended toward perfectionism and self-doubt but who did believe at some level that God had put him where he was instead of where he thought he'd be: Big Sur.

He was determined to become totally fluent in Italian, and also to get his PhD, which he did at Fordham between 1972 and 1976, flying back and forth to Italy each summer. His dissertation drew on his early spiritual formation with Yogananda plus Eastern Orthodox spirituality; it was called *Yoga and the Jesus Prayer,* a topic that did not pass muster at New Camaldoli and was not the Italians' favorite choice either, though he was ultimately given permission to write it. Perhaps they realized that Matus's work reflected the church's new attitude toward non-Christian religions and was thus worth pursuing. Like Griffiths and Merton, Matus was a pioneer exploring unknown territory

After receiving his doctoral degree, Matus went home to Camaldoli, where he began composing music for the Italian Camaldolese Psalter. He also taught Hindu and Buddhist monasticism in Rome. In the midst of all this satisfying work—at last he was seeing the shape of his unique vocation—he began making trips to India and most particularly, Shantivanam.

Pedro Rebello's quest to make a Camaldolese foundation in his native land ended almost before it began. On January 14, 1970, he set out in a jeep for Kurukshetra, a renowned Hindu shrine in Northern India, to see if he might find a potential site nearby for a new Camaldolese foundation. It was drizzling and the road was slick. The jeep began to skid, crossed the center line, and smashed into an oncoming bus. All three priests in the jeep were injured, but Rebello most seriously. He died in the hospital three days later and his sister arranged to have his body flown to Milagres, Mangalore, his native town, where he was buried in the sanctuary of the church. The driver of the jeep, a priest from Patiala, Punjab, sent word to the hermitage, adding in his letter that "Father Pedro's sufferings and death will lay the foundation for the noble work he had come to accomplish."[7] The Big Sur community felt badly that Rebello could not be buried in the little cemetery he himself had laid out at the hermitage. To honor this hardworking fund-raiser with the beautiful Malayalam script, a cross was erected on the hillside that overlooks much of the hermitage, just below a statue of Mary with her palms held open in blessing.

As it turned out, there would be another cross on this hillside. After the crisis of 1959 and Modotti's departure from the order, his fiercely loyal supporter Bishop Joseph Willinger highly recommended him to the bishop of Puerto Rico, who invited him to come help build a new seminary. Several years later, he returned to the States, where he became a diocesan priest in the farming town of Corcoran, California. By all accounts, he was a beloved pastor, admired and respected in much the same way he had been during his wartime years among the Italian immigrants of Australia.

But he had always struggled with a mysterious health problem, and sometime after he returned to California, he asked to be buried at the Big Sur hermitage when his time came. In 1971, he died in his bed in Corcoran and was laid to rest beside the cross marked "Pedro Rebello," below the statue of Mary. Though his grave was not among those of the monks he'd help form during those first pioneer years, from his place on the hillside, he instead overlooked them. He was seventy-four when he finally returned to New Camaldoli—a man who had lived several different lives, each of them dogged by conflict and grief, but also filled with adventure and accomplishment.

Though Bede Griffiths was desperately lonely during those first months at Shantivanam, by 1970 a small but stable community had developed. He continued the practices of Kurimsala; he and the other monks lived like Christian sannyasis, going barefoot, wearing the *kavi* habit, sitting on the floor and eating with their hands. They hoped to create an environment that allowed for maximum simplicity, humility, and peacefulness. Their daily practice centered around an hour of silent meditation each morning and evening, but they also maintained the full Benedictine schedule of morning, noon, mid-afternoon, and evening offices. Their day began at 4:30 a.m. and followed the Benedictine principle of *ora et labora*, or "prayer and work." In the hope of developing a truly Indian Christian liturgy, the monks sat cross-legged on the chapel floor in two facing lines, and visitors left their shoes on the threshold, just as they would at a Hindu temple. The basic prayers and lessons were in English, but there were also readings from the Vedas, the Upanishads, and the Bhagavad Gita, along with Sanskrit *slokas* (verses). A Latin Rite Mass was celebrated each day after morning prayer.[8]

Griffith's justification for this deliberate intermingling of two quite different religious cultures was to be found, once again, in the Vatican Council's Declaration on Non-Christian Religions: "This should mark the beginning of a new era in the history of the church. No longer need we have a negative attitude to other religions and philosophies; we can welcome the truth to be found in all alike and co-operate in common tasks for the welfare of mankind."[9] To this end, members of the Catholic hierarchy attended two All-India Seminars, the second taking place in 1969, a year after Griffiths arrived in Tamil Nadu. The seminars drew six hundred participants, and their goal was to help foster liturgical renewal and "to establish authentic forms of monastic life in keeping with the best traditions of the Church and the spiritual heritage of India."[10]

This new ecumenical openness on the part of the church came at a time when droves of young westerners, perhaps exhausted by a decade of social upheaval and protest, began heading eastward, both metaphorically and literally. Shantivanam became a magnet for spiritual seekers, and within the next ten years, Griffiths himself would become an international guru for people of all religious backgrounds, or with no religious background at all, who were genuinely seeking God. His openness to the spiritual beliefs and practices of others, coupled with his unwavering kindness and willingness to listen, turned Shantivanam into a sanctuary for those who had become disillusioned by the institutional church, yet still hungered for worship.

However, a backlash was building. As far as some more traditional Catholics were concerned, Griffiths was dangerously pushing the envelope if he really thought that one could be a serious Catholic who employed Hindu and Buddhist practices. By the late seventies, the uproar had grown so loud that Griffiths was forced to find another Benedictine congregation, one that would feel comfortable absorbing the controversial Shantivanam community.

And who was better suited for this challenge than the spiritually nimble Camaldolese with their marvelous threefold charism of community, solitude, and mission-martyrdom?

To be fair, the traditionalists' concerns about the direction Griffiths was going were neither frivolous nor necessarily wrongheaded. Though the great religions share a great many moral principles, such as compassion and self-restraint, and though they form their adherents in often similar ways—for example, through the creation of small communities and the practice of ascetical disciplines—there's a philosophical point at which Eastern religions part ways with Christianity. Yet too many eager young seekers, enthralled with the exotic elements of newly discovered spiritual paths, fell into syncretism, or the belief that "all paths lead to the top of the same mountain." Griffiths at times walked perilously close to that line. Unless people were prepared to read closely and think deeply, they could become confused, and the traditionalists worried that in the process, orthodox belief might become diluted or even abandoned.

Even ancient Camaldoli was swept up in the general frenzy. According to the former prior of San Gregorio in Rome, Innocenzo Gargano, in 1968 there were "young Italians, often disaffected culturally and even spiritually, who were among those—and there were thousands in those years —coming back from India, where they had embarked on extraordinary spiritual journeys indicated by gurus of Hinduism, and had been led to experiment with 'spiritual' techniques of every kind, not excluding erotic experiences or the use of drugs, more or less hard, of which many unfortunately became tragic victims. Camaldoli, thanks to the decisive appeal of its age-old sacred hermitage, attracted more than one of these young people, convinced that they could continue . . . that which they had tasted in India." Alas, however, the monks ("naive and fledgling guides," as Gargano puts it) were completely unprepared to deal with the problems the young seekers brought into the monasteries.

"Those young people were extremely sincere and, in their way, even generous, but their previous experiences had almost always left indelible marks on each one of them, and unfortunately very grave ones, which led some of them to death not only in soul, but also in body, making them the victims of the incipient tragedy of AIDS, and some others were influenced by psychophysical and psychedelic practices, seen as magical resources of full human realization." These young seekers did not stay on to become monks, but it took a few years for the community to figure out what in the world was going on.[11]

Adding to the general confusion of the era was the New Age philosophy that by now had fully entered the bloodstream of American culture. Originating at the very same Slate's Springs where Gabriel Dani once traded backbreaking labor for sacks of dried corn and peas, and seventy years later, Henry Miller floated in his favorite hot tub, the New Age philosophy born at Esalen Institute in the early sixties offered a compelling and attractive alternative to postwar American church life. Only eleven miles north of the hermitage, Esalen sat at the epicenter of a genuine spiritual revolution, one driven by the romantic notion that abiding by the rules of bourgeois society was the fastest way to stunt creativity and crush the spirit. Under this view of things, fuga mundi meant flight from a corporate world driven by a soul-sucking, competitive capitalism—and even more importantly, flight from unnecessary "hang-ups." The institute offered a spectacularly beautiful sanctuary for those seeking to throw off middle-class inhibitions, including sexual mores, in order to recapture the innocence and freedom of nature.

A 1969 gathering exemplifies how influential Esalen was at the dawn of a new decade. In a conscious nod to Woodstock, major rock musicians like Joan Baez, Joni Mitchell, and Crosby, Stills, and Nash performed for a large Big Sur Folk Festival crowd on the cliffs overlooking the Pacific. In the language of the musical *Hair,* which had debuted the previous year, it really did feel like the "dawning of the Age of Aquarius."

Meanwhile, just down the road from hot tubs jammed with naked celebrants of life and grassy meadows filled with wildly dancing hippies, the Italians were finally preparing to leave New Camaldoli in American hands. It had been nearly twelve years since Modotti first laid eyes on what had been Nesbitt's hideaway, Moore's dream ranch, the Dani family homestead, and the former home of the Salinan tribe. And despite the controversy of those initial years, much had been accomplished in this first decade. The American community, which began with the arrival of Philip Klee, had grown to the point that there was now a core group in place that would persevere through the coming decades. The extensive building project had been undertaken and completed. The church had been erected, the cells were occupied, and guests now had a place to stay.

More, Prior Clemente Roggi and Pedro Rebello had continued to build on the relationships first formed by Modotti; they had established a wide circle of supporters among local Catholic parishes and groups—particularly the Italian Catholic Federation—in Monterey/Carmel, Salinas, and San Luis Obispo County. As a mark of how quickly the reputation of the hermitage had grown, in June of 1969, the once-controversial but by now renowned theologian who had long ago inspired Giabbani, Calati, and Ignesti to move the Camaldolese out of the neoscholastic mindset and into the modern world, made a visit to the Big Sur hermitage. Fr. Henri De Lubac, SJ, whose theological writings had been suppressed under Pius XII only to be embraced by Vatican II, arrived with a couple of other Jesuits to see for himself the American hermitage envisioned by his admirer, Giabbani.

Clearly, it was time to turn the page. Given that Hale and Matus had transferred to Old Camaldoli, the natural choice for new prior was the introverted mystic and chemist, Bruno Barnhart. He was elected to the post in 1970, and along with his role as pastor and guide for the community, he continued to fly back and forth to Rome to meet with the commission that was drafting reforms of the congregation.

But he had not forgotten his remarkable mystical experience, never since repeated, of St. Teresa of Avila's Prayer of Union. And he continued his search for the path that would reconnect him to that moment.

17

Despite being a mere eleven miles down the road from the birthplace of the Age of Aquarius, life at New Camaldoli in the seventies, hippie camps and all, continued in much the same direction it had gone under Modotti in 1958. Waking hours were taken up by liturgy, contemplative prayer, and the endless labor required to maintain nine hundred acres in the Big Sur wilderness. The somewhat tongue-in-cheek March 1970 newsletter provides good insight into the dual nature of life during this period. The first heading deals with the profane: "Drainage Problems" informs friends of the hermitage that "the postulants' quarters were constructed near the edge of a steep ravine. Excessive rainfall has saturated the earth and caused the building to move slowly but surely toward destruction. Lest we lose both postulants and their quarters at one blow, we plan to dig a deep trench at the side of the ravine and fill it with coarse gravel. This, we hope, will allow the water to drain off and the Community to breathe more easily."

The next heading, "The Changing World," gives a nod to the sacred: "Like so many others, we are cringing before the impending changes in the ritual of the Mass. Perhaps we may be pardoned a certain nostalgic longing for the happy days when the Sacred Mysteries were celebrated with rites which we naively thought were forever unchangeable (and knew were sometimes unintelligible). But we have been gradually initiated into the new order of things and are now preparing to take the final plunge. Whatever we may say about it, we do appreciate the wisdom of Vatican II in taking the necessary steps to make the liturgy more meaningful—hence, more prayerful."[1]

   Though New Camaldoli still had trouble retaining people—many postulants came, few stayed—the community had managed to grow during the previous decade and now numbered well over twenty-five. However, new tensions had sprung up. The problem was twofold—theological disagreement generated by Vatican II was becoming more pronounced, while inadequate formation of new monks continued to impede the spiritual development of the group. Of the two, the formation issue was clearly the most pressing. Young men without any experience of monasticism would be sent up the mountain to spend a month in a trailer at the lake to see if they had a true eremitical calling. People would bring them food, but other than that, they were on their own, sometimes for a whole year.[2] In addition, some of them were contending with serious psychological issues that the discernment process either did not recognize or preferred not to address.[3] Things needed to change, but the new prior, Barnhart, had not yet figured out what to do and in fact, did not seem well-suited to the role he'd been charged with. Thanks to Hale's decision to transfer to Old Camaldoli, however, Barnhart felt he had no choice but to shoulder the mantle.

   But he had taken on a daunting task. Though the formation issue clearly took priority, the theological split was becoming serious. Barnhart and many of the others were very much in the postconciliar frame of mind, eagerly absorbing the work of Karl Rahner and other modern theologians. The "old guard" was most definitely not. The leader of the traditionalist camp was the former keeper-of-the-cows, Philip Klee. The very first American postulant to arrive at New Camaldoli in 1958, he had persevered all through the pioneer years and was aghast at the changes now being instituted in the hermitage church—the church he had helped to build. His sense of outrage would eventually boil over and affect the whole community.

   What helped the group cohere around a common goal during this troubled time was the 1975 vote by the Domestic Council to sponsor two Vietnamese refugee families and two single men. The men would live at the hermitage, the families in the Bay area, and the community would donate $500 a month toward each family's expenses. Everyone was involved in making the final commitment. According to Hale, the vote to sponsor the families would have been "unthinkable" before Barnhart took charge.[4]

Hale himself was still in Italy teaching at Sant'Anselmo. After visiting the Anglican Centre in Rome, he became friends with the chaplain, Canon Harry Smythe. The center, backed by Canterbury and the Anglican Communion, was committed to the ecumenical Anglican-Catholic dialogue. When he had a chance to accompany the new prior general's protégé, Emanuele Bargellini, on an official visitation to New Camaldoli, Hale took the opportunity to further these ecumenical ties with the Anglicans. He accompanied Bargellini on a tour of the US in March of 1975, one of their visits being to the Episcopalian monastic community of Holy Cross, West Park. There, they met with the superior, who welcomed them into yet another interdenominational friendship. This connection would eventually flower into a joint enterprise between Episcopalian and Roman Catholic monks, a project that would ultimately pull Hale away from the Italy he so loved and into a new adventure.

Meanwhile, young seekers kept discovering Big Sur. In the summer of 1970, a young Catholic named Kevin Joyce was driving down the coast with a friend and decided to drop in at the hermitage bookstore. The monk behind the counter was the charming French Canadian with the black beret, Bernard Massicotte, and the two of them had a lively conversation before Joyce continued on his journey. Less than a year later, Joyce underwent a "mini-crisis" while in seminary and realized he needed to get away to recover his balance. Back he headed to New Camaldoli, this time bringing with him a collection of writings by the medieval German mystic, Meister Eckhart. Though he still didn't get a chance to meet the new prior in person, he heard enough about Barnhart, no doubt from the loquacious Massicotte, to realize that, whatever its problems, the hermitage was clearly in the hands of a "beautiful soul."[5]

Joyce went on to graduate seminary, decided he did not have a vocation after all, then headed for Europe for nine months where he studied with Maharishi Mahesh Yogi. Though the practice of meditation had been drawing young westerners eastward in droves for at least a decade by now, Catholic seminaries did not teach it, and Joyce—intensely interested in the mystical path—was hungry to learn. He became an ardent practitioner of transcendental meditation, at the same time continuing to faithfully attend Mass. This was not an uncommon story in the seventies. The church was so preoccupied with incorporating the liturgical changes precipitated by Vatican II into its often resistant parishes that it failed to identify, prioritize, and address the obvious spiritual hunger of its youth. Longing for more, many left the pews altogether, while some, like Joyce, quietly inserted Eastern practices into the otherwise Catholic structure of their lives.

Indeed, some even took on dual religious identities. Griffiths, both Catholic priest and Hindu sannyasi, was a good example of this trend. Another was the Jesuit priest William Johnston, who developed a serious practice of Zen meditation while continuing to preside over the Mass each day. In 1970, Johnston published an influential book called *The Still Point*, whose title comes from T.S. Eliot's famous poem "Burnt Norton" in the *Four Quartets*. In his introduction, Johnston conjectured that "not only Zen but all forms of Buddhism are going to make an enormous impact on the Christianity of the coming century. If there has been a Hellenized Christianity (which is now about to succumb with the passing of the so-called Christendom), there is every likelihood that the future will see the rise of an Oriental Christianity in which the role of Buddhism will be incalculably profound."[6]

It appeared to those involved in the East-West dialogue of the day that one element Eastern and Western mysticism might have in common was negative theology or a kind of spiritual fuga mundi. The "via negativa," as it was called in the Christian tradition, requires that all images and symbols of religion, along with any attempt to name the attributes of God, are left behind so that the mind is no longer held back by its inability to grasp the nature of the divine and is thus freed up to enter a mysterious, radiant darkness. The apophatic, or imageless, way is most obvious in Zen, but negative theology also runs through the Hindu Upanishads. The via negativa is well-established in Christianity too, as exemplified by Meister Eckhart, the Spanish mystic St. John of the Cross, the anonymous medieval author of the *Cloud of Unknowing*—and of course, the holy man Romuald himself in the opening lines of his Brief Rule: "Sit in your cell as in a paradise. Put the whole world behind you and forget it."

Joyce was intrigued by all of it. After he returned to the States, he was invited to go to New Camaldoli by a carpenter friend who had been hired by Barnhart to put a new ceiling in the remodeled hermitage church. Joyce stayed for five days, and it was on this occasion that he finally got to meet the new prior in person. As he recalls, "I thought, this is one heck of a wise man. I'm going to keep him in my back pocket for when I really need help!"[7]

It was not only some famous Western mystics who embraced the apophatic way; Eastern Christianity also nourished strains of negative theology, particularly through the writings of John of Damascus and Maximus the Confessor. The Orthodox practice of *hesychasm,* or silent meditation, combined with a humble refusal to make statements about the divine, gave birth to a number of legendary charismatic elders over the centuries, particularly in the ancient monastic republic of Mount Athos. In November of 1972, Barnhart was offered a chance to visit this oldest bastion of monastic life in the Christian world, older even than the Sacro Eremo, if only by a few years. Barnhart and Massicotte were in Italy for the triennial meeting of the whole Camaldolese Congregation known as the "Consulta," and the prior of San Gregorio, Innocenzo Gargano, who had once lived and studied in Athens, suggested that they make the trip to the wooded peninsula east of Saloniki in northern Greece to see for themselves what Orthodox monasticism had to teach.

Though Athos is home to twenty monasteries, some of them quite large and at least one of them dating back to the tenth century, it is the charismatic holy elders, living in scattered hermitages and sketes on the great peninsula, who have long captured the imagination of pilgrims entranced by the fourth-century Desert Fathers of Egypt, Palestine, and Syria. Barnhart, Massicotte, and Gargano decided to forgo visits to the historic monasteries and instead seek out the "startzy," as the Russians call them. They were able to meet and converse with six of these holy elders and found that some bore all the marks of genuine "pneumataphors," or "Spirit-bearers."

André Louf, a Belgian Trappist who visited Mount Athos about this time, offers a rhapsodic description of what Barnhart and Massicotte were hoping to find: "Here and there in the world some places survive where prayer is everything. There are still men who pray as they breathe. He who has hiked under the burning sun of

Mount Athos will never forget certain monks whom he was able to encounter there: men of prayer with faces like flames and looks like fire, plunging deep down and yet so utterly gentle; men who from the innermost depths of their being go forward toward each thing and each person, attaining in each the secret flame, the hidden core, the deepest center, in a love and understanding without limits."[8]

The holy elders of New Camaldoli were, by definition, the recluses. They'd been given this special status a thousand years ago in Blessed Rudolph's constitutions: "When the [hermits] or other brothers at the Hermitage become sick or very weak, as often happens, they can be moved to the hospice of Fonte Buono and receive there with attentiveness the care necessary for their health. Cured of their sickness, they can return to the Hermitage. . . . The recluses, however, whether well or sick, should remain always in their cells and receive everything necessary for physical health, as though they were Christ."[9] Joseph Diemer had been a recluse at New Camaldoli since 1968, and now Anthony Barabe, who had made his simple profession the same year, was building a little metal cell in the hills, hoping to enter reclusion himself. But he was still needed as kitchen supervisor, so the Domestic Council came to a compromise: he could spend two to three days up in the hills and man the kitchen for the rest of each week.

But there were other ways besides total reclusion to participate in the divine life. According to Vatican II, which sought to make room for the unpredictable work of the Holy Spirit within the institutional church, spiritual transformation was not confined to Camaldolese recluses or the holy elders of Mount Athos. Even laypeople had been called:

> [T]he Holy Spirit not only sanctifies and guides God's people by the sacraments and the ministries, and enriches it with virtues, he also distributes special graces among the faithful of every state of life, assigning his gifts to each as he chooses. By means of these special gifts he equips them and makes them eager for various activities and responsibilities that benefit the Church in its renewal or its increase, in accordance with the text: To each is given the manifestation of the Spirit for a good purpose.

> These charisms, the simpler and more widespread as well as
> the most outstanding, should be accepted with a sense of grati-
> tude and consolation, since in a very special way they answer
> and serve the needs of the Church.[10]

This passage in *Lumen Gentium*, one of the four constitutions
produced by the council, helped trigger what became known as the
Catholic charismatic renewal. Catholics who had long believed that
personal spiritual experiences were only for Protestants began to
embrace the Pentecostal charismatic gifts: baptism of the Holy Spirit,
laying on of hands, speaking in tongues, faith healing, prophecy.
In August of 1966, a Catholic professor and a graduate student at
Duquesne University read two books that changed their lives, *The
Cross and the Switchblade* and *They Speak with Other Tongues*.
After they were baptized in the Spirit at an Episcopalian prayer
meeting, they began laying hands on other Duquesne professors,
who also experienced the phenomena. Then a whole chapel full of
students and teachers received the gifts. The professor sent news
to Notre Dame, and the renewal began to spread. The traditionalists were naturally made uneasy when they heard about what they
considered to be yet another outrageous postconciliar happening,
but in 1975, Pope Paul VI officially welcomed Catholic charismatics
into the fellowship of the church.

The charismatic renewal hit hard at New Camaldoli. Barnhart,
still hoping for a recurrence of the astonishing prayer experience
he'd had as a young man and just back from his conversations with
the charismatic startzy of Mount Athos, quickly became involved.
So did the French Canadian Massicotte, the humble Emmanuel
Wasinger from Diemer's Benedictine monastery in Colorado, and
the artist and guest-master Gabriel Kirby. They organized a charismatic prayer service every Sunday after Vespers in the small chapel
beside Mary and were so excited by what began to unfold that they
proposed a "revision of life" document for the whole community.
The Domestic Council, afraid of the Pentecostal label, said no. Instead, the renewal group was given permission to have a midweek
charismatic prayer service just for those who wished, no retreatants
or guests allowed. The Domestic Council's decision was summed
up thusly: "Let the Holy Spirit lead."[11]

To some degree, the church's new openness to the charismatic gifts could be laid at the door of Anselmo Giabbani's favorite ressourcement theologian, the brilliant Jesuit scholar Henri de Lubac. It was de Lubac's recovery of patristic spirituality and an authentically sacramental interpretation of Scripture that so fired up the young Prior Giabbani at Fonte Avellana in 1935. It was the work of de Lubac that, in part, enabled Giabbani to "re-see" the Camaldolese in light of the modern world. And it was de Lubac's intellectual influence that prompted newly elected Prior General Giabbani to rewrite the 1941 Camaldolese constitutions in the early fifties—a move that ignited the Modotti-led hermit rebellion at the Sacro Eremo.

De Lubac frightened the church in those days, and he was one of the scholars silenced after the dissemination of Pius XII's encyclical *Humane Generis.* Yet he and other ressourcement theologians were rehabilitated during Vatican II, where the concept of going back to the sources in order to understand the present became an operating principle.[12] Giabbani had recognized de Lubac's prophetic genius, and had paid a high personal price for attempting to reform the Camaldolese in light of his insights.

But Giabbani was ultimately vindicated, at least in the eyes of his own congregation. At some point after Paul VI had closed the last session of Vatican II, Thomas Matus was driving through Italy with another monk, who declared, "At the end of the Council, everybody began to realize that Anselmo had been right after all."[13]

18

In light of all the dramatic changes taking place in the church during the seventies and eighties, the fiery hermit-cenobite controversy that pulled Modotti out of his recluse's cell at the Sacro Eremo and several years later set him back down as a parish priest in a California farm town began to look almost quaint—more like an event from another century than recent family history. Though Modotti was gone, Giabbani, Catani, and the other principals involved were still alive—striving, as were Catholics everywhere, to understand and implement the revelations of Vatican II.

For some, like Philip Klee, the changes were almost unbearable. On March 21, 1977, he poured out his anguish in a long letter to Pope Paul VI. He recounted one of the more inspiring experiences of his life—a personal meeting with Pius XII when he was working in a hospital in Italy after the war. On his knees before the pope, he confided his dream of becoming a Trappist. Pius clapped his hands and said, "Oh, how wonderful! My fatherly blessing, my fatherly blessing!" Now, proclaimed Klee in his impassioned letter, he was metaphorically kneeling before another pope, begging for the same blessing, though not as a Trappist but as a Camaldolese monk.

Then he got down to business: "This comes to Your Holiness as a last resort to save our Hermitage Church from proposed alterations which will, to my mind, destroy the wonderful uniqueness of our cloistered choir where presently we have our Eucharistic Savior in our very midst—the King and Center of our hearts." He explained that the church had been consecrated on the feast day of St. Romuald only eleven years before, but now architects had been called in to remove the old altar.

The new altar would be placed where the tabernacle containing the Blessed Sacrament currently sat. "The Blessed Sacrament," he lamented, "will I suppose be relegated to some out-of-the way corner." But there was more. "Presently, we hermits are being homogenized with the Laity, who come to our Morning Prayer." Not only that, but "sometimes the Liturgy is held in our Chapter Room where the rank and file of the Laity—men and *women*—are invited to participate" (italics added). He explained that he had already complained about these travesties to the local bishop, now Harry Clinch, and when he didn't receive a reply, wrote to a cardinal at the Sacred Congregation of Religious.[1]

The cardinal's soothingly ambiguous response, encouraging him not to be disheartened, informed him that "some of the changes introduced today are unauthorized; others have the full approval of the Church." How could he possibly be satisfied with an answer like that? Therefore, Klee explained to the pope, he felt he had no choice but to send his plea directly to the highest level. He ended his lament on a surprisingly folksy note: "In God we trust. All others cash. . . . If we live smiling, we will die smiling, so smile your way into heaven, Your Holiness."[2]

On November 11, 1978, he wrote another letter, this time to Prior General Calati, just before the triennial Consulta in Italy. He reminded Calati that Cardinal Romoli of the Sacred Congregation of Religious had made it very clear during the Modotti era that New Camaldoli would always remain a hermitage and there would never be an attached cenobium. However, it "seems that the Trappists, or whatever is left of them, are itching to be hermits and we Camaldolese, if we can still be called such, are itching to be cenobites." How so? "With the recent auto-destruction of our Hermitage Church, our cloister was eliminated, our choir stalls removed to make place for the oriental mysticism that makes our former choir a place for all." Even worse, though monks were not supposed to leave the hermitage except for the most necessary of reasons, those in authority (Barnhart) were allowing them not only to present conferences outside the walls but to attend charismatic conventions and "to foster Pentecostalism in our midst."[3]

Klee's attempt to stop what he considered to be a shocking departure from "real" Catholicism was destined to fail, however. Vatican

II had not just given permission for Catholics to stop thinking of the church as an unshakeable fortress built to protect the faithful against Protestantism, Judaism, Islam, and the "pagan faiths" of the East. It also strongly encouraged them not only to learn about but to respect the religious beliefs of all.

Nowhere was this new spirit of openness more evident than in the words of Pope John Paul II, elected in 1978, to the members of what would eventually be called the Pontifical Council for Interreligious Dialogue. Referring to his first encyclical, *Redemptor Hominis*, published only a month before, he said that the Second Vatican Council had "given a view of the terrestrial globe as a map of various religions." He spoke of the "values enshrined in other religions" and assured his listeners that "the non-Christian world is indeed always before the eyes of the Church and of the Pope. We are truly committed to serve it generously."[4]

According to the new pope, Catholics had much to learn when they initiated "activity for coming closer together with the representatives of the non-Christian religions, an activity expressed through dialogue, contacts, prayer in common, investigation of the treasures of human spirituality, in which, as we know well, the members of these religions also are not lacking." In fact, Catholics might even be strengthened in their own faith when they were able to see the strength of faith displayed by many non-Christians.[5]

Barnhart was aware of the tensions that were swirling through the hermitage—some generated by Klee's alarm at unwelcome changes at the local level but others that came with rethinking what it now meant to be Catholics and Camaldolese monks. Kevin Joyce noticed a third problem. "By the time the seventies were in full bloom," he recalls, "this place had lost its eremitical character. It was definitely not a place of hermits—by default it had become a cenobium. They couldn't handle the solitude. There was one true hermit, the recluse Fr. Joseph Diemer."[6]

What had happened? In Joyce's view, it was all the activity in a monastery meant to foster deep contemplative prayer. "So much coming and going, wonderful men arriving and leaving. That really destabilized the place. Some of these men were very creative, even brilliant. But it was not an easy life, and many of them didn't stay."[7] And there was more. The East-West dialogue prompted by Vatican II was "really shaking up the place." Though he was intensely interested in the subject himself, Joyce could see that it was confusing some of the monks.[8]

At the 1978 Consulta, Barnhart candidly admitted that the hermitage in Big Sur was "not doing brilliantly," and that perhaps another presence in California—more communal than eremitical—might help.[9] But New Camaldoli had neither the men nor the resources to make another foundation. Innocenzo Gargano offered a potential solution: "Why not Robert Hale? He could go!" Hale, who was present at the Consulta in his role as visitor of the general's council, was at first startled, then perplexed. Why would Gargano, with whom he was working as assistant student master in Rome, suggest such a dramatic move? And what about his own teaching and his longtime, happy relationship with Old Camaldoli? Did he really want to return to California after transferring his stability to Italy? And did they understand that he knew absolutely nothing about founding a new house?[10]

However, there seemed to be a general consensus of voices urging him on, so he asked for time to ponder and pray. It took some days for the thought to come to him that he had always been close to Prior General Calati—had in certain ways been formed by him—and that in the process he had absorbed something of Calati's loving style of leadership. Calati truly believed in the guidance of the Holy Spirit, which came through constant attention to the word of God in daily *lectio divina*. He urged his monastic family to be faithful to the practice of common prayer, to be open to one and all, and to never forget the primacy of the person over every human law or custom. Calati's natural-born ecumenism extended to political differences besides; after Catholics were forbidden to join the Communist Party in Italy, he remained loyal to deep friendships he had formed with prominent leftists. Hale reflected that if he took on the task of making a new foundation and then challenges arose and difficult choices had to be made, he could simply ask himself, "How would Benedetto Calati respond?"

Within a month, Hale had drafted a proposal regarding the new American foundation and had received permission to proceed. He wrote to a friend, the prior of the Episcopalian Holy Cross house in Berkeley, explaining that he might be founding a Camaldolese house in the city and asking about the possibility of teaching at the Jesuit School of Theology after he arrived. He received a reply on April 27, 1979. Why, asked Fr. Roy Parker, superior of the Holy Cross Berkeley monastery, would you go to all the trouble and expense of establishing a new monastic presence here when we could cofound a joint community? Think of how ecumenically cutting-edge that would be!

In late 1979, Gargano and Hale flew to San Francisco from Rome to visit the Holy Cross monks of Incarnation Priory in Berkeley. They agreed that the joint monastery proposal was a great idea and that the inception date would be November 28. The two communities, Episcopalian and Catholic, each with its own superior and identity, would live under one roof, sharing the Divine Office and meals and witnessing to ecumenical dialogue. When Gargano went back to Camaldoli, Hale stayed on to teach spirituality at Holy Family College. By September of 1980, he was also teaching at the Jesuit School of Theology.

The following year, in a ceremony at Grace Cathedral in San Francisco, the new hybrid community received the joint blessing of the Episcopalian and Catholic archbishops. Incarnation Priory's Basic Statement read: "Since the Triune Life is itself the model for the unity in diversity which we seek ('That they may be one, Father, as You in Me and I in You') there is no pursuit of a lowest common denominator, but rather of communion in diversity which safeguards the distinctiveness of each heritage in the substance of unity we already share."[11]

Meanwhile, Calati had been encouraging Hale's friend and fellow monk, Andrew Colnaghi, to go to America for a year to practice his English. Before he joined the Camaldolese at the age of twenty-seven, Colnaghi had been a machinist in a huge factory in Milan where he was a member of a Catholic Christian workers' union. For fifteen years, he had labored beside 10,000 other employees, none of whom were ever called by their names but instead by their assigned numbers (his was 2036). He did not find out until much later what the factory was making: Beretta guns.[12] Colnaghi and Hale had in part become close because of their mutual interest in social justice, though after he became a monk, Colnaghi began to understand that a serious life of prayer could be just as powerful a force for good as his former activism had been.

Colnaghi arrived in the States in 1980 and spent all forty days of Lent at New Camaldoli, where he found little opportunity to improve his language skills. "I didn't see anybody. We had Vigils at 4:30 a.m., then Lauds, then you went into your cell, you had lunch by yourself. You got food twice a week. You cooked on your own. In the afternoon, you worked for a few hours. That was the only time you could talk a little bit and establish a friendship with the young people."[13]

Though Colnaghi returned to Italy after this first visit to America, Hale urged him to come back and help him run the new joint monastery in Berkeley. Calati at first said no, but then gave Colnaghi a check for the plane ticket and signed the documents letting him go. For the first few years, Hale and Colnaghi lived with their fellow Episcopalian monks in an old house owned by the Anglican seminary. Then they obtained a building on the corner of Cedar and Oxford, which served as Incarnation Priory's home for the following decade.

After the big move from Italy, Hale was once again happily settled in. But not for long.

Back at the hermitage, Barnhart was coming into his own as a thinker and spiritual guide, and the role of prior—which he had never sought and only accepted out of humility and a strong sense of duty—was becoming exhausting. He had thought there would be a replacement for him waiting in the wings, but in 1980, the most likely candidate—a gifted novice master who had already been at New Camaldoli for sixteen years—fell in love with one of his spiritual directees, a nun. Both left their respective communities in order to marry just at the time Barnhart was hoping to finally step down.

In spite of his many duties, however, Barnhart continued to work with his own group of directees. Kevin Joyce was one of them. Finally ordained in 1980, Joyce had a very difficult first year as a priest. "I was in a wonderful parish," he recalls, "but wasn't dealing with my own issues well. I came down here [to New Camaldoli] with John of the Cross and the *Ascent of Mt. Carmel*. I'd never read John of the Cross, though I'd heard about him for years. As I read the *Ascent of Mt. Carmel,* I thought, this is the truth, and I became very depressed. Because I realized how attached I was, which was giving rise to so much of my distress. I was attached to people's opinion of me, always trying to be the savior, the rescuer. But then I talked with Fr. Bruno [Barnhart]. He said, 'If you only read John of the Cross, you'll go out of your mind. You have to balance him out, that's why he and Teresa are such good companions on the spiritual journey. She's so different yet so complementary.' That's how I got to know him, and he was really helpful to me because I was in great distress spiritually at the time."[14]

Barnhart's appreciation of Teresa of Avila was rooted in his own youthful struggle with John of the Cross. Teresa's good sense had helped counterbalance John's idealistic vision, which was so entrancing yet so debilitating for a young monk. Barnhart became convinced that a purely masculine spirituality was deficient; it needed the feminine to become whole. This became an important theme for him, both in his role as prior and also in his future writings.

Joyce went on as a diocesan priest, but continued to struggle. He was, as he puts it, "kind of a contemplative type, and you just couldn't get that kind of life as a priest. I was exhausted and I was going to therapy and it was very helpful. The therapist, who was a Jesuit, really supported me in asking for a year off." Joyce approached his bishop, who told him to look around for a place to go during that time. Still very interested in the East-West dialogue, he immediately thought of Bede Griffiths and Shantivanam, which had become a Camaldolese house in 1980. He knew that Barnhart had spent six weeks there and that he and Griffiths had become good friends.

So he wrote to Griffiths, who sent back a simple, humble postcard, saying, "I don't know what we can offer you but you are more than welcome." Joyce's bishop, however, was not wild about this idea, so Joyce went back to New Camaldoli to consult with Barnhart. "And the way he described life there made me realize that I couldn't survive it—I couldn't survive in that kind of environment. Too much toughness, austerity, heat. He helped disavow me of this excitement I had about going to India. He helped release me from this attachment." Joyce instead became a chaplain at a retreat center for a year, which gave him the rest he needed, and then returned to diocesan life. He eventually wound up pastoring an enormous church—7,000 people—for thirteen years, but continued to make retreats at New Camaldoli and to talk with Barnhart every year or so from then on.[15]

Meanwhile, Klee had something new to worry about, a threat far more dangerous than the changes in the liturgy. It had long bothered him that women were allowed to be in the church during services. He could not understand the logic in it. Why would you give females the chance to distract young monks if you didn't have to? Women in a monastery were invariably trouble. Look at what had happened to the novice master who was meant to become prior. He'd gone and fallen in love with that nun and now both of them were excommunicated!

But instead of protecting the community from this baleful influence, the prior was not only welcoming female retreatants but was contemplating allowing a group of three nuns and four single laywomen to live together on the premises as an experimental religious community. Even Prior General Calati had approved! What was this world coming to? Where would it all end?

What Klee could not know was that there was no stopping the female invasion at this point; women would become increasingly involved in the life of New Camaldoli from this time forward, including one toward the end of his life whose friendship would miraculously transform his whole personality. And even as he fretted and stewed over the woman question, there was another, soon to be on her way, who would come and stay for decades and whose influence would help shape the theology and spirituality of more than one Camaldolese monk, including Barnhart.

Her name was Therese Gagnon, and like Massicotte, she was charmingly French Canadian. She was also married, an artist, and a passionate lover of nature—a woman who, like a number of hardy coastal women before her, would arrive in spectacular Big Sur only to find she had come home.

19

Just a year after the conflicted young seminarian Joyce first visited New Camaldoli, another youthful seeker made his initial visit to the hermitage. It was 1973, and Isaiah Teichert, both an avid student of the theater and a brand-new Catholic, was a mere nineteen when he arrived on the mountain. Like Hale, he had been raised Episcopalian, though from birth had one foot in the Roman Church. His mother, always intensely drawn to the Eucharist, had fallen in love with Catholicism while she was still in college and finally converted while she was pregnant with him, her fourth child. His father was not happy about her decision, and the two of them agreed that their children would continue to go to church with him while she went to Mass alone. But she made sure that her offspring were introduced to the rich traditions of Catholicism by establishing a kind of "home church" in which they celebrated the major feast days as a family, were taught to love and admire the saints, and learned Catholic prayers and devotions. One by one, in their own time and own ways, each of her five children eventually followed her into the Catholic Church.

Teichert's arrival at New Camaldoli was not merely a happy accident. One of his older brothers had already discovered the hermitage and was seriously exploring whether or not he might have a monastic vocation. Like Joyce and his own older brother, Teichert kept coming back—initially, for a few days at a time but already thinking about what might happen if he were to have a long, intense retreat experience. What might he learn about himself? He had so many interests, after all—acting, poetry, fine literature, music—but also this intense love of God and what seemed to be a natural capacity for deep prayer. He eventually asked permission to stay for an entire month, and about halfway through had a revelation: "I started to think, life is too short not to be living some kind of monastic life. It was so rich. But then I thought, what's going on here? This wasn't the plan!" The plan, he thought, surely had more to do with the arts in some way? "Yet when I took it to prayer, God seemed to be saying, this could be yours if you wanted it."[1]

Teichert's older brother made a formal observership in 1977 and realized at the end that in spite of how he had loved the experience, he was not cut out to be a monk. It appears he was right, as he would go on to marry and have eight children. Teichert himself became an observer in 1979 and, somewhat to his amazement, reached a different conclusion than his brother had: this was the life for him. He left the hermitage for a few more months of discernment before beginning his postulancy, but returned to a community in disarray. The novice master he'd come to count on had left to get married, and it was clear that Barnhart, the prior he so liked and respected, was now doubly burdened and suffering under the increased workload.

Teichert worried about him. The monk who everyone had assumed would replace him as the next prior was no longer part of the picture. And now Barnhart had the postulants to deal with as well. As Teichert recalls, he "had the help of one other senior monk, who wasn't yet a 'father' at the time—so we weren't as carefully supervised as we could have—should have—been. It was a hard time."[2]

Janet Walker was only twenty-five and mulling over a marriage proposal when she first visited the hermitage. She had heard about the place from a friend who'd been a worker there. It was 1978, and—despite Klee's horrified conviction that females were overrunning the place—women were still a relative rarity at New Camaldoli. But when she called to see if she could make a retreat, she was told she was welcome to come up the following week. One of the monks, Angelus, was in charge of delivering food to the guests, which was put through a little cupboard door that opened from both the inside and outside of the room. After setting her meal inside the cupboard, he knocked on her door. Was she all right? Did she have any troubles he could pray for? Always shy, she was nearly overwhelmed by this unexpected gesture of concern for a total stranger.

On her second visit to New Camaldoli, she had a conversation in the bookstore with the effervescent Massicotte. "He just put me under his wing immediately," she recalls. During subsequent visits, Massicotte began introducing her to people guests did not usually get to meet. Clearly, he thought that these experiences would benefit her, and also that she could be trusted to behave appropriately. "I guess it was because I was so quiet. He took me to see the two recluses [Diemer and Barabe] when he was saying Mass for them. I had to sneak when he took me inside the enclosure." Diemer, who was already losing his vision and in the coming years would go totally blind, took her hand and felt how rough it was. "You're a hard worker," he told her, then gave her a little wooden cross Barabe had made.[3]

After she married and had the first of her three babies, it was much harder to get away for a retreat. But Massicotte continued to check up on her. During these years, he served as cellarer for the community, which meant he was often on the road buying supplies for the fruitcakes the hermitage was now making and selling or driving one of his brothers to the doctor or dentist. When he was in the area, he would sometimes drop by her house for a short visit. On one occasion, he had the former British secret service agent Bede Janvrin with him, who was a "total English gentleman. He had a little hump on his back and was very humble—he also had a fantastic speaking voice, a beautiful baritone with an English accent. He was angelic; he made a deep impression on me."[4]

Teichert began his formal postulancy in 1980 and made his simple vows in 1981. By 1984 he was going to seminary at the Dominican School in Oakland, returning to the hermitage each summer for the next four years. As for his early conviction that this was the life for him, it didn't waver. "It was really like falling in love. But like any romance, it had its ups and downs. Yet I'm so intensely grateful for the vocation." At one point a friend said to him, "God suits you"— and this felt right, and jived with his sense that God was blessing his monastic life, even though it was not the path involving acting that he had once envisioned for himself.[5] This peaceful sense of assurance may be what allowed his own version of the Third Good to emerge early on: his ability to cheer the hearts of others, to help them laugh at themselves and their foibles, to lead them into the joy of God's presence through the one-on-one ministries he would take on for the community as a spiritual director, confessor, guest-master, and novice master. In the monastic world, and especially among young, idealistic monks who too often became their own worst task-masters, the gift of joy was both precious and rare and usually did not fully manifest until wise old age.

Teichert found inspiration in the life of the sixteenth-century St. Philip Neri, sometimes known as the "laughing saint." Neri believed that "[a] joyful heart is more easily made perfect than one that is sad."[6] He was famous for deliberately behaving foolishly at times, a method he'd developed to protect him from the pitfalls of pride. Neri's legendarily capacious heart beat so loudly that sometimes during confession, he would ask the penitent to place a hand on his breast to feel the strength of his love. Some said that his heart was so large it could not be contained within his chest—and an examination after his death confirmed that two of his ribs were indeed broken.

Teichert's keen appreciation for wit allowed Barnhart, the mystical chemist and overburdened prior, to indulge his own gift in that arena. For example, one New Year's Eve during the kiss of peace, he murmured to Teichert, "Try to do better next year." Once when they were discussing the peace movement, Barnhart declared, "We're going to break the back of the opposition." When Teichert asked him how he was doing after an illness, Barnhart responded, "Better—there are degrees of dead." When Teichert reported that there were two women visitors at the hermitage who were fighting like tigers and it was truly scaring him, Barnhart declared, "That's the feminine dimension that's missing from the church."[7]

Their mutual appreciation of irony allowed Barnhart to confide, in the middle of his most burdensome time as prior, that in truth, the job had been good for him. He was a classic introvert and it would have been easy for him to become a recluse. Yet serving as the face of the hermitage had forced him into meeting the wider world and engaging with it in a way he might not have otherwise. Given his natural inclinations, stretching himself this way meant for continual tension—but the energy generated by being pushed one way and pulled the other no doubt helped him navigate the difficult transition that was taking place throughout the seventies: the shift from Italian leadership to American. Barnhart was "always a lover of solitude and the Italians were always suspicious of that," recalls Teichert. But if the Italians were concerned about too great an emphasis on the eremitical side of monastic life, they had a reason: the not-so-long-ago clash between the hermit party and the cenobites that had so disastrously spilled over the ancient walls of the Sacro Eremo and nearly destroyed the infant American foundation in 1959.

According to Teichert, Barnhart ultimately came to see their wisdom. "We have to have fellowship with one another and be more human before we embrace solitude. . . . His long stint as prior was about shaping that and making that happen, and he was not always clear about how to do that. One of his sayings was, 'We just have to muddle along,' and he didn't mind doing that."[8]

Six years after Janet Walker's first visit, French Canadian artists Therese Gagnon and her husband, Eric, arrived at New Camaldoli. Like other women before her, Gagnon was drawn by the wild beauty of the coast. But the possibility of retreat from a distracting world was equally compelling. From pioneers Elizabeth Dani, Lulu Harlan, and Julia Pfeiffer Burns to writers Una Jeffers, Lillian Bos Ross, and Lynda Sargent, women were just as susceptible to the mystique of fuga mundi as the young men who sought out Henry Miller's Partington Ridge hideaway or became monks, and as a serious artist, Gagnon was no exception.

The Gagnons had a proposal for the community. What if the two of them were allowed to stay, make ceramics that could be sold in the bookstore, and train some of the younger monks in the art of producing earthly vessels for use in the liturgy? The idea appealed to Barnhart, who proposed it to the group. Gagnon did not have much hope the monks would allow her and her husband to remain, but, "You won't believe it!" Barnhart reported back enthusiastically. "The whole Chapter unanimously approved!"

The question was, where would this married couple live? Clearly, they could not be housed anywhere near the monastic compound or the guest quarters. The solution for the first year was a small travel trailer, parked below the hermitage in a canyon that first had to be cleared of big downed oaks. Emmanuel Wasinger, who had nearly lost his leg in a Kansas tractor accident when he was a child, operated all the heavy equipment at the hermitage; it was he who took on the oak removal project. Gagnon's husband had many skills but, thanks to his emphysema, was not particularly strong, so much of the heavy work involved in helping Wasinger fell to her—not an easy life for a woman almost sixty.

Then there was the question of deportment. What, Gagnon asked Barnhart, did he expect her to wear and where on the property was she allowed to go? She was told that she could not cross the cloister where the monks lived, and that he preferred her to always wear a long dress. Getting up to the church from down in the canyon required a lengthy hike and meant she arrived at Mass or prayer in skirts soaked by the dew-covered grass, so her husband built her a set of steep stairs to make the ascent a little easier.

Though *he* was welcome to work on his ceramics in the monastic compound, this was forbidden territory for *her*. However, Barnhart—"who was very perceptive" and knew how much she loved spending time alone in the forest—gave her permission to build her own studio in the canyon, allowing her to "open the creek" in the process. Since her husband was busy working with the ceramics, cooking for the community on Saturdays, and doing other jobs in the compound, this special project was for her alone. "So I set out into the wilderness with some tools," she recalls. She discovered that the creek was a shape-shifter, in one place a waterfall and in another, a cataract churning between two huge redwoods. She discovered magnificent boulders that eons ago had tumbled from the top of the mountain and now lay half-hidden by thick foliage. She stood in bars of light and named the wonders she found: the lightning-hollowed Womb Tree, the towering Moses Rock, the Trinity-with-the-Holy-Spirit-in-Between.[9]

As nature had worked its way into the soul of poet Robinson Jeffers, so it did in Gagnon, igniting within her an overpowering need to worship. And in much the same way that India had pushed Griffiths past the boundaries of his British Benedictine worldview, the wonders of the natural world began pushing her beyond her French Canadian Catholicism. Though she continued to hike out of the canyon to attend Mass and pray the liturgy in the church, over the next few years—now living in a mobile home perched on pilings instead of the tiny trailer—she began to create sanctuaries in the forest, shrines made out of pebbles and shells and twisted branches and her often whimsical ceramic statues: candlelit outdoor chapels among the dripping redwoods. One year she single-handedly cleared old stumps from a rare piece of flat ground overlooking the sea and planted the newly created meadow in blazing orange poppies.

Therese Gagnon

The joint monastery in Berkeley was going well, and Hale was especially happy with the ecumenical dialogue made possible by living together and sharing the Divine Office. Wasn't this how the Body of Christ was supposed to operate? What was making his role as prior even more interesting was the oblate program he had instituted in 1984. Old Camaldoli had once had oblates, but was now less enthusiastic about the idea; New Camaldoli was convinced that the eager involvement of non-monastics in the life of the hermitage could become a major distraction. So Hale was on his own with this experiment, and thankfully, he found the role of oblate chaplain a natural fit.

But as had already happened once before, the superiors of Camaldoli had other plans for him. In 1987, they began urging, "though not ordering," him to go to Big Sur so as to be available in case he was needed as the next prior. Barnhart was just completing his third six-year term and was openly admitting that every day in the job was "very heavy and painful" for him. A successor was desperately needed.

The prospect of giving up his satisfying life in Berkeley was made easier by the fact that Hale's good friend Andrew Colnaghi could most definitely carry on as prior there. Hale told the Italians that he would consider the move but that he would need to go to New Camaldoli well in advance of the election so the community had a chance to get to know him before it was time to vote. His superiors agreed. In June of 1987, Hale offered the community of New Camaldoli a retreat on a theme that would come to characterize his priorship: "The Primacy of Love." He considered it to be one of Benedetto Calati's most important teachings because it touched on so many important questions: who God was, why the incarnation, Christ as loving brother, friend, spouse, and the cross as a living out of Christ's love. More, it captured the essence of the First Good of the tripartite charism: community as "koinonia" (Christian communion).[10]

A few months later, Hale moved into the New Camaldoli cell called St. Gregory the Great that he would occupy for the rest of his life. He received a kind welcome by Barnhart and the brethren, though some were no doubt perplexed by this "ecumenicist cenobite" moving in on them. Shortly after he settled in, Bede Janvrin, the "English gentleman" who had so impressed Janet Walker with his obvious humility and beautiful baritone voice, died at the age of eighty-six. Janvrin had been one of the pioneers at the Big Sur hermitage, and his loss was felt deeply.

On March 9, 1988, with the new prior general, Emanuele Bargellini, present, Hale was elected prior of New Camaldoli. In his first address to the community, he spelled out his program, which he was rooting in the three major texts of the Camaldolese. Scripture, of course, came first, and was norming and decisive. The Rule of St. Benedict spelled out the basic Benedictine identity of the community, while the Camaldolese constitutions provided the specific identity of the hermitage monks. He also urged the group to be open to the signs of the times, to be constantly aware of the uniqueness of their particular situation, and to remain alert to the challenges they might face in the future. A few months after his installation, New Camaldoli voted to accept the monks of Incarnation as full members of the hermitage community. Barnhart's vision of a monastery linked to the hermitage had come to fruition.

Robert Hale, 1980s

With Hale's installation behind him, Barnhart was free to leave the hermitage on a much-deserved break. He headed for L'Arche Daybreak near Toronto, Canada, where he became the companion of a profoundly disabled young man named Adam. Henri Nouwen wrote about Adam in his book of the same name. Barnhart met Nouwen at L'Arche, who later described him in glowing terms: "He was a tall, thin man with a short beard, gentle eyes, and a peaceful disposition, very soft-spoken, but mostly silent and a little shy. A true monk . . . as soon I saw them [Barnhart and Adam] together, I thought 'What better companion could Adam have than this quiet, peaceful monk! Isn't Adam's life similar to his? Peace is speaking to peace. Solitude is greeting solitude. Silence is dwelling with silence. What a grace!' "[11]

For Barnhart, finally released from the arduous job he'd so humbly accepted eighteen years before, it was grace indeed.

Barnhart doing dishes

20

Thomas Matus, still in Italy, was beginning to see how he would live out the Third Good of the Camaldolese charism. If nothing else, he seemed to have evolved into a bridge between the old Camaldoli and the new. He'd lived at the motherhouse since the sixties; he spoke fluent Italian; he'd translated some of the most important foundational documents of the congregation. With his music degree and his talent for composition, he had been tapped to create a new Camaldolese Psalter, more reminiscent of Gregorian chant than the "guitar liturgies" that began to flower in parish churches post–Vatican II. He knew the road through the Apennines between Camaldoli and Ravenna, the birthplace of the holy man Romuald, like the back of his hand. Yet deep down, he also knew that his primary identity was American.

In 1987, he returned to New Camaldoli for a while to work on the English version of the Psalter. Though he was fairly sure that his time in Italy would come to an end someday—every time the monks there urged him to apply for Italian citizenship, he automatically resisted—being back in the place where he had begun his life as a Camaldolese confirmed that his intuition was right. He *would* return to New Camaldoli at some point. The only reason he had left in the first place was to protect his vocation, but sometime in the future—when, he did not yet know—he would finally come home for good.

Meanwhile, he had plenty of work to get done before he made that move. The new constitutions still needed translating. And there was the book that his friend and superior Giabbani had long ago urged him to write: the English translation of two of the most important early Camaldolese documents: *The Life of Blessed Romuald* by the eleventh-century cardinal Peter Damian, and *The Life of the Five Brothers* by Romuald's contemporary Bruno of Querfurt. Matus's job, according to Giabbani, was to make these men of a thousand years ago comprehensible to his brethren. He wanted Matus to show them that the ancient Romualdian legacy lived on within the congregation, and he suggested that Matus might be able to do that by interweaving the story of his own spiritual journey. "The more you know about Saint Romuald," Giabbani told him, "the more you will see how Camaldoli, precisely in its constant mutations, has inherited a good portion of his spirit. Of course the monks of today's Camaldoli do not live as Saint Romuald lived; perhaps we do not live as he would wish us to, were he here to tell us. But I would not be afraid to meet him."[1]

As a way to start thinking about this book project, Matus had been studying Peter Damian's account of Romuald's life and his reason for writing it: "For me, the most useful thing to do would have been to stay hidden in my hermitage, meditating on my sins, instead of telling a tale about somebody else's virtues. . . . But the fact remains that all through the year and especially on his feast day, crowds of believers from far and near flock to his tomb to see the miracles God works through him. They come eager to hear the story of his life, and they find nobody there to tell it. A worry has begun to gnaw at me, and not without reason: might it not happen that, as years go by, Romuald's fame will grow dim among the people, and they will forget him?"[2]

Clearly, Damian's fears had not come true. Clearly, the world—or at least the Camaldolese portion of the world—had never forgotten the long-ago holy man who had built the Sacro Eremo in the Apennines of Italy. But this was in part because of Damian himself, and his willingness to take on the job of writing the saint's biography.

Therese Gagnon, still tramping through the forest in her long skirts, was starting to understand what her version of the Third Good might be. It seemed to her that in their zeal for the life of contemplative prayer, at least some of the monks had lost their connection to the natural world—and especially to the female half. She was aware that some of the older, more traditional monks—Klee, in particular—automatically bristled in the presence of women; she'd felt this herself. One night one of her friends, the British historian Donald Nicholl, spoke at the hermitage. Head of the Tantur Ecumenical Institute for Theological Studies in Jerusalem and fluent in medieval Welsh, Irish, and Russian, he was considered a major modern Christian thinker by the time he made his visit to Big Sur.

But all this apparently didn't matter, for "when Donald came here to speak and brought his wife with him, the monks wouldn't even look at her. He told them that the marriage vocation was just as important as the monastic. But nobody clapped. Nobody said thank you." Gagnon was appalled at their ingratitude—and even more, at their attitude of hostile suspicion toward her friend's lovely wife. "So I went to the back of the church and held Donald around the waist—he was very tall, probably 6'6"—and I apologized on their behalf. We can blame some of this attitude toward women on St. Paul. Danger! Red light! Be careful! Fire!' "[3]

Thankfully, other monks seemed better balanced. One of them was already living at the hermitage when the Gagnons arrived. David Steindl-Rast, a Benedictine from Mount Saviour Monastery in New York, had been charged by his abbot in the early sixties with pursuing Christian-Buddhist dialogue. He soon began a serious study of Zen, and later the same decade, cofounded the Center for Spiritual Studies with Jewish, Buddhist, Hindu, and Sufi teachers. Now he lived half of each year as a hermit at New Camaldoli and spent the other half on the road, lecturing and teaching. But the hermitage was becoming crowded, and he got word that he might need to find another monastery to house him. Steindl-Rast and Gagnon had become friends. After the community was evacuated because of a fire, she was given permission to work on her ceramics up above in the compound, which meant that her little studio in the canyon was free. So her husband built a bathroom on the "Beehive," and Steindl-Rast had a place to live whenever he returned to the coast.

Meanwhile, she continued working on her forest sanctuaries and entertaining a small but steady stream of visitors to the mobile home that Steindl-Rast had named the "Treehouse." "I remember one time a priest from Ireland was here and he was depressed, so I invited him to put his forehead on one of the largest boulders that has been here for centuries, capturing the sunlight and vibrating with energy. And he could feel it, and it helped him."[4] She also played host to a visiting rabbi, a group of Sufis, and even some of the monks of New Camaldoli. As a fellow French Canadian, Massicotte regularly showed up at the Treehouse in his signature black beret for tea or lunch. Barnhart had long since become Gagnon's dear friend, one who understood her special connection to the forest and even felt it himself. One time, she "asked him to come bless this huge old tree that was so magnificent, and he said, 'Why should we bless this tree when the tree itself is a blessing?'"

Gagnon understood, however, that her reverence for gigantic boulders and towering trees might shock the rest of the community even more than her female presence in a male hermitage already did. So she had to be discreet. As she recalls, "I did not have a dull life—it was a very exciting life, but it was lived underground. I didn't let people know how exciting it was."[5]

Gagnon's personal relationships with individual rocks and trees and bodies of water are reminiscent of ancient animism, which is the belief that all created beings have souls of their own. The ressource-ment theologian Henri de Lubac, though clearly no animist, may well have understood Gagnon's compulsion to worship in the forest. De Lubac devoted much of his thinking to what he saw as a major problem in contemporary Christianity: the strict separation between nature and the supernatural that was introduced by the scholasticism of the late Middle Ages. He pointed out that, before Thomas Aquinas arrived on the scene, Christians had lived in an undivided universe. There was no such thing as a purely physical world standing dumbly on its own. And likewise, no such thing as a separate supernatural order of reality that occasionally penetrated the mundane in order to carry out some mysterious project on God's behalf.

Instead, the old understanding of the "supernatural" was *sacramental*: it referred to the "the sacramental means of grace that allowed nature to reach its divinely appointed end: eternal participation in the divine life itself (deification)."[6] In other words, the supernatural world of grace was not foreign to the world of nature but interpenetrated it; an ancient tree, a towering rock, a glittering waterfall had the power to make visible an invisible spiritual reality.

Hale was still finding his way into the role of prior of New Camaldoli, but there were some aspects of the job that came naturally to him. Where Barnhart had found the required travel to conferences and meetings to sometimes be a burden—they took him away from his cell and the contemplative life he had signed up for—Hale seemingly reveled in the social dimension of the work. Soon after becoming prior, he traveled to Rome for the Congress of Abbots at Sant' Anselmo for an in-depth conversation between priors and abbots about the mysterious work of the Holy Spirit in monastic life. A month later, he taught conferences at Bishop's Ranch in Healdsburg, California, for an event called "The Benedictine Experience." Soon after, he went to a meeting of the American abbots and priors at St. Joseph's Abbey in Louisiana. And in May of 1989, he attended the first International Thomas Merton Society Conference in Louisville, Kentucky. Hale, whose initial attraction to the Camaldolese had come through Merton's *The Silent Life*, served as a board member for the society.

Bede Griffiths (center, in prayer shawl), David Steindl-Rast to his right, and Philip Klee in wheelchair in front

In July, he led a chapter meeting discussion about the dire financial straits of Incarnation Monastery in Berkeley. The official minutes reflect the urgency of the situation: "This is the poorest house in our whole congregation. All who live there have to work to support themselves. The new Prior [Colnaghi] has to work full time and is away on weekends. He should be at home then."[7] The hermitage voted to try and raise an endowment for Incarnation—especially because the young monks said they'd like to spend some time there on "at least a temporary basis."

Hale knew he needed to officially transfer his stability from Italy back to Big Sur. But his first priority was to settle the oblate question; though the New Camaldoli community had been resistant to having an oblate program up until now, thinking it would become a distraction for the monks trying to live a contemplative life, he'd noticed a recent softening in their attitude. Perhaps this was because they could see for themselves that the program he'd started at Incarnation earlier in the decade seemed to be going well. Much to his delight, in the fall of 1989, the oblate program was extended to the hermitage.

As the people-loving Hale happily noted in his journal, "So now the oblates of Incarnation and New Camaldoli will be one expanding group. A real advance!"

Born in 1906, the World War II conscientious objector Philip Klee had been the very first American postulant to arrive in 1958 at the building site that would become the hermitage. He slept with the cow, rang the wheel rim that served as a bell, pushed wheelbarrows full of wet cement, laid tile, and defended the pre–Vatican II church with a fierce conviction that never wavered. But now he was sick with a stubborn, debilitating, and seemingly incurable colitis, and what was to happen next?

The veterans hospital informed him that he qualified for a VA home for the elderly if he wanted to go. But Hale would agree only if Klee was happy with this decision; otherwise, Hale said firmly, the community would care for him. Klee wanted nothing more than to go home to Big Sur. And so he was ensconced in Cell 18, with the monks acting as his caregivers during the weekdays and a VA nurse, Mary Ellen Shepherd, driving down the coast every weekend to check up on him.

Teichert, who spent many a recreation hike respectfully waiting up for the much older Klee and in the process "getting a huge earful about what was wrong with the church, what was wrong with the country, with the monastery, etc.," considers Klee one of his most important mentors. "Not so much by what he taught but what he modeled about how to die. He came back from the hospital in 1991 and was told he had a month to live. But he lasted five more years. He had the reputation of being a grumpy old sourpuss, especially back in the '80s. And I think the reputation was probably deserved. But as he was dying, in the last part of his life, he became so gentle, so appreciative, so patient with people. I really felt like God was using him to show the rest of us how it was done."[8]

Other members of the community, so used to Klee's endless diatribes about the abominations of the modern world, were mildly stunned at the transformation of their elderly brother in the last years of his life. Truly, this was the goal of the monastic life, its reason for being: genuine transformation—or, as the Orthodox at Mount Athos would put it, "deification." It didn't always happen, even in that most venerable of monastic republics. A lifetime of ascetical discipline, daily liturgy, the difficult praxis of community relationships, solitude, and silence did not guarantee that monks became better human beings; some simply became more pronounced versions of who they'd been from the beginning. But the change in Klee was unmistakable and, for many, truly inspiring. As Teichert puts it, "At the end he was just so sweet. . . . I think he was preparing for this his whole life. The maple sugar was just covered up."[9]

But the VA nurse Mary Ellen Shepherd also played an important role in Klee's late-life transformation. When his benefits ran out and he could no longer pay her, she faithfully continued to minister to him on her own. As Gagnon puts it, "Mary Ellen adored Philip. He loved tomatoes, so she would plant those. He loved hummingbirds, and she brought him a hummingbird picture. He loved sunflowers, so she planted a row of them inside his wall." Klee had never before experienced this kind of total devotion. He had always been the kind of man, Gagnon recalls, who would go to the kitchen to check whether the potato peels were thin enough. If not, he would gather them up and boil them and eat them to teach everyone a lesson about wastefulness. But now—"Close to his last days," recalls Gagnon, "they found him in tears. He said, 'I hated women but women are so beautiful.'"[10]

Then Klee developed cancer along with his colitis. Shepherd gathered the community, undressed Klee, and said, "Now I would like you to take care of my boy. He needs to be washed every day, and that includes his genitals!" They were stunned—but her forthrightness broke some ice that needed to be broken.[11]

For Teichert, Klee's humble embrace of helplessness, pain, and the powerlessness of old age was life-changing. "I remember one time expressing the fear to Thomas [Matus] about becoming an old monk and becoming a burden to those who would have to take care of me. Thomas reminded me of all the amazing old monks that have already been and gone—and how much we learned from them from caring for them. So that got me thinking about particular people who've been especially important to my own growth and development. Bruno [Barnhart]—a great spiritual director and confessor. He had a way of listening to you that let you know that he knew exactly what you were trying to say. Fr. Bede [Janvrin] was another. . . . He was definitely an inspiration—serene and upbeat and cheerful, even though he had severe dementia. . . . Except for the period during which he realized that he was losing his memory—that was extremely difficult for him. But once it was lost, he was once again cheerful."[12]

Klee, though, was special. "One time I was supposed to be bringing him some medication at 3:00 but forgot. I came rushing in at 4:00, apologizing. He said to me, 'You're like God in that way. He forgets our sins.' So sweet, and meaning it. He always ended our conversations with 'God bless you for your Christlike kindliness.'"[13]

A year or so before Klee finally died, Janet Walker made the winding, two-hour drive along the coast from her home to the hermitage. In a toddler booster seat behind her slept her youngest, three-year-old Emily. Walker wanted to visit Massicotte, go to Mass, and introduce her little girl to the community that had become so important in her own life. After Eucharist—Emily was fascinated by all the men in white—Massicotte led them through the cloister to the refectory, where they stood in line with the monks and waited for the lunch bell to ring.

Little Emily, as solemn and shy as her mother used to be, clung to Walker's leg and peered up at all the strange men crowding around her. Some of them looked down at her and smiled, but others were too busy talking to each other to notice she was there. Inside, there were long tables with a bowl of fat black olives on each. The olives made her feel better. She loved olives! After they got their plates and sat down, she tugged at her mother's arm and pointed at the bowl but before her mother could dish them out, Emily spotted an old wizard from a fairy tale sitting across the room. Even though she had never seen him before, except in a book, he was smiling at her like he knew her. Did he? Then someone was wheeling him over and he was parked right in front of their table. At first she was scared—his beard was too long! She hid her face for a minute against her mother's shoulder, shaking a little and feeling like she might cry. Then her mother patted her on the head and said, "Look, Emily! Look what Brother Philip is doing!"

The old wizard, still smiling, was holding up his hands like two stop signs, and on the end of every finger was an olive. He waggled his fingers at her and nodded at the bowl, and her mother dished some out for her and she put them on her own fingers and waggled back at him and somehow, everything was okay.

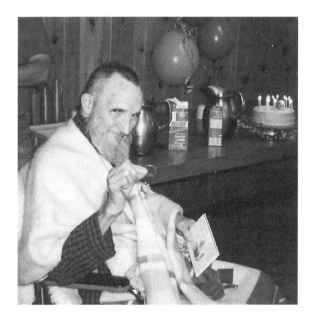

*Philip Klee
birthday party*

21

Helicopters have landed on the mountain before, though usually for emergency-related purposes. There was the national guard chopper from the military base on the other side of the ridge that in the early days flew over to make sure it could actually be done. If you were going to build a hermitage in the middle of nowhere, reasoned the two officers aboard, you needed to make sure you had a viable escape route.

Then there was the navy pilot who showed up a few years later to plant the cross on the top of the church cupola but could not pull off the job, no doubt because of capricious coastal weather. A different helicopter made food drops to the monks when a massive landslide blocked Highway 1 in both directions. During fires that forced the community to evacuate for weeks at a time, Cal Fire choppers sucked water from the hermitage lake and dropped it on burning redwoods and smoke-filled ravines. In years to come, rescue helicopters would transport the elderly, including Wasinger, Hale, and Gagnon, to hospitals up north.

But today, on the Third Sunday of Easter, 1990, a helicopter is landing at the hermitage for none of the reasons above. Instead, a brand-new priest, Fr. Isaiah Teichert, is about to celebrate his first Mass. At the base of the mountain, hundreds of marathon runners are clogging the coastal road, making it impossible for a group of his closest friends to get to the church on time. On board the descending chopper are four Dominicans—two deacons and two sisters—and one of them, permanently traumatized by a long-ago helicopter ride that made her so sick she thought she might die, is there for the sake of love and love alone. The stiff headwinds are increasing the suspense.

When a passenger asks the pilot, a twenty-two-year veteran, how long he has been flying, he jokingly replies, "Almost six months!"

The many relatives of the new priest are roused by the pounding of blades above them and flock from the church, their guest rooms, and scattered benches overlooking the sea. The children—and there are many, many children in the sprawling Teichert family—are beyond thrilled. They run toward the dust cloud kicked up by the craft and clap when the shaky but smiling Dominicans appear in the doorway. People tell them they should kiss the ground. Somebody suggests that next time, they should jump while they are still overhead and float down in their white robes playing "Gloria in Excelsis" on their tape recorders. Kids hop back and forth over the shadows cast by the slowly rotating blades. Friends laugh and hug.[1]

In this place where not so long ago interactions with relatives were almost entirely forbidden, where monks could not even return home when a parent was dying, this is a three-day family fest of unparal-leled dimensions. And it signals the beginning of yet another stage at New Camaldoli, one that will usher in a whole new generation of young men seeking fuga mundi. They will come from a different historical era than the pioneer generation, carry with them different cultural assumptions, and struggle with different attachments. But like Hale, like Barnhart, like Matus, they will arrive at the hermitage in order to find out what this urge

Isaiah Teichert (photograph by Kayleigh Meyers)

toward fuga mundi is all about. They will make their observerships, spend another year as postulants, be clothed as novices, and —Gloria in Excelsis!—fourteen of them will choose to stay, including two future priors.[2]

Gagnon had been thinking about a celebration of her own. It seemed that the older she got, the more creative energy she had and the more physically daring she was becoming—a potentially dangerous development for a woman of seventy-two. One day, for example, she came upon the faint outlines of the face of Christ on a rock at the edge of a deep ravine. As she peered down at the massive boulders below, half-hidden by the forest, one monolith caught her eye. "[The boulder] had two huge wings like a bird, and in the middle, a tiny redwood. . . . I came back and got a rope and tied it to a tree so I could rappel my way down. All of a sudden, I heard a noise. It was an underground river. When a person discovers underground water, it is a miracle. I began to rake the dirt, and then I saw the water coming and it looked like a little church."[3]

Gagnon invited Barnhart, back from his post-prior sabbatical as Adam's companion at L'Arche, to offer Mass in her "little church," which he did, telling her that it was "God's place." Over the next decade and a half, other priests would make their way down by a safer route to the place she named "the Cathedral." There, they would offer the Eucharist on a large, flat natural altar set among the stately redwoods and great boulders.

But now it was time to plan out her special festival. She would have to be careful: she and her husband had nearly lost their trailer to fire the first year they were there, and in 1985, the whole hermitage was evacuated for many weeks while the mountains blazed and choppers whirled overhead. So for her first attempt, she carried 250 candles down into the forest, making sure everything was thoroughly damp before she arranged them in patterns on the ground and lit them. Success! The second time, she used 500 candles, and the third, 750—a magical array of dancing lights among the redwoods.

Then she videotaped the entire spectacle, added Christmas music, and sent it to friends for the holidays.

The Year of the Helicopter—1990—brought with it a steady flow of new vocations. Hale had been prior for two years, from the beginning of his term working hard toward building a stronger community. One way was to avoid unnecessary rigidity. His attitude was "If you need to go, take a car and go. Don't go for stupid things, but go when you need to."[4] He also encouraged relationship-building. Where in the past, professed monks took their midday meal alone in their rooms while novices dined as a group, now everyone ate family-style in the refectory. Picnics had once been forbidden because they might lead to unnecessary talking and—God forbid!—actual friendships; now monks were *supposed* to get to know each other. But the most striking change he helped usher in was a new focus on the individual as a unique person with special gifts, in particular gifts that were hidden or undeveloped.

Hale had never forgotten his own beginnings at New Camaldoli, and the academic studies he was prepared to abandon in order to become a monk. If it hadn't been for the intervention of his Pomona professor and the willingness of Modotti to allow him to take his finals at the hermitage, he could have never gone on to earn his PhD at Fordham, written his many papers and books, taught his many classes, led his many seminars—all work that completed him and gave him joy.

He believed that there was something very beautiful about the Camaldolese charism in this regard: the natural formation that occurs through living in a close-knit community, combined with generous time given over to solitude and silence, almost invariably leads to a flowering of the Third Good in the life of an individual monk. Each expression of the Third Good is different, and each is linked to a person's particular gifts. As with a good family, Hale believed, the job of a good community is to support the expression of these gifts in whatever way it can.[5]

Though the men who entered New Camaldoli during the first years of Hale's priorship varied in age—some had been born in the mid-forties, most in the fifties—they brought with them similar beliefs and attitudes toward life. As children of the fifties, most had grown up in a time of unprecedented American prosperity, which meant that the making of money was not as high a priority as it had been for their Depression-era parents. As teens of the sixties, most had absorbed and believed in the notion that self-fulfillment was more important than social status. Thanks to the civil rights movement, the feminist revolution, the antiwar demonstrations, and the nascent gay rights movement, most of them had also acquired a strong sense of social justice. Perhaps most importantly, as young adults in the seventies, many had undergone profound awakenings that led them either to leave the institutional church altogether or to search for spiritual experiences beyond what those institutions could seemingly offer.

Unlike the pioneer generation, most of whom arrived at the hermitage in their early twenties, these new men were older—in their thirties and forties—and had done other things before deciding to test their vocations at New Camaldoli. Many transferred from more active orders: Daniel Manger and Arthur Poulin from the Franciscans, Joseph Wong from the Salesians, Michael Fish from the Redemptorists, David Meyers from the Missionary Brothers of Christ. Some came from larger, busier Benedictine monasteries: Joshua Monson, Bede Healey, Romuald Duscher. And some had given their all to careers in the world: Michael Harrington as an engineer, Healey as a psychologist at the Menninger Clinic, Cyprian Consiglio as a professional musician, Zaccheus Naegele as a cook for a captain of the Coast Guard. With the addition of Benedict Dell'Ossa, a first-generation Neopolitan from the wilds of Philadelphia, the hermitage finally had an Italian monk again. What united them was the desire for a more contemplative life—a freer, less distracted, more focused life of prayer.

But not just for themselves. As Teichert explains, "Prayer is what the world needs so intensely. We pray for ourselves, we pray for the world, we hope by transforming our own selves that this will impact the wider world too. It is mysterious. Our life here is a little more malleable than, say, the Trappists'. We have a certain freedom here. We can blow this, squander this, or make the most of this freedom to live this life in the Holy Spirit. It's a great privilege."[6]

Hale was trying to give the new men of the 1990s as much of this precious freedom as the community could safely bear. Says Teichert, "That's very Camaldolese—to give the individual some room. God is speaking to each one in his own way. And that can be abused. It can get squishy." Which for Hale meant there had to be certain non-negotiables in place. Teichert says, "The liturgy [was and is] a hard and fast rule. And meditation. You can't skip those. . . . If people don't participate in a good spirit, it's clear this isn't the life for them." Hale was also counting on a natural safeguard in place since the time of the holy man Romuald—the uncanny ability of the hermitage to winnow out those who should not be there: "If you don't really try to enter into the monastic life, the monastery will spit you out. You'll know it, we'll know it, there won't be any doubt about it."[7]

Raniero Hoffman, a diocesan priest from Baltimore, was in some ways typical of the new generation of the 1990s. Ordained in 1975, he went to New Camaldoli to visit a Franciscan friend and healer who couldn't make it to the ceremony. His friend asked for permission from Barnhart for the two of them—he and Hoffman—to go to the lake at the top of the mountain. There, his friend prayed a lengthy healing prayer for him, starting at the moment of conception and covering every aspect of his life up to that point. Says Hoffman, "He wanted to clear everything out that could get in the way of the grace of ordination. And it was an extremely powerful experience and I preached about it at my first Mass. Who would ever think that fifteen years later I would be back and joining the community?"[8]

Like so many of the other new postulants under Hale, Hoffman was not only involved in the charismatic renewal movement but had a strong interest in social justice issues. While still in seminary, he and five others served as bodyguards for Cesar Chavez during a march from Maryland to Washington, DC. After he became a priest, he served as associate pastor in three parishes before being assigned to St. Mary's Spiritual Center. During his last four years he was given permission to participate in a three-year internship in spiritual direction and retreat work at the Jesuit Center for Spiritual Growth in Pennsylvania. There, he went through, then guided, both eight-day, then full thirty-day Ignatian retreats.

Meanwhile, he recalls, "I was wanting more of God and he was wanting more of me." When he realized he was being called to the monastic life, the one thing he knew was that he couldn't go to California because it was going to fall into the ocean. So he went to Christ in the Desert Monastery in New Mexico instead, and knew after only a few months that it was not a good fit. The prior urged him to visit New Camaldoli, that this was what he was looking for. "And so I wound up in California on the earthquake fault."[9]

Seven years after he arrived at the hermitage, Hoffman found himself in a position he hadn't expected to be in. Hale, in the last year and a half of his second term, had developed heart trouble and was advised by his doctor to either step down or get help with the job. Hoffman was asked to take on the role of vice-prior. "I said to them, I don't think I'm a leader but I offer you my gifts and my talents. Use my gifts and my talents but don't ask me to do what I can't do." When Hale's term was officially up, Hoffman was elected to lead the community as it moved into the twenty-first century, a role that he would fill for the next twelve years. As he recalls, "I didn't have any particular ideas about what I would do as prior. . . . I feel like my two terms were about holding the community together during this time of transition."

Often, his work was more about the nitty-gritty than the numinous. "All those old carpets had to be pulled up and something new put down, the roof had to be repaired, the water tanks. . . . We had to build the infirmary. And in the middle of our Hopes and Dreams campaign, the stock market crashed. Plus, we had the fiftieth anniversary."

But the physical plant was not the only maintenance problem the community faced. In the early years, unaddressed psychological issues had too often culminated in abandoned vocations, so Hoffman made a commitment to find good counselors for the group. "We had to learn how to communicate. We'd have facilitators come in on a regular basis just to teach us that. [They helped take] us into our humanity."

Hoffman's particular expression of the Third Good turned out to be both simple and pure: a classic example of Benedictine humility. "On the Enneagram, I'm a 2," he says with a shrug and a smile. "I'm a helper. Let me help you."[10]

Like other men who arrived at New Camaldoli in the 1990s, Arthur Poulin entered into a serious spiritual search in midlife. Though faith had been at the forefront of his mind since he was a twenty-year-old junior studying fine arts at Loyola University in Rome, it

*Raniero Hoffman
(photograph by
Kayleigh Meyers)*

was not until he turned forty that the call to contemplative prayer began to manifest. His long-haired, bell-bottomed exploration of Catholicism via the great art and ancient sacred places of Italy had triggered his 1970s move from a nominal childhood faith to deep religious commitment—and eventually to becoming both a priest and a Franciscan—but this new call was clearly different.

What complicated the discernment process, but in other ways simplified it, was his longtime conviction that he was also meant to be a serious painter. After his junior year abroad, he returned to Chicago to complete his degree at Loyola. "I finished up my final year with just art classes and had a show. Art and theology coming together in a painting. Art and spirituality. It was all there, but it took awhile to see it. I was always doing artwork. . . . I'd get little jobs for illustrations in magazines, abstract art, portraits of friends.

I had a lot of experience but didn't take it seriously as a way to preach the gospel—I had to own that, really dig in."[11]

At this point in his life, however, it seemed that a more direct way to preach the gospel was to serve the poor. So he began living in a small, intentional Franciscan community in an impoverished neighborhood in uptown Chicago where he worked with emotionally disturbed boys. "My community had a very intellectual bent. Dorothy Day used to visit there. I once stayed in the room she'd stayed in the night before, which I thought was very exciting."[12] In time, he moved to California where he spent more years in the inner city, this time in Oakland and now as a Franciscan priest.

But in 1990, Poulin was strongly prompted to take a sabbatical, so he went to Europe again. "A lot of good things came out of that. When I came back, still as a friar, people started to recognize my work and acquire it. People would print it in magazines or book covers." He realized that he had to make a choice; there was no way he could be a parish priest and a serious artist at the same time. So he moved to one of the California missions, San Antonio, on the other side of the mountains from the Big Sur coast. There, he found the peace and quiet he needed to devote his time to painting. "But there was still the restlessness about the contemplative dimension. I always wanted to be an artist in community. Part of what I was saying was this has to either be an integral part of the community or I'm not interested in being a religious anymore. I need a witness from this community."[13]

Though it took him some time to figure it out, the community he was seeking and in fact had long ago visited was but an hour's hair-raising drive away, just on the other side of the ridge. The Camaldolese three-part charism offered the familial monastic bonds he knew he needed, provided the solitude and silence necessary for contemplative prayer, and most of all, might give him the "community witness" he required in order to preach the gospel through his paintings. If he could only navigate the transition from Franciscan friar to Camaldolese monk—not necessarily easy—New Camaldoli might prove to be the homeland of his heart.

Hale's friendship and wise guidance played a key role in this process. "He was so welcoming," recalls Poulin, "and so encouraging as I learned to live for the first time in a monastic community." In 1998, after five years at the hermitage, Poulin officially transferred his vows. Soon afterward, Andrew Colnaghi at Incarnation Monastery invited him to move north to the small house in Berkeley, now separate from the joint community established by Hale in the late eighties.

Though Poulin had loved his time in Big Sur—"I got to experience that solitude and hospitality and artwork and everything was thriving"—he felt spiritually free enough to re-enter a bustling urban setting after so many years in the "desert." His transition was made easier by Colnaghi. Like Hale, Colnaghi had been formed in the spirit of Benedetto Calati and was dedicated to the notion that a good community supports the development of a person's God-given gifts. "Andrew Colnaghi was an encouraging friend and 'brother-in-religion' for me," says Poulin. "And he was always wildly enthusiastic about my artwork, especially in getting it out there into the public realm." Poulin had found his home. The contemplative restlessness that triggered his midlife quest was gone; he had answered the call to fuga mundi and learned what it had to teach. With the full blessing of his monastic community, he was living out his own version of the Third Good.

What lay beyond the walls of the monastery, even though he could see all of it from his window, was no longer alluring. Nor did it have the power to draw him out of his solitude.

22

Unlike Robert Hale's professor in 1959, who was so concerned about his prize student's decision to become a monk at New Camaldoli that he jumped in his car and made the five-hour trip north to dissuade him, Cyprian Consiglio's seminary professor actually urged him to visit the hermitage. "I did not know a thing about them," recalls Consiglio. "I did know where Big Sur was. I didn't know they were Benedictine. I didn't know St. Romuald either, whose feast day was my birthday. . . . Then I met Fr. Romuald [Duscher] and I said, 'Your saint is my birthday.' And he said, 'What? Your saint is our founder!' And as it turned out, I was born on Romuald's feast day in the same year New Camaldoli was founded in Big Sur—June 19, 1958. That's kind of wild."[1]

As was typical of so many others who arrived at the hermitage in the nineties, Consiglio had been on a spiritual quest for years. Like Poulin, he'd been raised Catholic—even gone to high school seminary—but it was only when he underwent a powerful conversion experience at seventeen that God became real to him. There was nothing splashy about it. "It was one night with my spiritual director. I walked in one kind of person and walked out completely different. There was [suddenly] a personal relationship that has never gone away. Even during my most debauched years as a rock-and-roll guitar player, that haunted me. I knew something real had happened. What went along with it was a radical commitment to the gospel, to somehow live it as it was written down, which included a radical commitment to poverty. I thought, I have to live this way—I have to make this real."[2]

Like Poulin, he wound up with an intentional Franciscan community in an impoverished neighborhood in Chicago. "It was somewhat

173

associated with the charismatic renewal and also with the Catholic Worker. It was fiery—quite inspiring." Being with this community precipitated "a kind of bursting forth of charismatic prayer. And this was also the year I got involved with gospel music. . . . Some friends of mine were at a small African American church in the south of the city and I used to go there on weekends and spend time with them . . . and that's where I learned spirituals." Then he went to a workshop with Catholic gospel singers Clarence Rivers, Grayson Brown, and Avon Gillespie. "I told my mom that without them, I'd have grown up to be Dan Fogelberg. Whom I love, by the way!"[3]

Meeting musicians of their caliber helped point him in a new direction. "These guys just blew my musical circuits. It was like having a musical conversion too. So music has always been a part of it." Like Poulin with his painting, Consiglio had discovered that you can preach the gospel through the arts. But the excitement was almost too much for a passionate teenager like him, and he knew he wasn't handling it well. "After a year with this group, I decided I was too young to continue on with them and that I needed to continue my education, so I left and went on to college . . . and the whole thing just kind of fell apart." He blames his sense of disillusionment in part on his own immaturity. "So I left and spent my twenties doing music. I kept looking. . . . I never saw anything in the church that came close to what I'd experienced with the radical Franciscans—not until the Camaldolese. There, somehow, it was in the air. And I thought, this is it. I found it again."[4]

He arrived at New Camaldoli in 1992 and made his simple vows in 1994. During his first year there, the eighty-seven-year-old Bede Griffiths visited from India for the purpose of transferring all his papers to New Camaldoli. His visit would have major ramifications for the spiritual path of the young Consiglio. Bruno Barnhart had already become an important mentor for Consiglio, and Barnhart and Griffiths were good friends. In the same mysterious way that monks from other times and places had changed the lives of Merton, Hale, and Matus, these two older monks—Griffiths and Barnhart—would eventually inspire Consiglio to visit Shantivanam in India. And this experience would lead him into one aspect of his own unique, Third-Good work: the composing of Veda-inspired, liturgically rooted music that could communicate across religious cultures.

According to Thomas Matus, the primary conduit for monastic initiation from generation to generation is not the prior nor the abbot but the novice master. "We are the daughter house of the oldest religious community in the Western church." And for a thousand years, "uninterrupted religious monastic life at the holy hermitage of Camaldoli [has been passed on] from the novice master to the novices, and one of those novices becomes the next novice master, who passes it on to the next class of novices, and so on."[5]

This meant that Teichert, who had been made novice master shortly after his Year of the Helicopter ordination, automatically became a force in Consiglio's life. Though only a few years older, Teichert had nearly two decades of experience at New Camaldoli under his belt. He knew and loved the pioneer generation and was thus able to convey not simply the facts but the emotional timbre of the community's "family history." Plus, Teichert believed in the goodness of healthy laughter and Consiglio had a funny bone; he was an excellent mimic and a master of the droll monologue. "I was Cyprian's postulant master when he was just a baby-faced kid," Teichert deadpans. "I saw he had potential."[6]

Meanwhile, the pioneers themselves were entering a new phase of life. In 1994, the recluse Joseph Diemer went totally blind. Though caring for his basic needs might have been easier if he'd moved back into the community, he remained in uninterrupted reclusion until his death in 2005, broken only once when the community had to evacuate during a major fire.

Philip Klee, the fiery conscientious objector and first American novice to arrive at Modotti's infant hermitage in 1958, went home to God in 1995. Though the post–Vatican II transition had been a real struggle for him, sickness, suffering, and death were not. His last five years had proven to the community beyond any doubt that the goal of monastic life—putting on the mind of Christ—was not merely a lofty ideal but possible for any one of them.

Others from the early generation—Hale, Barnhart, Matus, Kirby, Massicotte, Wasinger—no longer had youthful energy to burn, but on the other hand, no longer suffered from the spiritual restlessness that invariably plagues young seekers. Instead, they were coming into their own. Hale's long mentorship under Benedetto Calati was producing good fruit in a once-divided community. Bruno Barnhart was finally writing the visionary books of theology he'd been too busy to work on during his long years as prior. Thomas Matus was deep into his own translating and writing, including a biography of Sr. Nazarena, the Camaldolese recluse in Rome he'd once prayed to for guidance about whether to enter the monastic life. Gabriel Kirby's poetry and photographs were more and more reflective of his joyful, charismatic spirituality. The whimsical little French Canadian Bernard Massicotte had become a pastoral anchor for many retreatants, especially those who were shy or suffering. And Emmanuel Wasinger, formed in the "old school" when talking was forbidden, had become so inspired by Hale's new focus on relationships that he'd committed himself to learning a skill he sorely lacked: the art of conversation.

For the elders, it was time for slowing down, reflecting on their many years as monks, and preparing to pass the baton.

Emmanuel Wasinger (photograph by Kayleigh Meyers)

The new men of the 1990s were also finding their places.

Joseph Wong, the first Chinese person to enter the Camaldolese in a thousand years, made his formal transfer of vows to the hermitage in 1997 in a beautiful ceremony that included his family from Hong Kong. Chinese banners, borrowed for the day from a museum in San Francisco, adorned the church. Chinese musicians sang the liturgy. Wong's Third Good vocation was blessed in advance by Pope John Paul II during a pastoral visit to the Sacro Eremo in 1993 when he asked the Camaldolese to take on the special task of ecumenical and interreligious dialogue on behalf of the church. Fluent in several Chinese dialects, plus English, Latin, and Italian, Wong would open this door to mutual understanding and respect even wider than Barnhart and Griffiths already had. In 2000, he would lead a week of meditation and conversation at New Camaldoli for Hindu, Zen and Chan Buddhists, Taoists, and Confucian monks, and would eventually end up serving as a special assistant to the prior general in Italy and forming young Chinese novices for a potential new foundation in China.

Bede Healey's years of experience as a psychologist at Menninger Clinic would be immediately helpful for a community committed to strengthening individual relationships. In the coming decades, he would become subprior under Hoffman, treasurer, and eventually—following the retirement of the faithful servant Andrew Colnaghi—resident prior of Incarnation Monastery in Berkeley, where he would teach, counsel clients, and continue to explore the connections between psychology and spirituality.

Daniel Manger's many years as a Franciscan included time spent in war-torn Central America, and this, combined with the practical skills and good sense he'd picked up on the family truck farm in Kentucky, would uniquely suit him for the role of acting prior when fifteen years later, New Camaldoli took on another daughter house. The Monastery of the Risen Christ in San Luis Obispo, California, would in some ways become the "bridge" monastery that Barnhart had envisioned so long ago—not urban, though on the edge of a small city, yet not completely rural either. If the monks were looking for a divine sign that this was the foundation they'd been seeking, they got more than they were bargaining for: the volcanic peak on which their new monastery sat had for the past 150 years been known as "Cerro Romualdo."

The old would slowly give way to the new. Benedict Dell'Ossa would take over both the supply runs from Kirby and the job of procurator from Massicotte, and would go on to serve as kitchen master for the next twenty-five years. Zaccheus Naegle would replace Massicotte in his other role—bookstore manager—and eventually become vice-prior for the community. Joshua Monson would take on the duty of obedience once filled by Kirby: the cleaning of the guest rooms. David Meyers would apprentice himself to the bulldozer-manuevering, backhoe-wrangling Wasinger, learning to clear fire hazards and maintain the generator. Michael Harrington would engineer some major remodels and become the water analyst for the community.

And Romuald Duscher, who once said that all he desired of monastic life was to become a "starets," the Russian term for "holy elder," would die of a rare and aggressive blood cancer at the age of fifty-six, continuing to play his silver flute, go to Mass, and generally astonish his brethren for nearly two weeks after his kidneys failed.

After the deaths of Diemer and Barabe, there would be no more recluses at New Camaldoli. On the contrary, interest in another ancient archetype began to surface: "monk as pilgrim," "monk on the road," monk following the Jesus who has no place to lay his head. The holy man Romuald was a good example of this kind of eremitical *peregrino*; in 975 he traveled to Spain, then returned to Italy and wandered through Tuscany, the Romagna district, and southern France. He embraced the walking life for some years, visiting monasteries and hermitages and reforming them when he found problems. Sometimes he established small houses of his own, only to move on when the community had been sufficiently formed.

This peripatetic hermit archetype showed up in Cyprian Consiglio a decade after his arrival at New Camaldoli. "The first ten years at the hermitage were about stripping away layer after layer of stuff and by the time it was over, I met someone I didn't even know, and that person had to leave. It was very clear to my spiritual director and to the prior and all the people who knew me and loved me best that this was the case. That what I thought was my vocation when I walked in—it turned out I didn't know who I was when I walked through the door."[7]

With the blessing of the congregation, he would spend the next ten years traveling the world, mostly outside of monastic and even Catholic Christian circles. In his many interreligious encounters, he would discover that people were starving for spiritual practice and what he thought of as the "great conversation." Thus, and somewhat to his surprise, he would wind up spending as much time giving retreats as giving concerts. When he finally returned, he would begin a new phase of the journey as prior of New Camaldoli.

Cyprian Consiglio (photograph by Kayleigh Meyers)

Several years before Consiglio's global trek began, a second pilgrim-monk arrived at New Camaldoli—again, having no idea about where God would eventually lead him. Michael Fish, born and raised in Johannesburg, South Africa, joined the Redemptorists at the age of twenty-three. He first served as a missioner, then was sent to the States for a one-year Jesuit course in how to become a good formator. While there, he made a friend who would eventually wind up at New Camaldoli. Fish himself returned to South Africa where the Redemptorist novitiate had been set up in a Zulu village so that the African postulants raised in the countryside did not have to move to a large monastery in an unfamiliar urban setting.

He spent ten years in that village. "We lived in mud huts, no running water or electricity. . . . Living that very simple rural life of back to basics, I realized I was happy. In me emerged a call to this deeper dimension of life that wasn't as active as I'd been as a parish missioner." But this peaceful interlude was destined to end when he was tapped for the role of vicar provincial and then provincial. "I tried to remind the province that we had this tradition as a contemplative and active order . . . and I felt this dissatisfaction as we became more and more active."[8]

Fish had a good spiritual director, a German Dominican nun. "She helped me discern that maybe there was a different call." So the next time he had to go to the States for a leadership meeting, he made a point of visiting his friend who'd become Camaldolese. He was particularly interested in the congregation because it had retained its three-part charism of community, solitude, and outreach. "I thought, Here's a community that's simple and small and with the mix of contemplation and ministry which initially attracted me to the Redemptorists. I went to New Camaldoli for two months (officially on sabbatical) but I was actually making an observership. At the end it was clear to me that I needed to give it a bash."[9]

Fish would transfer his vows in 2002 and be given the role of oblate chaplain. Under his tutelage, the roster would swell to 350. Then he would be asked to take on the canonical position of novice master, which in many ways was a natural fit for him, capitalizing as it did on his ten years in the Zulu novitiate. But despite the goodness and necessity of the work, something in him would powerfully resist—in his mind, the Holy Spirit.

Eventually, he would ask for permission to take a year off, which he hoped might allow him to think and pray more clearly about his next steps. During this extended time away from the hermitage, he would make his first Camino. The Camino de Compostela is a web of ancient European pilgrimage trails that extend anywhere from five hundred to twelve hundred miles, depending on the starting point. The endpoint is always the same: the Cathedral of Santiago de Compostela in Spain. Endless days on the trail would begin to reveal what Fish hadn't been able to discern in his cell at New Camaldoli. So many laypeople felt disenfranchised as Catholics. So many felt bitter and bereft. What if there was a way to help them reconnect with the richness and beauty of their tradition? What if he could give retreats to laypeople instead of to the monastic novices he had formed for so many years?

In time, and with the blessing of the congregation, Fish would live half the year in his own cell apart from the community, focusing on the Second Good of solitude and silence. During the other half, he would lead the kinds of retreats he had first envisioned on the Camino: his own version of the Third Good, known in the original language of the charism as "martyrdom," or "witness to the faith." As for the First Good of community, that took care of itself during regular visits with his beloved brethren of Big Sur.

Michael Fish
(photograph by
Kayleigh Meyers)

Fish's insight about how monastic wisdom might help laypeople find their way "back to the light," as he puts it, was validated many times over in the decades that followed. The urge toward fuga mundi would emerge in ordinary people from all walks of life, people who would never be monks but who were nevertheless drawn to the wilderness in order to find God and themselves. Many would begin their search by reading books by Thomas Merton, Bede Griffiths, and William Johnston. And eventually, thanks to the growth of the internet, some of them—including those who could not afford to travel to Big Sur for an in-person retreat —would discover the Camaldolese and their unique charism online.

During the next twenty years, 300 more oblates would make their public promises to live, with the help of God and their brother monks, a contemplative Benedictine life outside the walls of the monastery. Some of them would marry and have children, some would choose to remain single, but all of them would seek to comprehend the spiritual wisdom that comes to those who flee the world, yet continue to love and serve it.

And when the endless stress of work and kids and paying the bills threatened to overwhelm them, they would seek peace in the Brief Rule of the holy man Romuald: "Sit in your cell as in a paradise. Put the whole world behind you and forget it." When they found themselves confused and disillusioned by swirling political controversies and persistent religious scandals, they would pray the prayer of their Camaloldese brothers: "O God, come to my assistance, O Lord, make haste to help me." And when they found it nearly impossible, no matter how they tried, to discern the faint outlines of Christ's face in that of their fellow human beings, they would sigh and turn to the ancient Camaldolese symbol: two doves drinking from a single chalice, encircled by the words "I am yours, you are mine."

And they would be comforted.

Afterword

I first met the monks of New Camaldoli in 1991 when I was taken to the hermitage by one of the characters in this book, Janet Walker. I was not a Catholic—in fact, not even a Christian at that point, though my long-abandoned childhood faith had recently begun to stir uneasily within me. What would happen to my life if I started taking religion seriously again?

Janet led me into the hermitage church, where I proceeded to attend my first Mass. During the passing of the peace, a slender, dark-haired monk with oddly familiar features leaned over and whispered, "Um yah yah." Um yah yah? He nodded at my St. Olaf College sweatshirt and moved on. "Um! Yah! Yah!" was the St. Olaf fight song, and I had just made friends with my first monk, Joshua Monson—like me, a midwestern Norwegian. Though we weren't actually related, he looked a lot like family, which in that particular moment I found reassuring. It was Br. Joshua who eventually convinced me that a Norwegian could become a Catholic.

I'd soon make friends with another monk, the irrepressible Fr. Bernard Massicotte. Every time I made a retreat from then until he died of Parkinson's in his mid-eighties, we would take a long walk down the mountain together. On the way, he'd catch me up on hermitage gossip, tell French jokes he'd heard over his shortwave radio, and prod me to say the rosary, his way of introducing me to the culture of Catholicism. When we got to Highway 1, we'd walk to the middle of the road and touch our feet to the painted centerline, then trudge the two miles back up the hill. Many of the Massicotte stories in this book came from those hikes. His black beret hangs on the wall beside my desk.

Joshua Monson
*(photograph by
Kayleigh Meyers)*

A month after my father died in 1993, I made a grief-stricken retreat at New Camaldoli. That night was Holy Thursday, so when I went to evening services, there was the prior down on his knees, gently washing the feet of his brothers. My throat seized up— Robert Hale looked so much like the loving dad I had just lost, right down to the fifties-style haircut, the oversized horn-rim glasses, and the humble demeanor. Though I never told Fr. Robert that I had secretly adopted him as my substitute dad, I found his presence incredibly comforting during this hard time in my life.

Two days after Christmas of 1999, Janet Walker and I both made our oblations in the hermitage church. Our baffled husbands and kids were there, as was our dynamic oblate chaplain, Fr. Michael Fish, who read us the Oblate Rule with that marvelous South African accent of his. Fr. Michael has an amazing gift for seeing things in people that they can't see themselves—in this case, the archetype of the hermit that had been haunting me for so long, full-time university teacher and mother of four that I was. He encouraged me to take this contemplative call seriously, suggesting that I begin by making a list of my Most Important Activities, then cutting it in half. In *half*? Really? But somehow I did it.

As brand-new oblates, Janet and I both felt the need for a spiritual director, someone who could also hear our confessions. We put our heads together and—without consulting him ahead of time—decided on Fr. Isaiah Teichert, mainly because of his warm-hearted smile. Though he was a bit startled at getting "two directees for the price of one," he was a good sport about it. He has been hearing (and laughing at) my tortured confessions for nearly twenty years by now. I'm so glad I got to include the account of his ordination day, written by his mother, in the "Year of the Helicopter" chapter.

The day Fr. Cyprian Consiglio made his simple vows, I happened to be at the hermitage again (I was there often during the nineties, a particularly stressful time in my life). I'd never witnessed this ceremony, and it made a big impression. Later, when he left the monastery to hit the pilgrim trail, he sometimes stayed at our house when he had a concert in our area. No matter how early I got up, I always found him in the same place: in a rocking chair in front of our wood-burning stove with an open book across his lap. I'd just discovered Bede Griffith's *The Golden String*, and we had fascinating conversations about the connections between Christianity and the great religions of the East. Some of what we talked about—and also what he has written so much about—is in this book too.

When I first began visiting the hermitage in the early 1990s, Fr. Bruno Barnhart did not seem quite real to me, but instead like someone who permanently occupied a higher dimension. He was so tall, so quiet, so white of beard and hair that I was a little afraid to even speak to him. But then came a Sunday meal in the refectory, with its standing invitation for retreatants to help do the dishes afterward. And I found myself drying silverware for him—the legendary Fr. Bruno, who was hunched over the restaurant-style sink, up to the elbows in soapy bubbles, fishing out forks. Though he died before I began doing interviews for this book, I absorbed a lot from him, thanks to the many homilies he preached, the retreats he offered, the visionary books he wrote, and the stories others told about him.

I first got to know Fr. Andrew Colnaghi and Fr. Arthur Poulin when they led a small group of oblates on pilgrimage to Italy in 2002. They'd decided it would be a good idea for those of us who were now lay members of the family to see where it all began. We stayed at San Gregorio in Rome where Fr. Robert and Fr. Bruno lived when they were going to Sant'Anselmo in the early sixties. We saw the cell of Sr. Nazarena, the longtime Camaldolese recluse.

We stayed at Fonte Avellana, where Dom Anselmo Giabbani was prior in 1935. We spent three days at Fontebono—the cenobium at Camaldoli—which is where I met and became friends with Fr. Thomas Matus. He was still living in Italy then, and it seemed to me that he knew everything there was to know about . . . well, *everything*, but particularly Camaldolese history. The highlight of that pilgrimage was our day at the Sacro Eremo, where I got a chance to meditate inside the cell of St. Romuald himself.

It was this visit, and another in 2018—this time led by Fr. Thomas—that fixed in my mind the image of the ancient monasteries and made it possible for me to write about them here. Fr. Thomas gave me hours and hours of taped interviews for this book. We sat huddled in the chilly, windowless room that houses the archives while I coughed on clouds of book dust and he translated letters exchanged by Dom Anselmo Giabbani and Fr. Agostino Modotti in the 1950s.

I became friends with Fr. Raniero Hoffman when Fr. Bernard was dying. Fr. Raniero was not only the prior but the infirmarian by then, and Fr. Bernard, who'd become very difficult to understand because of his Parkinson's disease, whispered to me that "Fr. Prior is a very good mother." I saw the same tenderness in Fr. Raniero during the long dying of Br. Gabriel Kirby—

Thomas Matus (photograph by Kayleigh Meyers)

that enthusiastic, elfin character who loved nothing better than to pull me aside for a long disquisition on the Holy Spirit.

I was friends with Br. Emmanuel Wasinger for years before we ever had a conversation. His shy, tender smile conveyed his regard without his having to say a word. One day after Mass, he stayed back to ask if he could speak to me in the confessional. There, we sat in straight-backed chairs facing one another while he cleared his throat several times before confessing that he'd spent too many years not talking and would like to learn how to do it. Would I be willing to help him practice? For me, Br. Emmanuel was the quintessential monk, and his spirit pervades this book.

Given the focus on silence and solitude, friendships among monks and outsiders often grow more slowly than they do outside the walls. But grow they do, usually through one shared experience or a particularly deep conversation at a particularly important time. Br. Benedict Dell'Ossa, another monk with a funny bone, once took me and a couple of other women oblates on a wild ride to the lake at the top of the mountain, commanding us to "hit the floor" when another hermitage vehicle headed our way, and then cackling with glee when we obeyed—which at that somewhat dour time in my own life was exactly what the doctor ordered.

Engineer Br. Michael Harrington, a deeply spiritual monk who understands St. Elizabeth of the Trinity better than anyone I've ever met, once asked me for advice about his beloved grandchildren in a way that helped me figure out something important in regard to my own. Br. David Meyers, who is interested in bees and catapults and other wonders, once asked for permission to take his desert day at our house—which spurred a realization that we ourselves *never* took a desert day, even in this beautiful setting, simply because we'd never figured out how to stop working long enough to do so. And at a time when I was letting myself become obsessed about the safety and health of the hermitage community (it had been closed off for months in both directions after a major landslide), I experienced a monastic apparition in the aisle at Costco in San Luis Obispo: Fr. Zacc Naegele in T-shirt and jeans, pushing an overloaded cart and cheerfully hailing me: he'd figured out a way to get over the mountains and buy food for his brethren. These are the monks who keep the hermitage running, and I sincerely hope that their spirit of derring-do seeped into this book.

Fr. Daniel Manger, who by now has been prior at the Monastery of the Risen Christ in San Luis Obispo for nearly five years, is someone I see every week—or did, until the coronavirus lockdown began. He shares the little monastery on Cerro Romualdo with a relatively recent addition to the community, Fr. Stephen Coffey. I've known Fr. Steve since before he was a priest, which is to say, forever. Fr. Steve and I and a team of other oblates put on formation retreats at the Monastery of the Risen Christ every three months, as I did for years with Fr. Bede Healey, the present prior at Incarnation in Berkeley.

In fact, New Camaldoli's two daughter houses are beehives of oblate activity, and that is a real sign of hope during this time when new monastic vocations are few and far between. Along with our regular retreats and quiet days, we have been gathering for an annual assembly since 2012, where we have a chance to connect with fellow oblates and friends of the hermitage from around the world. After the pandemic made it necessary to offer our retreats via Zoom, even more oblates from England, Belgium, Scotland, New Zealand, Italy, and Australia have been able to participate. We're currently in the process of connecting the oblates of Transfiguration Monastery in New York (a Camaldolese women's community headed by Sr. Donald Corcoran) with our flourishing global family.

In order to help people discern whether the Camaldolese path is meant for them, fellow oblate Mike Mullard and I—relying on the help of ten other dedicated oblates—co-direct a one-on-one peer mentoring program for postulants going through their year of study, prayer, and reflection. I wish there was room in this book to tell the remarkable personal stories of these contemplatives-in-the-world. Though space limitations required that I had to single out one who could stand for all—Janet Walker—this global community of dedicated non-monastics is becoming a major vehicle for conveying the unique Camaldolese charism to countless seekers in far-flung places. I hope I've been able to get my love and appreciation for all of them across in these pages.

I met Therese Gagnon in 2003, after my first book about life at the hermitage was published. She liked it and invited me to visit her sanctuaries. Feeling as though I'd just been initiated into a secret society, I wandered through delightful forest gardens that had taken her years to build. Now ninety-five and just as wry and whimsical as ever, she good-naturedly sat for several days of interviews, shared her most precious picture albums with me, and gave me insights into the all-male community that I never would have stumbled onto by myself.

For all the reasons above, writing this book was—for me, at least—more like working on a family history than putting together a dispassionate account of the founding of a monastery. Yet I wanted to be as objective as possible, which means I had to create sufficient authorial distance from my subject. Thus the decision to call each character by his last name. This, I thought, would also help me avoid inflicting the "Russian novel syndrome" on readers in which every character has several names and in order to make sense of it all, you have to take notes on who is who.

But I couldn't leave it at last names only. At some point, I'd need to provide a first name, if only initially. Yet which one should I use? Each monk's birth name? Or the "glory name" he chose after joining the community? This was a tough call because frankly some birth names were so entrancing—"Francis Xavier Dell'Ossa," for example. However, I finally decided to go with monastic names, since these come only after a lot of reflection and prayer ("Francis Xavier," for instance, was transformed—presumably after a lot of reflection and prayer—into the humbler-sounding "Benedict"). In the same spirit, I also left off titles (i.e., simply "Giabbani" rather than Dom Anselmo Giabbani, or Dom Anselmo, or Prior General Anselmo Giabbani). I apologize if this technique causes any offense.

Sadly, I've had to leave some people out entirely. I did not talk about anyone who did not stay for the duration, even though there have been some brilliant and dynamic men who've come and gone over the years. I did not include monks who remained Camaldolese while living apart from the hermitage or its two satellites (Gregory Feltes, for example)—with the obvious exception of Fr. Michael Fish. I didn't mention wonderful people who joined after the year 2000, like Br. Martin Herbeck, Fr. Ignatius Tully, and Br. Ivan Nicoletto. And sadly, there was not enough room in these two hundred pages to include staff members, workers, and permanent residents from other communities, some of whom have been part of the family for decades.

Finally, I made the decision early on to forgo a strictly chronological structure. If historical accounts sometimes get bogged down in the middle, it's usually because the narrative arc gets buried under too many dates and facts. This is why there are so many flash-backs and flash-forwards, and also the shifts in tense and voice. Instead of following the dates, I chose to follow the themes. And this is also why I decided to end the story after roughly forty years rather than trying to cover everything up to the present. These past two decades have been remarkable, but to a large degree, they have been a working out of the big questions that arose early on. I sincerely hope nobody gets lost—and just to make sure, we've included a timeline at the end of the book.

Special thanks to Fathers Thomas, Cyprian, Raniero, Andrew, Arthur, Kevin, Michael, and Isaiah for allowing me to interview them. Thank you also to my fellow oblate, Jim Curtain of Melbourne, for helping me get access to some of Modotti's letters in the Jesuit archives there. Weeks after I finished the manuscript, he sent me new information about Modotti, courtesy of his archivist friend. A new book was out, written by a longtime Australian intelligence officer. And even though I'd finally concluded on my own that despite all the allegations, Modotti was no fascist spy, it was great to have this confirmed by a scholar with access to the letters and internal documents that proved beyond a doubt that he was innocent. The hermit from the Sacro Eremo who founded New Camaldoli was deliberately framed by a corrupt and bigoted (and since reformed) Australian Security Service. Contrary to the slanderous misinformation put out about him, Modotti was simply an Italian Catholic, trying his best in unbelievably difficult and complex circumstances to serve the Italian Catholic immigrants of wartime Australia.

Thank you to Katee Armstrong, who always found a room for me when I came to do research, and who even hid a key to the archives so we didn't have to go on a community-wide search each time I needed to get inside that chilly little room. Much gratitude to Vickie Conte for arranging the interviews with Therese and also for loaning

Church rotunda (photograph by Kayleigh Meyers)

me great books about Big Sur. Many thanks to Kayleigh Meyers for allowing me to use some of the spectacular photos she took for her book *Monks Inside Out: New Camaldoli Hermitage*. Everlasting gratefulness to Arthur Poulin for blessing this book cover with one of his amazing paintings. Thank you to my dear friend and fellow pilgrim Pico Iyer for his marvelous foreword. And to my beloved husband, Mike, who so cheerfully and patiently endured several years of my living in two worlds at the same time and handling neither of them very well: I could never have completed the task without you.

Most of all—more than I can ever say—thank you to Fr. Robert Hale, who kept notes for sixty years about his life at New Camaldoli, at Incarnation Monastery in Berkeley, and at Old Camaldoli in Italy, and who saved the hundreds of letters, documents, and photos that provided the bulk of my research material. Several years ago, he asked if I'd help him organize what he had saved for a possible book. He particularly wanted to answer a question that had lingered in the air since 1960—which was, What in the world happened at the beginning of the foundation? What was the conflict about and how did it finally get resolved? And did everything finally get healed? Sadly, Fr. Robert suffered a fatal fall at the hermitage only weeks after he sent me his last batch of notes. Though we never got a chance to talk about his vision for this book, I did try my best to answer those three questions for him.

As Merton said in *The Silent Life*, which inspired two young men of the late fifties— Robert Hale and Thomas Matus—to spend the rest of their lives in the white robes of the Camaldolese, "The monastery is neither a museum nor an asylum. The monk remains in the world from which he has fled, and he remains a potent, though hidden, force in that world . . . the monk acts on the world simply by being a monk. The presence of contemplatives is, to the world, what the presence of yeast is to dough."[1]

Dear brothers of New Camaldoli, you have been that yeast in my life and the lives of so many others. May you be blessed.

Camaldolese Chronology of Events

952—Romuald of Ravenna is born

1023—Sacro Eremo is founded

1027—Romuald dies

1072—Camaldolese Congregation is approved by Pope Alexander II

1080—Blessed Rudolph, fourth prior of the Sacro Eremo, writes the Book of the Eremitical Rule, followed by a shorter version in 1085

1212—St. Michael of Murano Monastery is founded on an island in the Venetian Lagoon

1295—Holy Mary of the Angels Monastery in Florence is founded; becomes famous during Renaissance for its miniaturists and painters

1320—Dante refers to Romuald in the *Divine Comedy*

1400s—Hermits of the Sacro Eremo defend themselves against an attacking battalion

1459—Blessed Ambrose Traversari, famous Camaldolese humanist philosopher, dies

1476—Birth of Blessed Paul Giustiniani, who enters the Sacro Eremo in 1510 and later, with the blessing of Pope Leo X, goes out to found new hermitages

1526—Giustiniani's purely eremitical congregation, known as the Hermits of Monte Corona, officially separate from Camaldoli

1528—Giustiniani dies

1569—Hermitage of Fonte Avellana, likely founded by Romuald in 1000, unites itself to Camaldoli

1616—Monks of St. Michael of Murano cut themselves off from Camaldoli to become purely cenobitical

1810—Napoleon represses monasteries throughout Italy

1831–1846—Reign of Pope Gregory XVI, Camaldolese monk

1857—Achille Ratti (to become Pius XI) born in Desio in province of Milan

1866—Religious orders are persecuted and monastic property seized by the secular government; King Victor Emmanuel suppresses 334 convents and monasteries, containing 4,280 religious men and 1,200 nuns

1870—*Il Risorgimento* (Italian Reunification); the church loses its Papal States; the Italian authorities deprive the religious of their legal existence and all they possess, without raising any obstacles to a possible reconstruction of regular communities; Camaldoli taken by Italian government

1873—Camaldolese monks allowed to return to monastery after working out a rental fee for the use of their own buildings

1876—Dani family arrives in Big Sur; Eugenio Pacelli (to become Pius XII) born in Rome

1882—Angelo Roncalli (to become John XXIII) born in Sotto il Monte near Bergamo

1883—Benito Mussolini (to become Il Duce) born in Dovia di Predappio in Romagna

1897—Giovanni Battista Montini (to become Paul VI) born in Concesio near Brescia; Ugo Modotti (to become Fr. Agostino Modotti) born in Udine, Friuli

1898—Four monks from Sacro Eremo make a new foundation in Brazil

1900—Mary Ellen Dani commits suicide in Big Sur

1901—Bede Janvrin born in England

1903—Pope Pius X is elected, serves until 1914

1906—Philip Klee is born

1907—*Lamentabili* issued against modernism; encyclical *Pascendi Dominici Gregis* calls modernism a heresy; in purge of modernists that follows, young Angelo Roncalli, future John XXIII, is investigated

1908—Anselmo Giabbani born in Stia; Pedro Rebello born in Mangalore, India

1913—Ugo Modotti enters Society of Jesus, studies philosophy at Gregorian University in Rome

1914—Benedetto Calati born in Pulsano; World War I begins; Robinson Jeffers lives with his wife, Una, in Carmel and travels extensively on Big Sur coast

1915—Aliprando Catani born; Thomas Merton born in eastern Pyrenees, France; Wlodzimizez Ledochowski is elected general of the Jesuits

1917—Code of Canon Law is issued; Battle of Caporetto lost by Italians; Modotti takes final Jesuit vows

1918—Joseph Diemer born; World War I ends

1919—Italian People's Party *(Partito Popolare Italiano)* founded by Luigi Sturzi, a Christian-democratic political party inspired by Catholic social teaching; Anselmo Giabbani enters Camaldolese at age eleven; British soldiers in India shoot over five hundred peaceful demonstrators in backlash against Gandhi

1920—Modotti is sent to the Malabar coast of India for the next sixteen years

1921—Mussolini wins seat in Italian Chamber of Deputies

1922—30,000 *squadristi* (Mussolini's Black Shirts) assemble in Rome to demand a new government; King Victor Emmanuel III hands reins of power to Mussolini, who becomes new prime minister; Achille Ratti is elected Pope Pius XI

1923—Modotti is ordained in India

1924—Mussolini's children are given First Communion in the Sacro Eremo by Camaldolese Prior Timoteo Chimenti and confirmed by Cardinal Vannutelli in the chapel of the Mausolea

1925—Mussolini declares himself "Head of Government no longer answerable to Parliament"; Giabbani makes solemn profession at age seventeen

1927—900th anniversary of Romuald's death; joint celebration with cenobites and hermits of order; monks from Sacro Eremo who made foundation in Brazil are recalled to Camaldoli

1928—Pius XI issues *Mortalium Animos*, his encyclical condemning ecumenism; Bernard Massicotte is born in Quebec

1929—Pius XI and Mussolini sign Lateran Treaties and Concordats; team of developers buys huge section of coastline, including the Dani homestead

1930s—Camaldolese begin discussing going to the US; group of cenobites go to Texas but new foundation fails; old ranch house (still standing at NCH) is built

1931—Bruno Barnhart is born in Long Island, NY; investor Edward Moore buys 10,000 acres of Big Sur land for his Circle M Ranch

1932—Giabbani is ordained

1933—Pius XI signs Reich Concordat with Hitler; Pedro Rebello enters Jesuits

1934—Old guesthouse is reopened at Camaldoli, first groups of students start arriving; Giovanni Battista Montini (future Paul VI) becomes part of this intellectual gathering place

1935—Camaldolese Cenobites (St. Michael's of Murano) are suppressed by the Vatican and monks are sent to Sacro Eremo for six-month novitiate, to St. Paul's Outside the Walls (Casseniese), or to become secular clergy; Giabbani is made prior of Fonte Avellana at age of twenty-seven; Mussolini invades Ethiopia in effort to rebuild Roman Empire—raises funds by asking all Italians to send him their gold, including wedding rings; Thomas Merton enrolls at Columbia University where he pickets the Casa Italiana in protest of Ethiopian invasion

1936—Mussolini forms Rome/Berlin Axis with Hitler and sends major support to Franco in Spain; Modotti becomes procurator in Italy of Italian mission in India; Ledochowski forms "Special Secretariat on Atheism" and summons Jesuits from around the globe to Rome for a summit on the battle against communism

1937—Pius XI's *Mit brennender Sorge* is smuggled into Germany; Robert Hale is born

1938—Kristallnacht is carried out by Hitler's Nazis; Modotti is sent to Melbourne to help Italian immigrants at request of Australian Archbishop Daniel Mannix; Thomas Merton meets the Hindu monk and academic Mahanambrata Brahmachari

1939—Mussolini signs Pact of Steel with Hitler; Pius XI dies; Eugenio Pacelli is elected Pope Pius XII

1940—Mussolini declares war on Britain and France, enters WWII with Axis powers; Australian government inters Italian immigrants as "enemy aliens"; Modotti is surveilled by Security Service; Australia takes on 18,500 Italian POWS sent by Britain; Thomas Matus is born

1941—Nazi Germany declares war on US; Japanese bomb Pearl Harbor; Merton enters Gethsemani as Trappist monk; Camaldolese monastery of San Gregorio Magno al Cielo in Rome hides Jews, antifascist political figures, and escaped prisoners; Philip Klee becomes conscientious objector; Modotti builds Lourdes Grotto in Australia

1943—Codice of Camaldoli is drawn up, becomes basis for Christian Democratic Party after war; Modotti is surveilled by Australian Military Intelligence and arrested by Security Service; Mussolini falls from power; Nazis set him up in a puppet government in northern Italy; Andrew Colnaghi born in Milan area

1944—Christmas Eve, Pius XII praises democracy for the first time in his radio address to the world; Henry Miller moves to Big Sur; Nazis carry out massacre in village of Moggiona near Camaldoli; Moore sells Circle M to John Nesbitt, "The Golden Voice of Radio"

1945—Germany surrenders to Allies in Northern Italy; Mussolini is assassinated by antifascist partisans two days before Hitler's suicide; Nazarena joins the Camaldolese with Anselmo Giabbani as her confessor; Bede Janvrin receives Order of the British Empire for work in secret service during war; Pedro Rebello is ordained

1946—Modotti goes to Italy to bring back more Jesuits, is forbidden to return to Australia; Nazarena goes into permanent reclusion at Sant'Antonio in Rome

1947—Merton muses in his journal about becoming Camaldolese

1948—Merton publishes *The Seven Storey Mountain;* Daniel Manger is born in Louisville, near Gethsemani

1949—Modotti interviews Francisco Franco in Spain for Vatican Radio

1950—Modotti leaves Jesuits, enters Sacro Eremo as Camaldolese monk; Arthur Poulin and Raniero Hoffman are born; Massicotte serves with Missionaries of the Holy Apostles; American student Jim Cottrell reads about Romuald in Butler's *Lives of the Saints* and writes to a hermit at the Sacro Eremo

1951—Modotti makes solemn profession; Anselmo Giabbani is elected prior general of the Camaldolese; Alan Watts publishes *The Wisdom of Insecurity*

1952—Merton write first letter to Giabbani; first issue of the journal *Camaldoli* is published

1953—Merton urges Giabbani to make an American foundation in California; Modotti enters reclusion; Aldous Huxley takes mescaline for the first time

1954—Merton writes journal entries that become *Thoughts in Solitude;* Aldous Huxley publishes *The Doors of Perception;* Thomas Matus reads Yogananda's *Autobiography of a Yogi;* Giabbani presents draft of new Camaldolese constitutions to hermits of Sacro Eremo

1955—John Nesbitt sells the Circle M Ranch to two ranchers from King City

1956—Merton writes last letter to Giabbani; Cottrell visits the Sacro Eremo and forms "Friends of the Camaldolese" after he returns to the States

1957—Merton's *The Silent Life* is published, with chapter on Camaldolese; Robert Hale reads it and is drawn to Camaldolese; Giabbani presents newly approved Camaldolese constitutions that start hermit-cenobite battle; Giabbani tours America looking for possible sites; Colnaghi works in huge factory; Massicotte is ordained; Thomas Matus reads *The Silent Life* by Thomas Merton; Henry Miller publishes *Big Sur and the Oranges of Hieronymous Bosch*

1958—Modotti and Aliprando Catani arrive in New York on liner *Constitution; Time* magazine publishes article on hermits' arrival; Modotti sees Lucia Ranch in Big Sur for the first time; Modotti enters into negotiations with Bishop Willinger for permission to build hermitage in diocese; section of Lucia Ranch is purchased for the site; Bishop Fulton Sheen writes letter encouraging Modotti; Pius XII dies; Angelo Giuseppe Roncalli is elected Pope John XXIII; Modotti writes to new pope complaining about Camaldolese constitutions, asking for a guarantee that new American foundation will be strictly eremitical; ground is broken for new hermitage; Philip Klee enters NCH; Pedro Rebello arrives at NCH; Andrea Agnoletti and Adalbert Paulmichel arrive from Italy to help Modotti; fire burns down Nesbitt's ranch house, most valuable building at NCH; Cyprian Consiglio is born on feast day of St. Romuald the same year NCH is founded

1959—John XXIII announces he will convoke Vatican II; Robert Hale and Bruno Barnhart arrive at NCH; Willinger visits NCH for first time and is displeased; Extraordinary Diet of Camaldolese meets to discuss problems with Modotti; Modotti goes to Rome at Bishop Willinger's urging and is put under monastic house arrest; Merton begins dialogue with D.T. Suzuki on Zen Buddhism

1960—Modotti is dispensed from vows, goes to Puerto Rico to start seminary; Clemente Roggi becomes prior; Hale, Barnhart, and Klee make simple vows; Rebello makes solemn profession; cornerstone of first cell is laid and blessed

1961—First fifteen cells, guesthouse, and retreat house at NCH are blessed by apostolic delegate to US, Archbishop Egidio Vagnozzi; Bede Janvrin arrives at NCH; Diemer makes simple vows; Matus becomes a Catholic

1962—Thomas Matus reads *Time* magazine story on Nazarena, prays to her to help him discern his vocation; Matus begins postulancy at NCH; Gabriel Kirby enters NCH; John XXIII opens Vatican II with 2,500 council fathers in attendance; Francis Gannon, Hale, and Barnhart study at S'ant Anselmo in Rome; Esalen Institute is founded in Big Sur by Michael Murphy and Richard Price; Henry Miller leaves Big Sur; Cuban Missile Crisis occurs

1963—Vatican blocks Giabbani's re-election; Aliprando Catani is made prior general; John XXIII dies; Giovanni Battista Montini is elected Pope Paul VI, oversees the rest of Vatican II; Janvrin makes solemn profession

1964—First Mass is celebrated in new NCH church at midnight on Christmas Eve; Bernard Massicotte enters NCH; Hale and Barnhart make solemn vows; Matus and Kirby make simple vows

1965—NCH church is consecrated by Auxiliary Bishop Harry Clinch; NCH acquires an additional 300 acres for a total of 900; Paul VI closes Vatican II

1966—Emmanuel Wasinger enters; Catani and Giabbani visit NCH; Janvrin makes solemn vows; first discussions of new constitutions and declarations are held

1967—Thomas Matus is sent to Rome for studies, Giabbani is his superior; NCH begins pouring slab for library; Matus, Hale, and Kirby make solemn professions; lessons are read in English for first time; Matus heads to Rome for studies; the Camaldolese become a congregation within the worldwide Benedictine Confederation

1968—Joseph Diemer goes into temporary reclusion; Philip Klee makes solemn profession; Merton dies of electrocution in Thailand; Paul VI publishes *Humanae Vitaea*; Rebello goes into reclusion at Sacro Eremo for a year; Bede Griffiths takes up the reins at Shantivanam

1969—Benedetto Calati is elected prior general; first fruitcake sale is held—1,600 are sold; Hale and Matus both ask for transfer to Old Camaldoli; Rebello goes to Mangalore to look for possible site for new Camaldolese foundation; Joan Baez, Joni Mitchell, and Crosby, Stills, and Nash perform at Esalen

1970—Bruno Barnhart becomes prior of NCH; Andrew Colnaghi enters Sacro Eremo; Poulin spends junior year abroad in Rome; Rebello is killed in car accident in Punjab; Klee makes solemn profession; Kevin Joyce makes first trip to NCH

1971—Modotti dies, is buried at NCH

1972—Hale receives PhD from Fordham; Barnhart and Massicotte visit Mt. Athos in Greece; Anthony Barabe goes into partial reclusion at NCH

1973—Diemer's reclusion officially becomes permanent; Isaiah Teichert makes first visit to NCH

1975—Catholic charismatic movement sweeps American church; Barnhart, Massicotte, Kirby, and Wasinger organize charismatic prayer service at NCH; Consiglio and Poulin live with different radical Franciscan communities in Chicago; Hoffman is ordained and visits NCH for the first time; NCH votes to sponsor two Vietnamese refugee families and two single men

1976—Poulin becomes Franciscan; Matus receives PhD from Fordham

1978—Paul VI dies; John Paul I is elected pope and dies within two weeks; John Paul II is elected, publishes encyclical *Redemptor Hominis* regarding other religions; Hale drafts proposal for new foundation in America, writes prior of Holy Cross House in Berkeley for advice; future oblate Janet Walker makes first visit to NCH

1979—Colnaghi is ordained; Hale and Gargano fly to America to visit Holy Cross monks of Incarnation Priory in Berkeley; Teichert becomes an observer

1980—Colnaghi arrives in America, works with Hale to help build joint community in Berkeley; Teichert begins formal postulancy

1981—Incarnation Priory (dual community, Episcopalian and Catholic monks) is blessed; Teichert makes simple vows

1984—Oblate program begins at Incarnation; Teichert goes to seminary at Dominican School in Oakland; Therese and Eric Gagnon arrive at NCH

1985—Bede Griffiths and Shantivanam become Camaldolese; NCH is evacuated because of fire

1987—Emanuele Bargellini is elected prior general; Bede Janvrin dies at NCH; Hale moves from Incarnation to NCH in advance of being elected prior; Matus spends time at NCH to work on English translation of Psalter

1988—Hale is elected prior at NCH; Colnaghi is elected prior of Incarnation Priory; Barnhart goes to Daybreak House at L'Arche and becomes companion of Adam

1989—Isaiah Teichert makes solemn vows; NCH accepts oblate program; Hale is elected to board of First International Thomas Merton Society Conference

1990—Teichert is ordained; Romuald Duscher transfers from St. Andrews in Valyermo; joint community in Berkeley separates and Incarnation Monastery is established as a Camaldolese house; Hoffman starts postulancy at NCH; Poulin takes a sabbatical in Europe

1991—Prior General Emanuele Bargellini visits NCH

1992—Cyprian Consiglio arrives; Joseph Wong begins transfer from Salesians; Joshua Monson, Michael Harrington, and Zaccheus Naegle make simple vows; Bede Griffiths visits, establishes the Bede Griffiths foundation for the Renewal of Contemplative Life

1993—Raniero Hoffman and Benedict Dell'Ossa make simple vows; Arthur Poulin arrives at NCH; Daniel Manger arrives at NCH to discern transfer from Franciscans; Incarnation Monastery community acquires the house in Berkeley at 1369 La Loma; Barnhart publishes *The Good Wine*

1994—Consiglio makes simple vows; Joseph Diemer goes blind; Sr. Donald Corcoran, Prioress of Transfiguration Monastery, Windsor, NY, gives annual retreat on "Monastic Life and Wisdom"

1995—Harrington and Monson make solemn vows; Fr. William Johnston gives annual retreat on contemplative prayer (Zen/Christian dialogue); Philip Klee dies

1996—Naegle makes solemn vows; Bede Healey from St Benedict's Abbey, Atchison, Kansas, makes observership; Hoffman and Dell'Ossa make solemn vows

1997—Wong transfers vows from Salesians and he and Consiglio make solemn vows; Aelred Squire dies

1998—Consiglio is ordained; Michael Fish arrives at NCH; David Meyers becomes postulant; El Nino causes major damage to Hwy 1, cutting off road in both directions; Hale develops heart trouble, Hoffman becomes vice-prior; Poulin transfers vows from Franciscans and is invited to move from NCH to INC (Incarnation Monastery) in Berkeley

1999—Barnhart publishes *Second Simplicity*; Janet Walker makes oblation; Manger makes solemn vows

2000—Benedetto Calati dies; Raniero Hoffman is elected prior NCH; Joseph Wong leads weeklong conversation at NCH between Hindu, Buddhist, Taoist, and Confucian monks

2002—Colnaghi and Poulin lead oblate pilgrimage to Italy; Consiglio leaves with blessing of congregation for ten years on the road, performing and leading retreats; Fish transfers vows and becomes oblate chaplain at NCH

2003—Lauds and Vespers Office book, translated by Matus and Consiglio, is published

2004—Anselmo Giabbani dies

2005—Aliprando Catani dies; Bernardino Corrazini is elected prior general; Joseph Diemer dies at NCH

2008—Barnhart publishes *The Future of Wisdom*

2011—Alessandro Barban is elected prior general; Bernard Massicotte dies at NCH

2012—Robert Hale is elected prior of NCH; Hale participates in ecumenical liturgies of Pope Benedict with Archbishop of Canterbury Rowan Williams; Consiglio returns to NCH; Hoffman goes on sabbatical to Shantivanam, Tanzania, and the Sacro Eremo; prior of Shantivanam visits NCH; board meeting of Monastic Interreligious Dialogue held at NCH; Ivan Nicoletto transfers from Old Camaldoli to INC

2013—Benedict XVI steps down; Jorge Mario Bergoglio becomes Pope Francis; INC purchases twin house next door: first Camaldolese

Oblate Assembly held at Asilomar in Pacific Grove gathers 150 oblates from around the world; Hale steps down as prior; Consiglio is elected; Ignatius Tully makes simple vows; Ora et Labora Program is launched at NCH for young men to explore contemplative life

2014—The Monastery of the Risen Christ in San Luis Obispo enters a three-year transition from the Olivettans to the Camaldolese; Daniel Manger becomes prior

2015—Bruno Barnhart dies at NCH; Camaldolese oblates establish peer mentor program

2016—Soberanes Fire threatens NCH; first peer mentor formation retreat is held at NCH

2017—MRC officially becomes Camaldolese; Stephen Coffey becomes Camaldolese; Emmanuel Wasinger dies; torrential rains cause bridge collapse and massive mudslides on Hwy 1 that close NCH for months; Ignatius Tully makes solemn vows

2018—Consiglio is confirmed to six more years of priorship at NCH; Andrew Colnaghi steps down as prior of INC after 24 years; Bede Healey becomes local prior at INC; Gabriel Kirby dies; Robert Hale dies; Matus leads oblate pilgrimage to Italy

2020—COVID-19 forces lockdown; Dolan Fire causes monthlong evacuation of NCH; annual Oblate Assembly is held via Zoom; oblate Zoom groups are established in various parts of the country; Martin Herbeck makes simple vows

2021—Atmospheric river weather event occurs, with thirteen inches of rain in three days, 150-foot section of Hwy 1 collapses into ocean; NCH once again closed off

Notes

Chapter 1

1. Belden Lane, *The Solace of Fierce Landscapes* (New York: Oxford, University Press, 1998), 41.

2. Edward Gibbon, "Origins of the Monastic Life," in *Decline and Fall of the Roman Empire*, ed. David Reed (n.p.: Gutenberg Edition, 2010), https://www.gutenberg.org/files/25717/25717-h/25717-h.htm#chap37.1.

Chapter 2

1. Henry Miller, *Big Sur and the Oranges of Hieronymus Bosch* (New York: New Directions Publishing, 1957), 237.

2. Miller, *Big Sur*, 12.

3. Miller, 7.

4. Miller, 25.

5. Miller, 26.

6. Rudolf Otto, *The Idea of the Holy* (London: Oxford University Press, 1971), back cover.

7. Belden Lane, *The Solace of Fierce Landscapes* (New York: Oxford University Press, 1998), 114.

8. Alan Watts, *The Wisdom of Insecurity: A Message for an Age of Anxiety* (New York: Vintage Books, 2011), 34.

9. Watts, *Wisdom of Insecurity*, 60.

10. Thomas Merton, *The Seven Storey Mountain* (New York: Harcourt, Brace, 1948), 316.

11. Merton, *Seven Storey Mountain*, 316.

12. Robert Giroux, "Thomas Merton's Durable Mountain," *The New York Times*, October 11, 1998, http://movies2.nytimes.com/books/98/10/11/bookend/bookend.html.

Chapter 3

1. Thomas Matus, OSB Cam, *The Mystery of Romuald and the Five Brothers: Stories from the Benedictines and Camaldolese* (Trabuco Canyon, CA: Source Books, 1994), 11.

2. Thomas Matus, interview with the author, New Camaldoli Hermitage, August 26, 2019.

3. Matus, *Mystery of Romuald*, 47.

4. Matus, 88.

5. Peter-Damian Belisle, ed. and trans., *Camaldolese Spirituality: Essential Sources* (Bloomingdale, OH: ErCam Editions, 2007), 241.

6. Matus, interview, August 26, 2019.

7. Thomas Matus, interview with the author, New Camaldoli Hermitage, January 6, 2020.

8. Emanuele Bargellini, "The Renaissance of the Camaldolese and the Word of God," AIM (France: AllianceInterMonasteres, 2012).

9. Bargellini, "Renaissance of the Camaldolese."

10. Roberto Forniciari, "The Institutional Evolution of Italian Monasticism from Unity to the Present Day," in *Christians of Italy; Church, History, State, 1861-2011*, vol. II (Rome: Institute of the Italian Encyclopedia, 2011), 911–27.

11. David Kertzer, "A New Pope," in *The Pope and Mussolini: The Secret History of Pius XI and the Rise of Fascism in Europe* (New York: Random House, 2014), Kindle.

Chapter 4

1. Thomas Matus, interview with the author, New Camaldoli Hermitage, August 26, 2019.

2. Roberto Forniciari, "The Institutional Evolution of Italian Monasticism from Unity to the Present Day," in *Christians of Italy: Church, History, State, 1861-2011*, vol. II (Rome: Institute of the Italian Encyclopedia, 2011).

3. Donald Grayston, *Thomas Merton and the Noonday Demon: The Camaldoli Correspondence* (Eugene, OR: Cascade Books, 2015), 56.

4. Grayston, *Thomas Merton*, 55.

5. Grayston, 70.

6. Grayston, 75.

7. Grayston, 82.

8. Robert Hale, "New Camaldoli Hermitage: Notes Towards a History" (unpublished manuscript, April 15, 2018).

9. Hale, "New Camaldoli Hermitage."

Chapter 5

1. David Kertzer, "Rising from the Tomb," chap. 5 in *The Pope and Mussolini: The Secret History of Pius XI and the Rise of Fascism in Europe* (New York: Random House, 2014), Kindle.

2. Kertzer, "The Pact," in *Pope and Mussolini*.

3. Kertzer, *Pope and Mussolini*.

4. Jorge Dagnino, "The Royalty of Christ the King and Its Enemies," in *Faith and Fascism: Catholic Intellectuals in Italy, 1925–43*, Histories of the Sacred and Secular series, 1700–2000, ed. David Nash, Oxford Brookes University Department of History (London: Palgrave MacMillan, 2017), Kindle.

5. Dagnino, *Faith and Fascism*.

6. Dagnino.

7. Bernardo Ignesti, "La Congregazioni Camaldolesi," *Monachesimo E Vita Religiosa: Rinnovamonto e Storia Tra Secoli XIXX-XX* (Verona: El Signo Gabrielli Editori, 2002).

8. Ignesti, "La Congregazioni Camaldolesi."

9. Cardinal V. Vannutelli to Cardinal P. Gaspari, September 9, 1924, Mausolea di Camaldoli.

10. Kertzer, "The Fatal Embrace," chap. 3 in *Pope and Mussolini*.

11. Emma Fattorini, *Hitler, Mussolini, and the Vatican: Pope Pius XI and the Speech That Was Never Made*, trans. Carl Ipsen (Cambridge: Polity Press, 2011), 65–66.

12. Fattorini, *Hitler, Mussolini, and the Vatican*, 67.

13. Anthony Cappello, "Italian Australians, the Church, War and Fascism in Melbourne 1919–1945" (master's thesis, Department of Social Inquiry and Community Studies St. Albans Campus, 1999), 30.

14. Kertzer, "Crossing the Border," chap. 16 in *Pope and Mussolini*.

Chapter 6

1. Ernest Hemingway, *A Farewell to Arms* (New York: Scribner, 1995), 198–99.

2. Hemingway, *Farewell to Arms*, 199.

3. Archives of the Society of Jesus in Australia.

4. Retrieved from https://www.shmoop.com/passage-to-india/setting .html%20#:~:text=The%20first%20two%20parts%20of,part%20taking %20place%20in%20Mau.

5. E. M. Forster, *A Passage to India* (New York: Harcourt, Brace, Jovanovich, 1984), 202.

6. Shirley De Boulay, *Beyond the Darkness: A Biography of Bede Griffiths* (New York: Doubleday, 1998), 122.

7. Anthony Cappello, "A Brief Survey of the Italian Catholic in Australia until the Second World War: An Italian Problem?," in *The Pastoral Care of Italians in Australia: Memory and Prophecy*, ed. Anthony Paganoni (Victoria: Connor Court Publishing, 2007), 38.

8. Anthony Cappello, "Italian Australians, the Church, War and Fascism in Melbourne 1919–1945" (master's thesis, Department of Social Inquiry and Community Studies, St. Albans Campus, 1999), 40.

9. Cappello, "Italian Australians," 41.

10. Cappello, "Brief Survey of the Italian Catholic," 32.

11. Cappello, "Brief Survey of the Italian Catholic," 32.

12. Gianfranco Cresciani, "The Second Awakening: The Italia Libera Movement," from *Labour History*, no. 30 (Liverpool University Press, May 1976), 22–37, https://www.jstor.org/stable/27508214.

13. Cappello, "Brief Survey of the Italian Catholic," 33.

14. Ilma Martinuzzi O'Brien, "Italian Australians and the Australian Catholic Church through War, Internment and Mass Migration," in *The Pastoral Care of Italians in Australia*, ed. Anthony Paganoni (Victoria: Connor Court Publishing, 2007), 58.

15. Anthony Cappello, "To Be or Not to Be an Italian: Culture, Descent, and the Social Exclusion of Italian-Australians" (thesis, Institute for Community, Ethnicity and Policy Alternatives, Victoria University, 2009).

16. Cappello, "To Be or Not to Be."

17. Cappello.

Chapter 7

1. Robert Hale, OSB Cam, "New Camaldoli before the Monks: Some Data and References" (unpublished manuscript, 1988).

2. John Walton, "The Poet as Ethnographer: Robinson Jeffers in Big Sur," in *California History*, vol. 87, no. 2, Robinson Jeffers (University of California Press in Association with the California Historical Society, 2010), 22–41, 66–67.

3. Robinson Jeffers, "The Coast Road," chap. 7 in *The Collected Poetry of Robinson Jeffers*, vol. 2, ed. Tim Hunt (Stanford, CA: Stanford University Press, 1989), 522–23.

4. Walton, "Poet as Ethnographer," caption under photograph.

5. Walton, 34.

6. Hale, "New Camaldoli before the Monks," remembrance by Judith Goodman.

7. Modotti to Anselmo Giabbani, December 24, 1958.

8. Modotti to Lena Santospiritu, August 5, 1954, Lena Santuspiritu Collection Inventory, SP-00455.

9. Modotti to Fr. Stan Kelly, SJ, March 8, 1946, Archives of the Society of Jesus in Australia.

10. Anthony Cappello, "Mannix, Modotti, and the Italian POWs," *Quadrant*, vol. XLVIII, nos. 7–8 (July–August, 2004).

11. Anthony Cappello, "Italian Australians, the Church, War and Fascism in Melbourne 1919–1945" (master's thesis, of Social Inquiry and Community Studies, St. Albans Campus, 1999), 114.

12. Cappello, "Italian Australians," 114.

13. Modotti to Kelly, March 8, 1946.

14. Paolo Monelli, quoted in Giuseppe Bottai, *Diario* (Milano: Rizzoli, 1935–1944).

15. Janet Kincaid Dethick, *The Arezzo Massacres: A Tuscan Tragedy, April–September 1944* (self-published and translated, 2008), 118.

16. Robinson Jeffers, "Evening Ebb," from *The Selected Poetry of Robinson Jeffers*, ed. Tim Hunt (Stanford, CA: Stanford University Press, 2001).

Chapter 8

1. Jeff Norman and the Big Sur Historical Society, *Big Sur: Images of America* (Charleston, SC: Arcadia, 2004), 56.

2. Stanley Harlan, *My Mom and Dad on the Coast South of Big Sur: A Historical Recollection of the Big Sur Area Experienced Through the Toils and Labor of the Harlan Family* (self-published, 2019), 69.

3. Harlan, *My Mom and Dad*, 73.

4. Robert Hale, OSB Cam, "New Camaldoli before the Monks: Some Data and References" (unpublished manuscript, 1988).

5. Hale, "New Camaldoli before the Monks."

6. Modotti to Fr. Joseph Klinglesmith, May 9, 1958, New Camaldoli Hermitage archives.

7. Thomas Matus, interview with the author, New Camaldoli Hermitage, November 12, 2019.

8. James Fox to Modotti, January 8, 1958, New Camaldoli Hermitage archives.

9. Modotti to Joseph Willinger, May 27, 1958, letter no. 200 in Robert Hale's correspondence file, New Camaldoli Hermitage archives.

10. Modotti to Willinger, June 17, 1958, New Camaldoli Hermitage archives.

11. Peter-Damian Belisle, ed., trans., *Camaldolese Spirituality: Essential Sources* (Bloomingdale, OH: ErCam Editions, 2007), 233.

12. Belisle, *Camaldolese Spirituality*, 227.

13. Belisle, 225.

14. Lino Vigilucci, OSB Cam, *Camaldoli: A Journey into Its History and Spirituality*, trans. Peter-Damian Belisle (Trabuco Canyon, CA: Source Books, 1995), 63.

Chapter 9

1. Thomas Merton, *The Silent Life* (New York: Farrar, Straus and Giroux, 1957), chap. 2, section III, Kindle.

2. Robert Hale, OSB Cam, "New Camaldoli Hermitage: Notes Toward a History" (unpublished manuscript, 2018).

3. Hale, "New Camaldoli Hermitage."

4. Hale.

5. Hale.

6. Anselmo Giabbani to Modotti, June 23, 1958, New Camaldoli Hermitage archives.

7. Modotti to Willinger, January 20, 1959, New Camaldoli Hermitage archives.

8. Michael Burke to Robert Hale, September 6, 1997, New Camaldoli Hermitage archives.

9. Modotti to Francis McGinley, December 4, 1958, New Camaldoli Hermitage archives.

Chapter 10

1. Modotti to John XXIII, December 24, 1958, New Camaldoli Hermitage archives.

2. Modotti to Willinger, January 29, 1959, New Camaldoli Hermitage archives.

3. Willinger to Modotti, March 12, 1959, New Camaldoli Hermitage archives.

4. Valeri to Giabbani, March 23, 1959, New Camaldoli Hermitage archives.

5. Giabbani to Modotti, June 20, 1959, New Camaldoli Hermitage archives.

6. Willinger to Valeri, July 7, 1959, New Camaldoli Hermitage archives.

7. Valeri to Willinger, plus handwritten note Willinger to Modotti, August 12, 1959, New Camaldoli Hermitage archives.

8. Giuseppe Cacciamatti to Benedetto Calati, July 24, 1959, New Camaldoli Hermitage archives.

9. Robert Hale, OSB Cam, "New Camaldoli Hermitage: Notes Toward a History" (unpublished manuscript, 2018).

10. Hale, "New Camaldoli Hermitage" (no extant copies of letters, but they are described in detail in Robert Hale's timeline).

11. Monsignor Culleton's letter to Aliprando Catani, October 19, 1959, New Camaldoli Hermitage archives.

12. Culleton to Catani, October 9, 1959, New Camaldoli Hermitage archives.

13. Willinger to Modotti, plus handwritten note by Modotti on bottom of last page, December 1, 1959 (copy not extant but described in detail on Robert Hale's timeline of events).

14. Jim Cottrell to Robert Hale, no date, in New Camaldoli Hermitage archives.

Chapter 11

1. Robert Hale, OSB Cam, "New Camaldoli Hermitage: Notes Toward a History" (unpublished manuscript, 2018).

2. Hale to David Burke, October 21, 1959, New Camaldoli Hermitage archives.

3. Hale to Burke, October 21, 1959.

4. Hale to Burke, October 21, 1959.

5. Hale to Burke, October 21, 1959.

6. Hale to Burke, October 21, 1959.

7. Pius XII, quoted in John W. O'Malley, *What Happened at Vatican II* (Cambridge: Belknap Press of Harvard University Press, 2008), 83.

8. Pius XII, quoted in O'Malley, *What Happened at Vatican II*, 86.

9. Pius XII, in O'Malley, 88.

10. Pius XII, in O'Malley, 89.

11. Pius XII, in O'Malley, 90.

12. Pius XII, in O'Malley, 91.

13. Thomas Matus, interview with the author, January 6, 2020, New Camaldoli Hermitage.

14. *Growth of a Hermitage*, Immaculate Heart Hermitage (Big Sur, CA, 1966).

15. Matus, interview with the author, January 6, 2020, New Camaldoli Hermitage.

Chapter 12

1. Thomas Matus, interview with the author, October 28, 2019, New Camaldoli Hermitage.

2. Matus, interview, October 27, 2019.

3. Robert Hale, OSB Cam, "New Camaldoli Hermitage: Notes Toward a History" (unpublished manuscript, 2018).

4. Bruce Ariss, "Saints and Sinners," *Monterey Peninsula Herald*, July 22, 1961.

5. John W. O'Malley, *What Happened at Vatican II* (Cambridge: Belknap Press of Harvard University Press, 2008), 93.

Chapter 13

1. "A Nun's Story," *Time* (April 13, 1962): 54.

2. "An American Enigma: Sister Nazarena," by Thomas Matus, OSB Cam, http://bvd-serralunga.com.

3. John W. O'Malley, *What Happened at Vatican II* (Cambridge: Belknap Press of Harvard University Press, 2008), 2.

4. O'Malley, *What Happened at Vatican II*, 2–3.

5. O'Malley, 4–5.

6. O'Malley, 9.

7. Thomas Matus interview with the author, October 27, 2019, New Camaldoli Hermitage.

8. Matus interview, October 27, 2019.

9. Robert Hale, OSB Cam, "New Camaldoli Hermitage: Notes Toward a History" (unpublished manuscript, 2018).

10. Hale, "New Camaldoli Hermitage."

Chapter 14

1. Robert Hale, OSB Cam, "New Camaldoli Hermitage: Notes Toward a History" (unpublished manuscript, 2018).

2. Hale, "New Camaldoli Hermitage."

3. Hale.

4. Roberto Forniciari, "The Institutional Evolution of Italian Monasticism from Unity to the Present Day," in *Christians of Italy; Church, History, State, 1861-2011*, vol. II (Rome: Institute of the Italian Encyclopedia, 2011), 911–27.

5. Hale, "New Camaldoli Hermitage."

6. Fornicari, "Institutional Evolution of Italian Monasticism," quoting Bargellini, 115.

7. Fornicari, quoting Bargellini, 115.

8. United States Conference of Catholic Bishops, explanation of devotionals, https://www.usccb.org/prayer-and-worship/prayers-and-devotions.

9. Handwritten note in file labeled "Vice Archivist," New Camaldoli Hermitage archives.

10. Thomas Matus, interview with the author, October 27, 2019, New Camaldoli Hermitage.

11. John W. O'Malley, *What Happened at Vatican II* (Cambridge: Belknap Press of Harvard University Press, 2008), 239.

12. Mary Judith O'Brien and Mary Nika Schaumber, "'Perfectae Caritatis': Renewal of Religious Life Is a Continual Process," https://www.ncregister.com/news/perfectae-caritatis-renewal-of-religious-life-is-a-continual-process.

13. O'Malley, *What Happened at Vatican II*, 239.

14. O'Malley, 95.

15. Emanuele Bargellini, "The Renaissance of the Camaldolese and the Word of God," AIM (France: AllianceInterMonasteres, 2012).

Chapter 15

1. Robert Hale, OSB Cam, "New Camaldoli Hermitage: Notes Toward a History" (unpublished manuscript, 2018).

2. Shirley Du Boulay, *Beyond the Darkness: A Biography of Bede Griffiths* (New York: Doubleday, 1998), 145.

3. Du Boulay, *Beyond the Darkness*, 148.

4. Du Boulay, 149.

5. Du Boulay, 150.

6. Thomas Matus, OSB Cam, *The Mystery of Romuald and the Five Brothers: Stories from the Benedictine and Camaldolese* (Trabuco Canyon, CA: Source Books, 1994), 7.

7. Hale, "New Camaldoli Hermitage."

8. Hale.

9. Hale.

10. Bernard Massicotte, as told to the author, 1999, New Camaldoli Hermitage.

11. Du Boulay, *Beyond the Darkness*, 155.

Chapter 16

1. Kevin Joyce, interview with the author, July 30, 2019, New Camaldoli Hermitage.

2. St. Teresa of Avila, *Interior Castle*, trans. and ed. E. Allison Peers (New York: Doubleday/Image, 1961), 101.

3. Robert Hale, OSB Cam, "New Camaldoli Hermitage: Notes Toward a History" (unpublished manuscript, 2018).

4. Hale, "New Camaldoli Hermitage."

5. Hale.

6. Thomas Matus, OSB Cam, *The Mystery of Romuald and the Five Brothers: Stories from the Benedictines and Camaldolese* (Trabuco Canyon, CA: Source Books, 1994), 27.

7. Hermitage Newsletter, 1970, New Camaldoli Hermitage archives.

8. Shirley Du Boulay, *Beyond the Darkness: A Biography of Bede Griffiths* (New York: Doubleday, 1998), 155.

9. Du Boulay, *Beyond the Darkness*, 159.

10. Du Boulay, 159.

11. Innocenzo Gargano, "Eroticism, Drugs, AIDS, '68 at Camaldoli," from introduction to Giovanni Dalpiaz, "'Volete andarvene anche voi?' La fede dei giovani e la vita religiosa," EDB, Bologna, 2018.

Chapter 17

1. Hermitage Newsletter, 1970, New Camaldoli Hermitage archives.

2. Andrew Colnaghi, interview with the author, December 2, 2019, Incarnation Monastery.

3. Kevin Joyce, interview with the author, July 30, 2019, New Camaldoli Hermitage.

4. Robert Hale, OSB Cam, "New Camaldoli Hermitage: Notes Toward a History" (unpublished manuscript, 2018).

5. Joyce interview, July 30, 2019.

6. William Johnston, *The Still Point: Reflections on Zen and Christian Mysticism* (New York: Fordham University Press, 1970), x.

7. Joyce, interview, July 30, 2019.

8. Raphael Brown, "Athos on the Pacific: The Silent Message of Big Sur's Fathers of the Desert," quoted in *The Way,* vol. XXX, no. 5 (June 1974): 2.

9. Peter-Damian Belisle, ed. and trans, *Camaldolese Spirituality: Essential Sources* (Bloomingdale, OH: ErCam Editions, 2007), 217.

10. "Mission and Gifts of the Holy Spirit—Vatican II," Crossroads Initiative, May 8, 2016, https://www.crossroadsinitiative.com/media/articles/mission-and-gifts-of-the-holy-spirit/, excerpts from *Lumen Gentium* 4, 12.

11. Hale, "New Camaldoli Hermitage."

12. John W. O'Malley, *What Happened at Vatican II* (Cambridge: Belknap Press of Harvard University, 2008), 42.

13. Thomas Matus, interview with the author, October 27, 2019, New Camaldoli Hermitage.

Chapter 18

1. Philip Klee to Pope Paul VI, March 21, 1977, New Camaldoli Hermitage archives.

2. Klee to Paul VI, March 21, 1977.

3. Klee to Paul VI, March 21, 1977.

4. Michael L. Fitzgerald, M.Afr., "Pope John Paul II and Interreligious Dialogue," EWTN, https://www.ewtn.com/catholicism/library/pope-john-paul-ii-and-interreligious-dialogue-1658.

5. *Redemptor Hominis* 6, Vatican website, http://www.vatican.va/content/john-paul-ii/en/encyclicals/documents/hf_jp-ii_enc_04031979_redemptor-hominis.html.

6. Kevin Joyce, interview with the author, July 30, 2019, New Camaldoli Hermitage.

7. Joyce interview, July 30, 2019.

8. Joyce interview, July 30, 2019.

9. Robert Hale, OSB Cam, "New Camaldoli Hermitage: Notes Toward a History" (unpublished manuscript, 2018).

10. Hale, "New Camaldoli Hermitage."

11. Hale.

12. Andrew Colnaghi, interview with the author, December 2, 2019, Incarnation Monastery.

13. Colnaghi, interview, December 2, 2019.

14. Joyce, interview, July 30, 2019.

15. Joyce, interview, July 30, 2019.

Chapter 19

1. Isaiah Teichert, interview with the author, July 29, 2019, New Camaldoli Hermitage.

2. Teichert, interview, July 29, 2019.

3. Janet Walker, interview with the author, November 15, 2019, New Camaldoli Hermitage.

4. Walker, interview with the author, November 15, 2019.

5. Teichert, interview, July 29, 2019.

6. Philip Kosloski, "Why St. Philip Neri Is Known as the 'Humorous Saint,'" May 26, 2018, https://aleteia.org/2018/05/26/why-st-philip-neri-is-known-as-the-humorous-saint/.

7. Teichert, interview, July 29, 2019.

8. Teichert, interview, July 29, 2019.

9. Therese Gagnon, interview with the author, October 29, 2019, New Camaldoli Hermitage.

10. Robert Hale, OSB Cam, "New Camaldoli Hermitage: Notes Toward a History" (unpublished manuscript, 2018).

11. Henri Nouwen, *Adam: God's Beloved* (Maryknoll, NY: Orbis, 1997), 69.

Chapter 20

1. Thomas Matus, OSB Cam, *The Mystery of Romuald and the Five Brothers: Stories from the Benedictines and Camaldolese* (Trabuco Canyon, CA: Source Books, 1994), 2.

2. Matus, *Mystery of Romuald*, 170.

3. Therese Gagnon, interview with the author, October 29, 2019, New Camaldoli Hermitage.

4. Gagnon, interview, October 29, 2019.

5. Gagnon, interview, October 29, 2019.

6. Hans Boersma, *Heavenly Participation: The Weaving of a Sacramental Tapestry* (Grand Rapids, MI: Eerdmans, 2011), 104.

7. Robert Hale, OSB Cam, "New Camaldoli Hermitage: Notes Toward a History" (unpublished manuscript, 2018).

8. Isaiah Teichert, interview with the author, July 29, 2019, New Camaldoli Hermitage.

9. Teichert, interview, July 29, 2019.

10. Gagnon, interview, October 29, 2019.

11. Gagnon, interview, October 29, 2019.

12. Teichert, interview, July 29, 2019.

13. Teichert, interview, July 29, 2019.

Chapter 21

1. Wendy Teichert, "The Priestly Ordination of Father Isaiah Teichert, April 28, 1990" (unpublished manuscript, 1990).

2. Robert Hale, OSB Cam, "New Camaldoli Hermitage: Notes Toward a History" (unpublished manuscript, 2018).

3. Therese Gagnon, interview with the author, October 29, 2019, New Camaldoli Hermitage.

4. Andrew Colnaghi, interview with the author, December 2, 2019.

5. Colnaghi, interview, December 2, 2019.

6. Isaiah Teichert, interview with the author, July 29, 2019.

7. Teichert, interview, July 29, 2019.

8. Raniero Hoffman, interview with the author, May 11, 2019, New Camaldoli Hermitage.

9. Hoffman, interview, May 11, 2019.

10. Hoffman, interview, May 11, 2019.

11. Arthur Poulin, interview with the author, December 2, 2019.

12. Poulin, interview, December 2, 2019.

13. Poulin, interview, December 2, 2019.

Chapter 22

1. Cyprian Consiglio, interview with the author, July 7, 2019, St. Francis Retreat Center.

2. Consiglio, interview, July 7, 2019.

3. Consiglio, interview, July 7, 2019.

4. Consiglio, interview, July 7, 2019.

5. Thomas Matus, interview with the author, July 30, 2019, New Camaldoli Hermitage.

6. Isaiah Teichert, interview with the author, July 29, 2019, New Camaldoli Hermitage.

7. Consiglio, interview, July 7, 2019.

8. Michael Fish, interview with the author, phone call, January 6, 2020.

9. Fish, interview with the author, January 6, 2020.

Afterword

1. Thomas Merton, *The Silent Life* (New York: Farrar, Strauss and Giroux, 1957), epilogue, Kindle.

Bibliography

Books

Alighieri, Dante. *The Divine Comedy: Inferno, Purgatorio, Paradiso.* Translated by Henry Wadsworth Longfellow. Charlotte, NC: IAP Publishing, 2010.

Atkinson, Rick. *The Day of Battle: The War in Sicily and Italy, 1943-1944. Vol. 2 of the Liberation Trilogy.* New York: Henry Holt, 2007.

Barnhart, Bruno, OSB Cam. *The Future of Wisdom: Toward a Rebirth of Sapiential Christianity.* Rhinehart, NY: Monkfish, 2018.

Belisle, Peter-Damian, ed., trans. *Camaldolese Spirituality: Essential Sources.* Bloomingdale, Ohio: ErCam Editions, 2007.

Belisle, Peter-Damian, ed. *The Privilege of Love: Camaldolese Benedictine Spirituality.* Collegeville, MN: Liturgical Press, 2002.

Boersma, Hans. *Heavenly Participation: The Weaving of a Sacramental Tapestry.* Grand Rapids, MI: Eerdmans, 2011.

Cappello, Anthony. "A Brief Survey of the Italian Catholic in Australia until the Second World War." In *The Pastoral Care of Italians in Australia: Memory and Prophecy,* edited by Anthony Paganoni. Victoria, Australia: Connor Court Publishing, 2007.

Casey, Michael, OSCO. *Strangers to the City: Reflections on the Beliefs and Values of the Rule of St. Benedict.* Brewster, MA: Paraclete Press, 2005.

Catechism of the Catholic Church. 2nd ed. United States Catholic Conference—Libreria Editrice Vaticana, 1997.

Consiglio, Cyprian. *Prayer in the Cave of the Heart: The Universal Call to Contemplation.* Collegeville, MN: Liturgical Press, 2010.

Consiglio, Cyprian. *Spirit, Soul, Body: Toward an Integral Christian Spirituality.* Collegeville, MN: Liturgical Press, 2015.

Cowan, James. *Desert Father: A Journey in the Wilderness with Saint Anthony.* Boston: New Seeds Books, Shambhala Publications, 2006.

Cummings, Charles, OCSO. *Monastic Practices*. Rev. ed. Monastic Wisdom Series: Number Forty-Seven. Collegeville, MN: Cistercian Publications, Liturgical Press, 2015.

Dagnino, Jorge. *Faith and Fascism: Catholic Intellectuals in Italy, 1925-43*. Histories of the Sacred and Secular Series, edited by David Nash, Oxford Brookes University Department of History. London: Palgrave MacMillan, 2017.

Delatte, Paul, OSB. *Commentary on the Holy Rule of St. Benedict*. Translated by Dom Justin McCann. Latrobe, PA: The Archabbey Press, 1959.

Dethick, Janet Kinrade. *The Arezzo Massacres: A Tuscan Tragedy, April-September 1944*. Self-published and translated, 2008.

de Vogue, Adalbert. *The Rule of Saint Benedict: A Doctrinal and Spiritual Commentary*. Cistercian Studies Series, Number Fifty-Four, translated by John Baptiste Hasbrouck. Kalamazoo, MI: Cistercian Publications, 1983.

Du Boulay, Shirley. *Beyond the Darkness: A Biography of Bede Griffiths*. New York: Doubleday, 1998.

Duncan, Bruce. *Crusade or Conspiracy? Catholics and the Anti-Communist Struggle in Australia*. Sydney, Australia: University of New South Wales Press, 2000.

Fahey, John. *Traitors and Spies: Espionage and Corruption in High Places in Australia, 1901-50*. Crow's Nest, Australia: Allen and Unwin, 2020.

Fattorini, Emma. *Hitler, Mussolini, and the Vatican: Pope Pius XI and the Speech That Was Never Made*. Translated by Carl Ipsen. Cambridge: Polity Press, 2011.

Fichera, Sebastian. *Italy on the Pacific: San Francisco's Italian Americans*. New York: Palgrave MacMillan, 2011.

Flynn, Gabriel, and Paul D. Murray, eds. *Ressourcement: A Movement for Renewal in Twentieth-Century Catholic Theology*. Oxford: Oxford University Press, 2012.

Forniciari, Roberto. "The Institutional Evolution of Italian Monasticism from Unity to the Present Day." In *Christians of Italy: Church, History, State, 1861-2011*, Vol. II. Rome: Institute of the Italian Encyclopedia, 2011.

Forster, E. M. *A Passage to India*. New York: Harcourt, Brace, Jovanovich, 1984.

Fry, Timothy, ed. *RB 1980: The Rule of St. Benedict in English*. Collegeville, MN: Liturgical Press, 1982.

Goodman, Judith, ed. *Big Sur Women*. Big Sur: Big Sur Women Press, 1985.

Grayston, Donald. *Thomas Merton and the Noonday Demon: The Camaldoli Correspondence*. Eugene: Cascade, 2015.

Griffin, James. "Mannix, Daniel (1864–1963)." *Australian Dictionary of Biography*, vol. 10 (MUP), 1986.

Griffiths, Bede. *The Golden String: An Autobiography.* Springfield, IL: Templegate Publishers, 1980.

Gruen, Anselm. *Heaven Begins within You: Wisdom from the Desert Fathers.* New York: Crossroad, 1995.

Hale, Robert, OSB Cam. *Love on the Mountain: The Chronicle Journal of a Camaldolese Monk.* Trabuco Canyon, CA: Source Books, 1999.

Harlan, Stanley. *My Mom and Dad on the Coast South of Big Sur: A Historical Recollection of the Big Sur Area Experienced through the Toils and Labor of the Harlan Family.* Self-published, 2019.

Hayne, Donald. *Batter My Heart.* New York: Knopf, 1963.

Hemingway, Ernest. *A Farewell to Arms.* New York: Scribner, 1995.

Hermitage Chronicles, 1960-1968. Author unknown (probably Clemente Roggi).

Huxley, Aldous. *The Perennial Philosophy.* New York: Harper and Row, 1944.

Ignesti, Bernardo. "La Congregazioni Camaldolesi." *Monachesimo E Vita Religiosa: Rinnovamonto e Storia Tra Secoli XIXX-XX.* Verona: El Signo Gabrielli Editori, 2002.

Isaacs, Harold R. *Scratches on Our Minds.* New York: John Day Company, MIT, 1958.

Jeffers, Robinson. "The Coast Road." In *The Collected Poetry of Robinson Jeffers*, vol. 2, edited by Tim Hunt. Stanford, CA: Stanford University Press, 1989.

Jeffers, Robinson. "Evening Ebb." In *The Selected Poetry of Robinson Jeffers,* edited by Tim Hunt. Stanford, CA: Stanford University Press, 2001.

Johnston, William. *The Still Point: Reflections on Zen and Christian Mysticism.* New York: Fordham University Press, 1970.

Kertzer, David. *The Pope and Mussolini: The Secret History of Pius XI and the Rise of Fascism in Europe.* New York: Random House, 2014.

Lane, Belden C. *The Solace of Fierce Landscapes: Exploring Desert and Mountain Spirituality.* New York: Oxford University Press, 1998.

Maguire, Nancy Klein. *An Infinity of Little Hours: Five Young Men and Their Trial of Faith in the Western World's Most Austere Monastic Order.* New York: PublicAffairs, 2006.

Martin, Malachi. *The Jesuits: The Society of Jesus and the Betrayal of the Roman Catholic Church.* New York: Simon and Schuster, 1987.

Matus, Thomas, OSB Cam, trans. *The Constitutions and Declarations to the Rule of Saint Benedict.* 1985. https://fdocuments.net/document/the

-constitutions-and-declarations-to-the-rule-of-saint-from-disciplinary
.html.

Matus, Thomas, OSB Cam. *The Mystery of Romuald and the Five Brothers: Stories from the Benedictines and Camaldolese.* Trabuco Canyon, CA: Source Books, 1994.

Matus, Thomas, OSB Cam. *Nazarena, an American Anchoress.* New York: Paulist Press, 1998.

McNary-Zak, Bernadette. *Seeking in Solitude: A Study of Select Forms of Eremitic Life and Practice.* Princeton Theological Monograph Series 210. Eugene, OR: Pickwick Publications, 2014.

Merton, Thomas. *The Seven Story Mountain.* New York: Harcourt, Brace, 1948.

Merton, Thomas. *The Silent Life.* New York: Farrar, Strauss and Giroux, 1957.

Merton, Thomas. *Thoughts in Solitude.* New York: Farrar, Strauss and Giroux, 1999.

Meyers, Kayleigh. *Monks Inside Out: New Camaldoli Hermitage.* Self-published, 2015.

Miller, Henry. *Big Sur and the Oranges of Hieronymous Bosch.* New York: New Directions Publishing, 1957.

Norman, Jeff, and the Big Sur Historical Society. *Big Sur: Images of America.* Charleston, SC: Arcadia, 2004.

O'Brien, Ilma Martinuzzi. "Italian Australians and the Australian Catholic Church through War, Internment and Mass Migration." In *The Pastoral Care of Italians in Australia,* edited by Anthony Paganoni. Victoria, Australia: Connor Court Publishing, 2007.

O'Malley, John W. *What Happened at Vatican II.* Cambridge: Belknap Press of Harvard University Press, 2008.

Otto, Rudolph. *The Idea of the Holy.* London: Oxford University Press, 1971.

Pollard, John. *The Papacy in the Age of Totalitarianism, 1914-1958.* Oxford History of the Christian Church Series, edited by Henry and Owen Chadwick. Oxford: Oxford University Press, 2014.

Posner, Gerald. *God's Bankers: A History of Money and Power at the Vatican.* New York: Simon and Schuster, 2015.

Salvemini, Gaetano, and George LaPiana. *What to Do with Italy.* New York: Duell, Sloan and Pearce, 1943.

Smith, Cyprian, OSB. *The Path of Life: Benedictine Spirituality for Monks and Lay People.* York, UK: Ampleforth Abbey Press, 1995.

Vigilucci, Lino, OSB Cam. *Camaldoli: A Journey into Its History and Spirituality,* translated by Peter-Damian Belisle. Trabuco Canyon, CA: Source Books, 1995.

Watts, Alan. *The Wisdom of Insecurity: A Message for an Age of Anxiety.* New York: Random House (Vintage), 1951.

Interviews

Colnaghi, Andrew, OSB Cam. Interview with the author, Incarnation Monastery, December 2, 2019.

Consiglio, Cyprian, OSB Cam. Interview with the author. St. Francis Retreat Center, July 6, 2019.

Fish, Michael, OSB Cam. Phone interview with the author, January 6, 2020.

Gagnon, Therese. Interview with the author, New Camaldoli Hermitage, October 29, 2019.

Hoffman, Raniero, OSB Cam. Interview with the author, New Camaldoli Hermitage, May 11, 2019.

Joyce, Fr. Kevin P. Interview with the author, New Camaldoli Hermitage, July 30, 2019.

Matus, Thomas, OSB Cam. Interview with the author, New Camaldoli Hermitage, July 29, 2019.

Matus, Thomas, OSB Cam. Interview with the author, New Camaldoli Hermitage, October 27, 2019.

Matus, Thomas, OSB Cam. Interview with the author, New Camaldoli Hermitage, October 28, 2019.

Matus, Thomas, OSB Cam. Interview with the author, New Camaldoli Hermitage, January 6, 2019.

Poulin, Arthur, OSB Cam. Interview with the author, Incarnation Monastery, Berkeley, December 2, 2019.

Teichert, Isaiah, OSB Cam. Interview with the author, New Camaldoli Hermitage, July 29, 2019.

Walker, Janet, OSB Cam Obl. Interview with the author, New Camaldoli Hermitage, October 27, 2019.

Magazine Articles

"Eremitical U.S." *Time, the Weekly Magazine.* March 3, 1958.

"A Nun's Story." *Time, the Weekly Magazine.* April 13, 1962.

Journal Articles

Bargellini, Emanuele. "The Renaissance of the Camaldolese and the Word of God: Experience, Witness, and Perspective." AIM (AllianceInter-Monasteres), 2012.

Cappello, Anthony. "Mannix, Modotti, and the Italian POWs." *Quadrant* XLVIII, no. 7-8 (July-August, 2004).

Consiglio, Cyprian. "Community, Solitude and Mission: The Dynamism of the Camaldolese Charism." *American Benedictine Review* 66, no. 2 (2015): 199–212.

Cresciani, Gianfranco. "The Second Awakening: The Italia Libera Movement." *Labour History,* no. 30. Liverpool University Press, May 1976, 22–37. https://www.jstor.org/stable/27508214.

Giannone, Richard. "Flannery O'Connor Tells Her Desert Story." *Religion and Literature* 27.2, (Summer 1995).

Kilcourse, George A. Jr. "Thomas Merton's Contemplative Struggle: Bridging the Abyss to Find Freedom." *CrossCurrents* 49, no. 1, Conversation, Conflict, and Community (Spring 1999): 87–96.

"Rigorous Camaldolese Order Thrives in First U.S. Home." *The Catholic Advocate* 12, no. 28 (July 4, 1963).

Seven Hermits of St. Romuald. "The Camaldolese Come to America." *The American Benedictine Review* XII (March 1961): 1.

Taylor, Eugene. "Desperately Seeking Spirituality." *Psychology Today* (November 1, 1994).

Walton, John. "The Poet as Ethnographer: Robinson Jeffers in Big Sur." *California History* 87, no. 2, Robinson Jeffers (2010). University of California Press in association with the California Historical Society, 22–41, 66–67.

Wink, Paul, Michele Dillon, and Adrienne Prettyman. "Religiousness, Spiritual Seeking, and Authoritarianism: Findings from a Longitudinal Study." *Journal for the Scientific Study of Religion* 46, no. 3 (September 2007): 321–35.

Pamphlets

Birth of a Hermitage. Big Sur, CA: Immaculate Heart Hermitage, 1962.

Growth of a Hermitage. Big Sur, CA: Immaculate Heart Hermitage, 1966.

Unpublished Papers

Cappello, Anthony. "Italian Australians, the Church, War and Fascism in Melbourne 1919–1945." Master's thesis, Department of Social Inquiry and Community Studies St. Albans Campus, 1999.

Hale, Robert, OSB Cam. "New Camaldoli Before the Monks: Some Data and References." Unpublished manuscript, 1988, typescript.

Hale, Robert, OSB Cam. "New Camaldoli Hermitage: Notes Toward a History." Unpublished manuscript, 2018, typescript.

Hale, Robert, OSB Cam. "Some Notes Regarding the Camaldolese Residence of Incarnation Priory, 1978–1988." Unpublished manuscript, 1988, typescript.

Harlan, Stan, and Irene Harlan. *The History of Ownership of the Camal-doli Hermitage.* Monterey, November 15, 2011.

Online Articles

Catalunya Religio. Excerpt from *The Devil in the Convent: An Original Mem-oir of the Catholic '68.* February 23, 2018. http://magister.blogautore .espresso.repubblica.it/2018/03/23/the-devil-in-the-convent-an-original -memoir-of-the-catholic-68/.

Jenkins, Philip. Review of *After Heaven: Spirituality in America Since the 1950s* by Robert Withnow. H-AmRel, H-Net Reviews. November 1998.

Jordison, Sam. "The Doors of Perception: What Did Huxley See in Mes-caline?" *The Guardian.* January 26, 2012. www.theguardian.com/ books/2012/jan/26/doors-perception-huxley-mescaline-reading-group.

Markoff, John. "Fear and Loathing in Big Sur." Alta. January 22, 2018. https://altaonline.com/fear-loathing-big-sur.

Matus, Thomas. "An American Enigma: Sister Nazarena." September 18, 2018, https://owlcation.com/humanities/An-American-Enigma-Sister -Nazarena-of-Jesus.

Reading Guide. *On the Road* by Jack Kerouac. Penguin Random House. https://www.penguinrandomhouse.com/books/540750/on-the-road -by-jack-kerouac/9780142437254/readers-guide/.

Index

Abbey of Gethsemani, 10–12, 24,
  53, 118
Acuti, Alessandra, 49
Adriatic Sea, 14
aggiornamento, 72, 79, 107
Agnoletti, Andrea, 61, 66, 67,
  70–73, 87
alternative medicine, 9
America, 23–27, 57, 65–66, 67–
  70, 74, 118, 140–41
Amritsar Massacre, 37
Anderson Creek, 6
Angelus, monk, 145
Anglican Centre, 130
antifascists, 29–30, 39, 48
Antoniutti, Ildebrando, 46, 48,
  74, 99
Apennines, 14–15, 87, 111, 154–55
apophasis, 131–32
Aquinas, Thomas, 90, 157
Arabian Sea, 36
Arezzo, 14
Arizona, 22
Armstrong, Katee, 190
asceticism, 82, 120, 124
Asia, 117–18

atheism, 32–33, 39, 78
Athens, 132
Atlantic Ocean, 26, 71, 109
Augustus, Emperor, 30
Australia, 2, 34, 38–42, 46–48, 65,
  97, 122, 190

Baez, Joan, 126
Bank of Rome, 29
Barabe, Anthony, 133, 146, 178
Bargellini, Emanuele, 130, 151–52
Barnhart, Bruno, 61, 63, 88, 90–
  91, 94, 103, 106, 113, 119–20,
  127, 129–32, 134, 137–39,
  141–43, 145, 147–48, 151–53,
  157–58, 161, 164–65, 168,
  174–77, 185
Battle of Caporetto, 20, 35–36
beard, 64, 77, 114–15
Beatles, 9
Bede, Michael, 86
Benedict, St., 25, 105
Benedictine Confederation, 114
Benedictines, 17, 38, 58, 77, 83,
  90, 104–7, 112, 116, 123–24,
  152, 167, 169, 182

Berkeley, 141, 151
Bernard, St., 85
Big Creek, 51
Big Sur (coast), 2–3, 7–10, 14, 26,
    43–45, 50, 58, 77, 86, 105–6,
    109, 148
Big Sur Folk Festival, 126
Bishop's Ranch (California), 158
Black Shirts, 20, 28, 39
Blessed Rudolph, 23, 54–56, 62,
    65, 72, 105, 108, 133
Bolshevik Revolution, 29, 32
bookstore, ix, 98, 130, 146, 148,
    178
Brahmachari, Mahanambrata, 10
Brazil, 23, 70, 91
Britain, 7, 40–41, 48
British Empire, 36, 38, 40–41
Brown, Grayson, 174
Bruno of Querfurt, 155
Buddhism, x, 118, 122, 131, 177
Buffadini, Pierdamiano, 26, 48–49
Buonsollazzo, 18
Burke, Michael, 61

Calati, Benedetto, 24, 26, 55, 79,
    81, 90–91, 99–100, 107, 127,
    137, 139–41, 143, 151, 172,
    175
California, 2, 14, 22, 26, 43, 53,
    85, 123, 136, 139, 168–69, 171
Calwell, Arthur, 47
Camaldolese Cenobitic
    Congregation, 17, 132
Camaldolese order, x, 2, 11, 13,
    16–18, 23, 26, 37, 43, 55,
    58, 70–72, 74, 76, 89–90, 94,
    96–97, 99–100, 104–8, 111,
    154, 177
Camaldolese Psalter, 122, 154

Camaldoli, Italy, 14, 17, 20, 28,
    31, 49, 56, 64–65, 70, 73, 76,
    80–81, 82, 91, 113–14, 116,
    121–22, 125, 127, 139, 151,
    154, 186
Cambria, 50
Camino de Compostela, 181
Campbell, Joseph, 9
Capuchins, 46
Carmel, 44, 52, 126
Carthusians, 11, 120
Catani, Dom Aliprando, 21–22,
    32, 53, 68, 70–73, 76, 85, 87,
    90, 97, 99–100, 102–4, 106–7,
    113, 115, 121, 136
Cathedral of Honolulu, 85
Catholic Action, 28
Catholic charismatic renewal,
    134–35, 137, 168, 174
Catholicism, 10, 19, 28–32, 40,
    84–85, 109, 124, 137–38, 144
Catholic Worker, 174
Cavery River, 111
Ceccherini, Aurelio, 49
cells, 1, 14, 16, 25, 53, 82–83,
    86–89, 110–11, 131, 133, 136,
    151, 159, 181–82
cenobites, 16–18, 23, 26–27,
    55–56, 65, 67–69, 71–72, 102,
    107, 117, 137
Center for Spiritual Studies, 156
Central America, 177
Chavez, Cesar, 168
Chenu, Marie-Dominique, 79
Chimenti, Timoteo, 31–32, 97
China, 177
Christ in the Desert Monastery
    (New Mexico), 168
Circle M Ranch, 51–52, 58, 87,
    103

Cistercians, 11
Classe, 17
Clinch, Harry, 89, 137
Coffey, Stephen, 188
Cold War, 12
Colnaghi, Andrew, 121, 140–41,
    151, 159, 172, 177, 185, 190
Colorado, 22
communism, 5, 28–29, 32–33, 39,
    80–81
community, 16–18, 104–5, 112,
    124, 151, 166, 171, 180
Confucianism, 118, 177
Congar, Yves, 18, 79
Congregation of Religious, 54,
    68–72, 99, 137
Congress of Abbots, 158
Consiglio, Cyprian, 167, 173–75,
    178–79, 185, 190
Constantine, 95
constitutions, 24–26, 55–56, 65,
    68–69, 71–72, 108–9, 113,
    120, 133, 135, 152, 154
construction, 87–89, 102, 106,
    110, 115
Conte, Vickie, 190
contemplation, 4, 12, 17, 23–27,
    37, 53, 58, 82, 107, 111–12,
    117–18, 120, 128, 138, 142,
    155, 158–59, 167, 170–71,
    182, 184
contemptus mundi, 5
conversatio morum, 16
Corcoran, Donald, 188
corona, 114–15
Cottrell, Jim, 26–27, 52, 57, 61,
    73, 88
Coulson, John, 61
Crosby, Bing, 52
Crosby, Stills, and Nash, 126

Cuban Missile Crisis, 96
Curtain, Jim, 190

Damian, Peter, 55, 154–55
Dani, Alvin, 44
Dani, Elizabeth, 43–44, 148
Dani, Gabriel, 43–44, 125
Dani, Mary, 44
Dani, Mary Ellen, 45
Dani family, 51, 87, 126
Dante, 55
Dartmouth, 119
Day, Dorothy, 171
de Boynes, Norbert, 47
Dell'Ossa, Benedict, 167, 178, 187
de Lubac, Henri, 18, 79, 127, 135,
    157
DeMille, Cecil B., 52, 63, 86
democracy, 78–81, 97, 120
Desert Fathers and Mothers, 3, 18,
    96, 112, 132
desire, 4
devotionals, 104–5
Diemer, Joseph, 82, 103, 107, 117,
    133–34, 138, 146, 175, 178
discipline, 62, 105
Divine Office, 15, 63, 77, 102,
    114, 123, 140, 150
Dom Ambrogio, 26
Domestic Council, 133–34
Dominican School (Oakland), 146
Duce, Il. *See* Mussolini, Benito
Duquesne University, 134
Duscher, Romuald, 167, 173, 178

Eastern Orthodoxy, 121–22
ecumenism, 80, 113, 124, 130,
    139–41, 177
Egypt, 3, 132
Eliot, T. S., 131

Elizabeth of the Trinity, St., 187
Emilia-Romagna, 28
Enclosure, x
Engels, Friedrich, 32
England, 36–37
Episcopalians, 130, 144
eremitical life, 3, 16, 18, 23, 26,
    55, 64, 67, 69–72, 76, 82, 91,
    105, 114–15, 138–39, 148
Esalen Institute, 8–10, 15, 125–26
Ethiopia, 33
excommunication, 73, 80–82

family, 102, 105, 164
farming, 115–16
fascism, 5, 10, 19–20, 28–33,
    38–39, 48, 80–81, 97
Feltes, Gregory, 189
fire, 66, 156, 163, 165, 175
Fish, Michael, 167, 179–82, 184,
    189–90
Florence, 14, 56, 113
Fogelberg, Dan, 174
Fonte Avellana, 18, 24, 135, 186
Fontebono, 14, 17, 55–56, 186
Fordham University, 120–21, 166
formation, 129
Forster, E. M., 37
Fort Ord, 87, 89, 97
Fox, James, Abbot, 53
France, 40, 80, 113
Franciscans, 10, 38, 89, 106, 167–
    68, 170–71, 173–74, 177
Franco, Francisco, 38, 48, 80
Free Masons, 33
French Revolution, 78, 92, 95
Fresno, diocese of, 67, 69, 71–72
Friends of Camaldoli, 52, 57, 61,
    64, 66, 72–73, 88
Friuli, 35

fuga mundi, 3–5, 6, 9–11, 14, 16,
    20, 24, 27, 37, 42, 49, 50, 58,
    72, 82, 85–86, 105, 108, 117,
    126, 131, 148, 164–65, 182

Gagnon, Eric, 148–49, 165
Gagnon, Therese, 143, 148–50,
    155–57, 160, 163, 165, 188–90
Gandhi, Mahatma, 36–37
Gannon, Francis, 61–62, 88, 90–
    91, 94, 106
Gargano, Innocenzo, 125, 132,
    139–40
Gasparri, Pietro, Cardinal, 32
Germany, 91
Gestalt therapy, 9
Giabbani, Dom Anselmo, 13, 15,
    17–18, 20, 24–26, 48, 52–53,
    55–57, 63–66, 67–74, 76, 79,
    81, 86, 90–91, 94, 96–97,
    99–100, 103–4, 106–7, 114–15,
    118, 121, 127, 135, 136, 154–
    55, 186
Gibbon, Edward, 4–5, 54
Gillespie, Avon, 174
Gilson, Etienne, 10
Giroux, Robert, 12
Grace, Peter, 27
Grace Cathedral, 140
Great Depression, 51
Greece, 132
Gregorian University, 36
Gregory XVI, Pope, 56
Griffiths, Bede, 38, 111–13, 117,
    122–25, 131, 142, 149, 158,
    174, 177, 182, 185
Gruppo Cattolico Femminile, 39
guests, 89, 99, 103, 105, 109, 126,
    134, 145–46, 149, 164, 178
Gunther, Professor, 90

Hale, Robert, 58–63, 75–77, 81–83, 86–88, 90–91, 94, 103, 105–7, 109, 113, 117–18, 120–21, 127, 129–30, 139–41, 144, 150–53, 157–59, 163–69, 171–72, 173–75, 184–85, 192

Harcourt Brace, 12

Harlan, Esther, 52

Harlan, George, 51–52, 58

Harlan, Lulu, 148

Harrington, Michael, 167, 178, 187

Harvard Psilocybin Project, 9

Hayne, Donald, 52, 86

Healey, Bede, 167, 177, 188

Hearst, William Randolph, 50

Hemingway, Ernest, 35–36

Herbeck, Martin, 189

hermitage, ix, xi, 2, 8, 27, 52–53, 57, 60–61, 64, 67–69, 75–76, 85–87, 89, 97–99, 102–6, 109, 110–11, 113, 116, 120, 122–23, 126–27, 129–30, 132, 136–39, 141, 144–47, 149, 151–53, 156, 159, 163–69, 173, 175, 177, 183–85, 187–89

hermit life, 3, 16–18, 25–26, 53–55, 60, 67–68, 73–74, 75, 82, 117, 148

hermit rebellion, 56, 64, 96, 135, 136

hermits, 23, 26–27, 56, 64–65, 67, 87, 99–100, 102, 107–8, 137–38

Hermits of Monte Corona, 17

Hermits of Tuscany, 17

hesychasm, 132

Highway 1, 2–3, 6, 44, 51, 97, 163, 183

Hinduism, 10, 36–37, 112–13, 118, 122–25, 131, 177

Hiroshima, 95

Hitler, Adolf, 31, 38, 40, 48–49, 78

Hoffman, Raniero, 168–70, 177, 186, 190

Hollins, Marian, 51

Hollywood, 2, 52, 84

Holy Cross Abbey (Colorado), 82, 103, 134

Holy Cross (Berkeley), 139–40

Holy Cross (West Park), 130

Holy Family College, 140

Holy Mary of the Angels (Florence), 55

Holy Office for the Doctrine of the Faith, 71, 80, 94

Holy See, 18, 28, 46–47, 65, 73

Holy Spirit, 69, 78, 96, 133–34, 139, 158, 167, 180, 187

Hope, Bob, 52

horarium, 76–77

hot springs, 6, 8

Huston, Mike, 192

Huxley, Aldous, 9, 10

Ignesti, Bernardo, 24, 26, 32, 55, 79, 107, 127

immigrants, 34, 38–40, 46–48, 122, 190

Incarnation Monastery, 158–59, 172, 177, 188

Incarnation Priory, 140–41, 150–52

India, 2, 20, 33, 36–38, 52, 91, 111–12, 122–25, 149, 174

Indigenous people, 8, 43

International Thomas Merton Society Conference, 158

Islam, 138

Italian Catholic Federation, 86, 126

Italy, 2, 14, 15–16, 19–20, 22,
    29–33, 36, 38–41, 46–49,
    53–54, 65, 67–69, 72–73, 80,
    90, 99–100, 103, 111, 113–14,
    120–21, 125, 130, 132, 136,
    140–41, 185–86
Iyer, Pico, ix–xi, 192

Jainism, 118
Janvrin, Bede, 89–90, 103–4, 146,
    151, 161
Jeffers, Robinson, 44–45, 49, 50,
    149
Jeffers, Una, 44–45, 148
Jesuit Center for Spiritual Growth
    (Pennsylvania), 168
Jesuits, 2, 32–33, 36, 38, 46–47, 56
Jesuit School of Theology, 140
John, Harry, 27, 53
John XXIII, Pope, 67, 74, 92, 94,
    108
John of Damascus, 132
John of the Cross, St., 73, 82, 131,
    141–42
John Paul II, Pope, 138, 177
Johnston, William, 131, 182
Joyce, Kevin, 130–32, 138–39,
    141–43, 144, 190
Judaism, 138

Karnataka, 111
Kerala, 37–38, 111
Kierkegaard, Soren, 60
Kirby, Gabriel, 94, 103, 110, 134,
    175–76, 178, 186–87
Klee, Philip, 61, 88, 98, 103, 105–
    6, 126, 129, 136–38, 143, 145,
    155–56, 158–62, 175
Klinglesmith, Joseph, 1, 52, 67–68
Kurimsala, 123

Kurseong, 36
Kurukshetra, 122

laity, 27, 28, 89, 95, 108, 133,
    137, 181–82, 185
landslides, 2, 50, 98, 163, 187
Lane, Belden, 3, 7–8
L'Arche Daybreak (Toronto), 153,
    165
Lateran Treaties and Concordats
    (1929), 30–31
Laureati, 80–81
Leary, Timothy, 9
lectio divina, 83, 139
Ledochowski, Vlodzimierz, 32–33,
    38
Lenin, Vladimir, 32
Lewis, C. S., 113
liturgical movement, 78
liturgy, 83, 105, 128, 131, 143,
    148, 168
logging, 116
London, 29
Los Angeles, 87
Louf, André, 132
Lourdes Grotto, 40
Loyola University (Rome), 169
Loyola University Chicago, 170
Luce, Clare Booth, 27
Lucia, 51

Madera, 87
Madonna, Alex, 87
Maharishi Mahesh Yogi, 130
Malabar, 36
Mangalore, 111, 122
Manger, Daniel, 167, 177, 188
Manhattan, x, 22
Mannix, Daniel, Archbishop,
    38–41, 46–47

Manressa, 40–41, 47–48

Marino, 61

Maritain, Jacques, 79

Marx, Karl, 32

Massicotte, Bernard, 103, 115–17, 130, 132, 134, 143, 146, 157, 161, 175–76, 178, 183, 186

Matus, Thomas, 84–86, 93–94, 96, 103, 105–7, 109, 113–14, 117–18, 121–22, 127, 135, 154–55, 161, 164, 174–75, 186, 190, 192

Maximus the Confessor, 132

McGinley, Francis, 66

meditation, 9, 76–77, 113, 123, 130–32, 168, 177

Meister Eckhart, 130–31

Melbourne, 38–40, 46–47

Menchini, Placito, 68

Merton, Thomas, 10–13, 20, 24–27, 32, 52–53, 58, 72, 77, 84–86, 96, 113, 117–18, 122, 158, 174, 182, 192

mescaline, 9

Meyers, David, 167, 178, 187

Meyers, Kayleigh, 164, 170, 179, 181, 183, 191–92

Milan, 49

Military Council of Catholic Women, 87

Miller, Henry, 6–8, 10, 44–45, 50, 125

mind-body interventions, 9

Missionary Brothers of Christ, 167

missionary-martyrdom, 18, 124, 180

Mission San Jose, 103

Mitchell, Joni, 126

modernism, -ity, 18, 31, 78, 90, 95

Modotti, Dom Agostino (Fr. Ugo), 2–3, 5, 6, 8–11, 15, 20, 22, 26–27, 32–33, 36–42, 45–47, 49, 52–54, 56–57, 59–66, 67–74, 75–76, 79, 81–82, 85–86, 89, 91, 94, 96–97, 99–100, 104–5, 111–12, 117, 120, 122–23, 126, 128, 135, 136–37, 166, 186, 190

Moggiona, 48–49

Monaco, Lorenzo, 55

monasteries, 3, 16

Monastery of the Angels, 52

Monastery of the Risen Christ (San Luis Obispo), 177, 188

monasticism, 4–5, 16–18, 26, 75, 82–83, 84–85, 96–97, 102, 104–5, 108, 110, 122, 129, 160, 175

Monelli, Paolo, 48

Monson, Joshua, 167, 178, 183–84

Monterey, 86, 98, 126

Montini, Giovanni Battista. *See* Paul VI, Pope

Moore, Edward S., 51, 126

Morales, Manuel, 119

Mount Athos, 132–34, 160

Mount Saviour Monastery (New York), 156

Mullard, Mike, 188

Murphy, Michael, 8, 86, 97

Musolea, 32

Mussolini, Benito, 10, 20, 23, 28–34, 36, 38–41, 48–49, 54, 78, 80–81, 97

Mussolini, Bruno, 31

Mussolini, Edda, 31

Mussolini, Rachelle, 31

Mussolini, Vittorio, 31

mystagogy, 62
mysticism, 9–10, 130–31

Naegele, Zaccheus, 167, 178, 187
Nagasaki, 96
Napoleon, 16
Nazarena, 93–94, 117, 176, 185
Nazis, 48, 95
Nebraska, 22
negative theology, 131–32
Neoscholasticism, 90, 127
Neri, Philip, St., 147
Nesbitt, John, 51–52, 66, 87, 126
New Age movement, 9, 125–26
New Camaldoli, 62, 64, 67–69,
    71–72, 75, 81, 85–86, 94, 97,
    99–100, 102–3, 105–6, 109,
    110, 112–14, 116, 119–21, 123,
    126, 128–31, 133–34, 137, 139,
    141–43, 144–46, 148, 151–52,
    154, 156–57, 159, 164, 166–69,
    171, 173–75, 177–81, 183–84,
    188, 190, 192
New Mexico, 22
Nicholl, Donald, 156
Nicoletto, Ivan, 189
Niebuhr, Reinhold, 60
Nouwen, Henri, 153
novices, 61, 69, 77, 81–82, 87–88,
    94, 100, 102–5, 110, 165–66,
    175, 181
numinous, 7–8, 37, 169

Oakland, 89, 146, 171
obedience, 2, 60, 74, 90, 178
oblates, 151, 159, 180, 182, 184,
    188
Occidental College, 84, 93
Old Camaldoli. *See* Camaldoli,
    Italy

olives, 1, 87, 97, 99, 103–4, 106
ora et labora program, x
Otto, Rudolf, 7, 37, 45
Oxford, x

Pacelli, Eugenio, 32, 38
Pacific Ocean, 8, 45, 98
Palestine, 3, 132
Panico, Giovanni, 46–47
Papal States, 19, 29
Parker, Roy, 140
Partington Ridge, 6, 10, 50
Partito Populare. See Popular
    Party of Italy (PPI)
passion, 4
Paul VI, Pope, 17–18, 80–81,
    94–95, 134–35, 136–37
Paulmichel, Adalbert, 61, 66, 67,
    70–73
Pearl Harbor, 12
Perl, Fritz, 9
Pfeiffer, Mary Ellen. *See* Dani,
    Mary Ellen
Pfeiffer Burns, Julia, 148
Piazzele Loreto, 49
pilgrim, 178, 181
Pius X, Pope, 18, 78
Pius XI, Pope, 18, 20, 28–31,
    77–78
Pius XII, Pope, 47, 65, 77–79, 92,
    95, 127, 135, 136
Point 16, 51
Pomona College, 58–59, 75, 88
Pontifical Council for
    Interreligious Dialogue, 138
Popular Party of Italy (PPI), 28–30
postulants, 1–2, 61–64, 67–68,
    75–77, 86, 89, 94, 99, 102,
    104, 110, 128–29, 145, 165,
    188

Poulin, Arthur, 167, 169–72, 173–74, 185, 190, 192
Price, Richard, 8
priests, 75, 82, 100, 102, 114, 141–42, 163–65, 168, 170–71
Prinknash Abbey, 38, 111
Protestantism, 134, 138
Puerto Rico, 122
Punjab, 122
purity of heart, 4–5

Quebec, 103
Quirinil Palace, 19

Ragged Point, 50
Raheen (Kew), 41
Rahner, Karl, 79, 129
Ravenna, 14, 17, 35, 154
Rebello, Pedro, 52, 86–88, 103–4, 110–11, 117, 122, 126
recluse(s), 11, 27, 56, 73–74, 93–94, 114, 133, 136, 146, 175–76, 178, 185
reclusion, 2, 9, 70, 89, 104, 111, 117, 133–34
Redemptorists, 167, 180
Reformation, 19, 95
religious dialogue, 9
ressourcement, 18, 26, 72, 79, 96, 107, 135
retreat ministry, 98
Rice, Edward, 77
Risorgimento, Il, 19, 29, 43
Rivers, Clarence, 174
Rockwell, Norman, 21
Roggi, Clemente, 82, 85–87, 89, 90, 94, 99–100, 102, 115–16, 126
Roman Empire, 10, 19–20, 30, 33, 54, 95

Roman Question, 19–20, 29
Romantics, 7
Rome, 14, 19–20, 29, 33, 36, 47–48, 57, 69–70, 72–73, 77, 90–92, 106, 109, 110, 121–22, 127, 140, 158
Romoli, Dino, Monsignor, 71, 73, 94, 137
Romuald, 15–18, 23–26, 35, 76, 87, 108–9, 111, 131, 154–55, 168, 173, 178, 186
Roosevelt, Theodore, 21, 85
Ross, Lillian Bos, 148
Rule of St. Benedict, 17, 61–62, 112, 152
Russia, 29, 80, 93

Sacro Eremo of Camaldoli, 2, 8–9, 11, 13, 15, 17–18, 23–27, 32, 48–49, 54–56, 62, 65, 69, 82, 90, 97, 100, 111, 113, 117, 121, 132, 135, 136, 148, 155, 177, 186
Salazar, António de Oliveira, 80
Salesians, 167
Salinan tribe, 43–44, 87, 126
Salinas Valley, 63, 86, 126
Saloniki, 132
San Bernardino Public Library, 84
San Francisco, 43, 88, 140, 177
San Gregorio, 90, 94, 113–14, 121, 125, 132, 185
San Luis Obispo, 86–87, 126
San Miguel Mission, 89
Santa Lucia Mountains, 43
Santa Maria Novella, 113
Sant'Anselmo, 90–91, 94, 113, 121, 130, 158, 185
Sant'Antonio, 94
Sant'Apollinare, 17

Sargent, Lynda, 148
Sartre, Jean-Paul, 5, 60
Second Vatican Council, 79,
    90–92, 94–97, 100, 104–5,
    107–8, 114, 118, 123–24, 127,
    128–29, 131, 133–35, 136–39,
    154
self-flagellation. *See* discipline
Serra, Junipero, 87
Shakespeare, x
Shantivanam, 38, 111–12, 122–
    24, 142, 174
Sheen, Fulton, 22, 53
Shepherd, Mary Ellen, 159–61
Siberia, 93
Sikhism, 118
silence, 11, 22, 25, 74, 82, 107,
    115, 153, 160, 166, 171, 181,
    187
Simoni (POW), 42
Simplon Pass, 113
Sisters of the Poor, 89
Slate, Tom, 44
Slate's Springs, 6, 8, 125
Smythe, Harry, 130
social justice, 28, 140, 167–68
solitude, 6, 11, 16–18, 24, 26,
    58, 74, 82, 100, 104–5, 107,
    117, 124, 148, 153, 160, 166,
    171–72, 180–81, 187
Sontag, Frederick, 60
South Africa, 180
Soviet Union, 96
Spain, 38, 46
Stalin, Joseph, 80, 93
Steindl-Rast, David, 156, 158
St. Aloysius College (Mangalore),
    36
St. Andrew's Abbey (Valyermo),
    75

St. Benedict's Monastery
    (Minnesota), 120
St. George's Church (Carlton), 40
St. John's University (Minnesota),
    106, 109, 120
St. Joseph's Abbey (Louisiana), 158
St. Joseph's College (Callicut), 36
St. Mary's College (Michigan), 26
St. Mary's Spiritual Center, 168
St. Meinrad Abbey, 89
St. Michael of Murano, 18, 56, 70
St. Vincent de Paul Society, 88
Sturzo, Luigi, 28–30
Sufism, x, 118
Supreme Congregation of the
    Holy Office, 79
Suzuki, D. T., 118
Swiss Alps, 113
syncretism, 125
Syria, 3, 132

Tamil Nadu, 38, 111, 124
Tantur Ecumenical Institute for
    Theological Studies (Jerusalem),
    156
Tanzania, 91
Taoism, 118, 177
Teichert, Isaiah, 144–48, 159–61,
    163–64, 167–68, 175, 185, 190
Teilhard de Chardin, Pierre, 60–
    61, 79, 121
Teresa of Avila, St., 82, 119–20,
    127, 142
Thailand, 118
Three-Fold Good. See *Triplex
    Bonum*
Tillich, Paul, 60
totalitarianism, 30–31, 78, 93
Transfiguration Monastery (New
    York), 188

Trappists, 10–13, 48, 68, 120, 136
Traversari, Ambrogio, 55
Treehouse, 156–57
Tre-Fontane, 48
Triplex Bonum, 18, 24, 27, 71, 82,
91, 107, 124, 147, 151, 154,
166, 169, 171, 174, 177, 180
Tully, Ignatius, 189
Tuscany, 28, 32

Udine, 35–36, 46, 48, 62
Umbria, 18
United States, 96. *See also* America

Vagaggini, Cyprian, 75
Vagnozzi, Egidio, 89
Valeri, Valerio, Cardinal, 68–69
Vannutelli, Vincenzo, Cardinal, 32
Vatican, 18–19, 29, 31, 46–47,
99–100, 102
Vatican II. *See* Second Vatican
Council
Vatican Radio, 33, 48
Venice, 18, 56
Victor Emmanuel II, King, 19
Victor Emmanuel III, King, 20
Vina, 89
Vincerelli, Raphael, 75
visitation, 103, 130

Walker, Emily, 161–62
Walker, Janet, 145–46, 148,
151, 161–62, 183, 184–85,
188
Wasinger, Emmanuel, 103, 134,
149, 163, 175–76, 178, 187
Watts, Alan, 8
Welk, Lawrence, 52
wilderness, 3–5, 6, 8, 14, 20, 105,
128, 148–49
wildfires, 2
Willinger, Aloysius, Bishop, 53–54,
64–65, 67–73, 76, 81, 87, 89,
99, 122
women, 137, 143, 145, 148–49,
155–56, 160
Wong, Joseph, 167, 177
Wordsworth, William, 4
World War I, 15, 20, 23, 35–36,
54, 82
World War II, 7, 24, 26, 40, 52,
78, 95, 159

Yevtushenko, Evgeny, 93
yoga, x, 9, 84
Yogananda, 84, 113, 121

Zen Buddhism, 8, 118, 131, 156
Zen *sangha*, x